Leading a Board

Stanislav Shekshnia • Veronika Zagieva
Editors

Leading a Board

Chairs' Practices Across Europe

Editors
Stanislav Shekshnia
INSEAD
Fontainebleau, France

Veronika Zagieva
Ward Howell Talent Equity Institute
Moscow, Russia

ISBN 978-981-13-3196-1   ISBN 978-981-13-3197-8   (eBook)
https://doi.org/10.1007/978-981-13-3197-8

This Palgrave Macmillan imprint is published by the registered company Springer Nature
Singapore Pte Ltd.
The registered company address is: 152 Beach Road, #21-01/04 Gateway East, Singapore
189721, Singapore

Preface

Relatively little is known about board chairs as most of their work is done behind closed doors. They deal with highly sensitive matters but rarely appear in public. They have no executive power but preside over the most powerful body in the organization—the board of directors. Their performance is critically important for every company, but they still need help to improve it. Yet they have no boss, no peers and no one to turn to for advice. They learn mostly by trial and error.

To shed light on the workings of board chairs in different European countries we undertook a large-scale research project supported by INSEAD Corporate Governance Centre and Ward Howell Talent Equity Institute. During the first stage (2014–2015) we conducted a survey of more than 600 chairs in different countries, including more than 400 in Europe. During the second stage (2016–2018), ten experts from eight European countries interviewed 80 chairs and 118 CEOs, directors and shareholders to detect and compare specific practices and instruments that chairs use to deal with the challenges identified in the first part of the project. To compare chairs' practices through a lens of national cultures we used the "Culture Map" model developed by our INSEAD colleague, Professor Erin Meyer. At the end we identified key trends that will define the work of the board leader in the next decade (see Appendix A for a detailed description of our methodology).

This book is based on our research. It presents a conceptual framework for understanding the work of a board chair. It describes the core roles of a chair—leading the board, maintaining relationships with the CEO and interacting with shareholders—establishes a "typology" of chair-CEO and chair-shareholder relationships and identifies emerging trends. Most importantly, the book identifies specific practices—iterative behaviour strategies or ways to get things done—that chairs use to perform their duties. We conclude by presenting a number of pan-European trends in the work of a board chair, which we believe will develop over the next decade.

Chapter 1 builds on the existing literature and findings of the research project. It offers a conceptual model of the environment in which board chairs operate, combining three macro factors—business context, laws and soft laws and societal norms—and three micro factors—company, board and chair. The unique combination of these factors defines what a particular board chair does (roles) and how he/she goes about it (practices).

There are strong similarities in the way chairs from various countries define the job itself and the way they go about it. Board leaders play three specific roles: engaging, enabling and encouraging, which we call "the 3Es of effective board leadership". While these roles intertwine and reinforce each other, we have identified and classified specific practices that board chairs use to perform them individually. We also present typologies of chair-CEO and chair-shareholder relationships and supporting behaviours.

Chapters 2, 3, 4, 5, 6, 7, 8, and 9 describe in detail specific contexts for chairs' work and their practices in eight European countries—Denmark, Germany, Italy, the Netherlands, Russia, Switzerland, Turkey and the UK—identifying cross-country similarities and context-bound differences.

Chapter 2 reveals that effective chairs of boards of directors in the UK are accomplished professionals with strong views, who lead the board without "taking up much space" and avoid the limelight. They engage directors in a collective effort, creating an environment for effective collaboration and encouraging productive behaviours by providing feedback and opportunities for collective and individual learning and development. They do not give orders or issue directives; instead, they steer or nudge followers by setting agendas, framing discussion items, soliciting opinions and seeking and providing feedback. They set clear expectations and establish rules, but the latter serve as guidelines rather than laws set in stone. They delineate their spheres with the CEOs—"I run the board—you run the company"—and strive to strike a fine balance between "equal-distancing" and proactivity in relationships with shareholders.

Chapter 3 uncovers the particularities of the chair's work in the Netherlands, such as growth orientation and focus on building consensus (*polderen*). Board leaders make sure that value creation and business development are permanent fixtures on board agendas. They encourage CEOs to think big and take reasonable risks and when necessary help the business by working with customers, vendors and regulators. Chairs of Dutch companies use a variety of consensus-building strategies to prepare and make decisions that satisfy every director: equal treatment and equal allocation of airtime; proactive facilitation of discussions, involving silent directors and containing talkative types; and self-restraint. They do not mind pre-agreed schedules overrunning to achieve consensus and they reach out to board members before meetings to create common platforms and avoid surprises.

Chapter 4 portrays board chairs from Switzerland as diligent professionals working for the long-term development of their companies and considering an effective board of directors as a core element of such development. Swiss board leaders describe themselves as "first among equals", "shepherds", "conductors" and "the link between the board and the CEO". They plan for the long term, ensure quality of board materials and combine discipline and freedom of expression during board discussions. They work proactively with shareholders and executives on behalf of the board and bring the information they gather back to the directors.

Chapter 5 demonstrates that in Denmark board leaders operate as facilitators, striving for harmony and consensus—and effectiveness at the same time. They are informal, candid and accessible. They encourage everyone to speak their minds with vigour and determination, are not afraid of conflicting views and deal with disagreements in a proactive way. Board chairs work proactively with all stakeholders and, most importantly, shareholders—yet they fiercely protect their independence and authority over board matters.

Chapter 6 shows that board chairs in Italy operate under two types of constraints: law and tradition. While legal regulations define the role of a chair in a similar way to other European countries, Italian tradition emphasizes the functions of conflict resolution and communication. Thus board leaders not only organize the work of the board and ensure compliance, but also interact intensely with key stakeholders, often in informal settings.

Chapter 7 describes the distinctive context for the work of a chair in Germany, which has a two-tier board system and, for large companies, mandatory employee representation on the supervisory board. Board leaders deal with these and other challenges by being very diligent with regard to the law and corporate governance guidelines, focusing the board's work on a limited number of issues, maintaining order and discipline in the board room and making specific efforts to reach out to employees' representatives on the board.

Chapter 8 shows how globalization and tradition shape the working practices of board chairs in Turkey. Board leaders there pay a lot of attention to the social status of those they work with—board members, shareholders and executives. They maintain a focus on performance and relationships, rely heavily on social contacts and informal relations to get things done and place a high value on social events such as dinners, outings and conferences. At the same time chairs take on the role of facilitators and mentors vis-à-vis their boards and their members.

Chapter 9 is dedicated to board chairs in Russia, where relationships are more important than institutions. It depicts board leaders as pragmatists working both within institutional and informal contexts to get their job done. They balance authoritative and facilitating modes of operating and use a range of practices from "traditional" conversations behind closed doors to "modernist" coaching sessions with directors. Chairs in Russia work proactively with significant shareholders, whom they often consider to be their ultimate masters. Engagement with CEOs is also high on their agenda, but it takes various forms—from dominant mentoring to advising—depending on the social status of the parties involved and their relationship to ownership.

Chapter 10 synthesizes the findings presented in the previous nine chapters on individual countries. We highlight five of the most common practices of European board chairs, identify five potential traps a European chair should be aware of and describe five personal attributes that make a chair effective in the European context. We conclude the chapter by presenting one highly original chair practice from each of the nine countries.

Chapter 11 offers the research team's view on how the chair's role and function in Europe will evolve in the next decade. The changes will be evolutionary rather than revolutionary, but their impact will be felt across multiple dimensions. In ten years there will be (a few) more female chairs in European companies than there are today and the average age of the chair will fall (slightly). "Celebrity chairs"—people chairing many boards thanks to their personal prestige—will disappear. External pressures on chairs will increase and their work will intensify. Technology will actively move into the boardrooms of Europe and become one of the main tools of the chair's trade.

We tried to write this book in a reader-friendly way, keeping in mind business practitioners as our main target audience. For those with an interest or background in research, we include a description of our methodology and processes in a separate appendix. We also list bibliography at the end of each chapter.

There are different ways to read this book. "Traditional" readers may go through all the chapters in order. "Busy" readers may limit their efforts to Chap. 1, which summarizes our research and the theory on which it was built, and Chaps. 10 and 11, which synthesize our findings and predictions—and their practical implications. People interested in a particular country may read just the corresponding section of the book. Indeed, Chaps. 2, 3, 4, 5, 6, 7, 8, and 9 are each designed to be stand alone. To further assist the busy reader, the chair practices identified in this research—matched with the challenges that emerged from the INSEAD Global Chair Survey 2015—are listed in Appendix B.

This is the essential guidebook for new and seasoned chairs, as well as for directors, shareholders and executives who want to understand how board leaders operate and how to interact with them more effectively. This book also helps regulators, educators, corporate governance scholars and experts develop unique insights into the work and mind-set of a board chair.

Fontainebleau, France   Stanislav Shekshnia
Moscow, Russia   Veronika Zagieva

ACKNOWLEDGMENTS

We are grateful to the many anonymous respondents from eight European countries—busy professionals who gave us their time and shared with us their priceless insights about the work of a board chair. Without their contributions, this book would not have been possible.

Many people helped us imagine, design, research and write this book. We are grateful to Ludo Van der Heyden, INSEAD Chaired Professor of Corporate Governance and founding Academic Director of INSEAD Corporate Governance Centre (ICGC), for supporting the project, advising on the early stages and making recommendations on improving the draft, and Professor Jose-Luis Alvarez, Academic Director of ICGC, for his encouragement and support. We thank also Muriel Larvaron, formerly Assistant Director of the ICGC, and Sonia Tatar, Executive Director of the ICGC, for identifying and contacting respondents, managing the technical side of the project and giving us encouragement. Special thanks go to Alexandra Matveeva from Ward Howell Talent Equity Institute for her invaluable help with data collection and analysis and to Alexey Ulanovsky from Ward Howell and Vincent H. Dominé from INSEAD and DOMINÉ & PARTNERS for their great contribution to the first part of the project. We would be remiss if we did not express our gratitude to Elin Williams for her unfaltering enthusiasm in editing the manuscript. We would like to thank our assistants Tatiana Shuvalova and Aurelia Merle for keeping us focused and meeting deadlines.

Many colleagues from academia have given us feedback and advice after reading the manuscript or parts of it and hearing our ideas. We would particularly like to thank Professors Manfred Kets de Vries, Alena

Ledeneva, Erin Meyer, Subi Rangan and Tim Rowley. We are very grateful to our clients, partners and friends from the corporate world who helped us develop the concepts presented in this book by listening, sharing and providing critique, especially George Abdushelishvili, Kirill Androsov, Gleb Frank, Pavel Kiryukhantsev, Alexander Saveliev, Vitaly Vassiliev, Maxim Vorobiev and Sergey Vorobiev.

Stanislav Shekshnia
Veronika Zagieva

Contents

Notes on Contributors[1]

Elena Denisova-Schmidt is a research associate at University of St. Gallen (Switzerland) and research fellow at Boston College's Center for International Higher Education (USA). Previously, she held appointments at the Humboldt University of Berlin, Kennan Institute of Woodrow Wilson International Center for Scholars, German Institute for International and Security Affairs, UCL School of Slavonic and East European Studies, Edmond J. Safra Center for Ethics at Harvard University and Aleksanteri Institute of University of Helsinki. Before moving into academia, Elena Denisova-Schmidt worked for the VSMPO-AVISMA Corporation in Russia.

Peter Firnhaber is an executive coach and coaching supervisor. He works globally with all industries, private and public, governments and non-governmental organizations, with all functions and hierarchical levels. Peter's business education includes a B.Sc. in marketing and an MBA from INSEAD.

Rolf Frey is Managing Partner of DOMINÉ & PARTNERS, a Swiss-based international leadership consultancy firm advising executive teams and boards. He is a member of the coaching faculty at IMD Business School in Singapore and Switzerland and at the European School of Management and Technology (ESMT) in Berlin. Rolf is also chair of a company, offering cloud-based personal leadership development for professionals and

---

[1] This book is a product of a collective effort and we wish to present and thank our co-authors.

teams. Rolf holds a Master of Science in Consulting and Coaching for Change from HEC Paris and University of Oxford.

Steen Buchreitz Jensen is the CEO and an owner of Scandinavian Executive Institute. He worked for over 25 years as a senior executive in consumer goods and fashion companies. He has served as a board member or chair for several organizations and has supported business transformations in his board capacity and as an independent consultant.

Andrew Kakabadse joined Henley Business School in July 2013 after 30 years at Cranfield School of Management, where he was Professor of International Management Development and was awarded the honour of Emeritus Professor. He was also Vice Chancellor of the International Academy of Management and Chairman of the Division of Occupational Psychology, British Psychological Society. His current areas of interest focus on improving the performance of top executives, top executive teams and boards, excellence in consultancy practice, leadership, corporate governance, conflict resolution and international relations.

Filipe Morais has joined Henley Business School as a post-doctoral fellow in governance, leadership and directorship. Filipe spent ten years as an HR professional for a variety of multinational firms. His research examines how CEOs and chairs respond to strategic tensions in contexts of far-reaching change. He currently directs a large-scale research programme on governance and director independence in various sectors. He is also interested in the performance of top teams, CEO and chair leadership, chair-CEO relations, strategic change and shareholder engagement. Some of Filipe's research has been published as book chapters, articles and case studies and presented at prestigious academic and practitioner conferences.

Mik van den Noort is an executive coach and team facilitator for INSEAD (Fontainebleau and Singapore) and ESMT (Berlin), as well as for the Kets de Vries Institute (Paris and London). Her clients include international companies in publishing, aviation, retail and biotechnology, as well as professional firms in the fields of strategic consulting, tax and law.

Ekaterina Ryasentseva is Head of Leadership Development at Ward Howell Talent Equity Consultancy in Moscow. She is responsible for a wide range of projects: from corporate culture transformations and corporate governance to team and individual effectiveness. As an associate executive coach at INSEAD's Global Leadership Centre, she works with top management across various industry sectors for both Russian and multinational clients.

Stanislav Shekshnia is Professor of Entrepreneurship at INSEAD, a director of the "Leading from the Chair" executive development programme and a senior partner at Ward Howell. His research concentrates on leadership, leadership development and effective governance in regions and organizations.

Hande Yaşargil is an international executive coach based in Istanbul and London. She is coaching for INSEAD Global Leadership Centre (IGLC), and also Leadership Development Practice Director for International Directors Programme (IDP) at INSEAD Business School. Hande served in board member roles in Turkish Personnel Management Association (PERYOD) and the founding President role in European Mentoring and Coaching Council (EMCC), Turkey. She is also the founding chairperson of "Women on Board Association of Turkey". Hande holds a BA in Psychology and an Executive Master's degree from INSEAD in Coaching and Consulting. Hande has lately been working on "Group Dynamics at Board Level" at Tavistock Institute.

Veronika Zagieva is a director of Ward Howell Talent Equity Institute, an internal research and development division of the Ward Howell Group. Her research is focused on leadership development, CEO effectiveness, CEO succession and board dynamics.

Anna Zanardi is a board advisor for several boards of directors of listed and unlisted companies. She also acts as executive coach to the chairs and directors in their decisional processes. Anna is a board member in a charity board and in a Zurich Stock Exchange–listed multinational company.

LIST OF FIGURES

LIST OF TABLES

CHAPTER 1

Work of a Chair in Europe: Context, Content and Evolution

Stanislav Shekshnia and Veronika Zagieva

A Brief History of Chairing the Board in Europe

Some forms of boards of directors existed in Europe as early as the Middle Ages,[1] and they have become a permanent feature of European business life since the seventeenth century. At that time, investors in Western Europe began to form joint stock companies to finance trading expeditions to the newly discovered lands in the East and the West. In 1600 Queen Elizabeth I of England granted a Royal Charter to 215[2] aristocrats and merchants to become "a body politic and corporate"[3] under the name of "Governor and Company of Merchants of London trading into the East Indies", known

---

[1] Cawston, G. and Keane, A.H. (1968). *Early Chartered Companies: A.D. 1296–1858.* New York: B. Franklin, p. 15.

[2] In some sources—218.

[3] Cawston, G. and Keane, A.H. (1968). *Early Chartered Companies: A.D. 1296–1858.* New York: B. Franklin, pp. 86–87.

S. Shekshnia (✉)
INSEAD, Fontainebleau, France

V. Zagieva
Ward Howell Talent Equity Institute, Moscow, Russia
e-mail: v.zagieva@wardhowell.com

© The Author(s) 2019
S. Shekshnia, V. Zagieva (eds.), *Leading a Board*,
https://doi.org/10.1007/978-981-13-3197-8_1

1

later as East India Company. The charter stated that shareholders of the company would annually elect 24 people called "committees" to oversee its business. Two years later, the Dutch government sponsored the foundation of Dutch East India Company (*Verenigde Oost-Indische Compagnie* or VOC), which became the first multinational enterprise to offer its stock to the public. The company had two types of shareholders—*participanten* (non-managing members) and 60 *bewindhebbers* (managing members). However, the 60-person body was too cumbersome, so later the VOC formed a smaller board with 17 members called the Collegium.[4] In both companies, "committees" and the "Collegium" were responsible for choosing a chief executive (or "governor"), distributing profits and raising capital from shareholders for new voyages. The term "director", used to describe a member of a governing body, was mentioned for the first time in 1694 in a charter of the Bank of England, which prescribed a "court of proprietors" to elect 24 directors to oversee the Bank's operations.

Today, in all the European countries we have studied, the board of directors is the highest decision-making body in a corporation. It consists of experienced individuals who may or may not be employees of the company (executive vs non-executive directors) and may or may not have a financial interest in it (affiliated vs independent directors). The directors meet periodically to debate and make decisions. Every director has the same rights and responsibilities, except in special cases (such as a conflict of interest).

Directors elect one of their number to preside over their joint work. At different times and in different countries, this person may be called a "chairman", "chairwoman", "chairperson", "president" or—our preferred term—simply "chair". The chair is one of the directors but is responsible for the smooth functioning of the board and communicating on its behalf with the firm's key stakeholders—shareholders, management, regulators and so on. Just like academics who research boards, the participants in our research project repeatedly referred to the chair as "the leader of the board".[5] Since leadership is a highly contextual

[4] Gevurtz, F. (2004). The European Origins and the Spread of the Corporate Board of Directors. *Stetson Law Review*, 33, pp. 925–954.

[5] Bezemer, P., Peij, S., Maassen, G. and van Halder, H. (2010). The Changing Role of the Supervisory Board Chairman: the Case of the Netherlands (1997–2007). *Journal of Management & Governance*, 16(1), pp. 37–55; Garratt, B. (1999). Developing Effective Directors and Building Dynamic Boards. *Long Range Planning*, 32, pp. 28–35; Furr, R. and Furr, L. (2005). Is Your Chairman A Leader? *The Corporate Board*, 26(154), pp. 11–15.

business, in order to understand the work of a chair, it is also important to understand the impact of key contextual factors and the interplay between them.

The Chair's Work in Context

In order to understand the context of the chair's work, we used a two-level model inspired by the work of Professor Alena Ledeneva and her colleagues, and informed by the respondents in our research project[6] (see Fig. 1.1).

Formal rules are the **laws and "soft laws"** (regulations, including corporate governance guidelines) that constitute the legal framework within which the chair's work is carried out. In all of the countries that we studied, corporate governance is developing significantly, with more and more aspects of the work of the board and the chair becoming regulated (directly

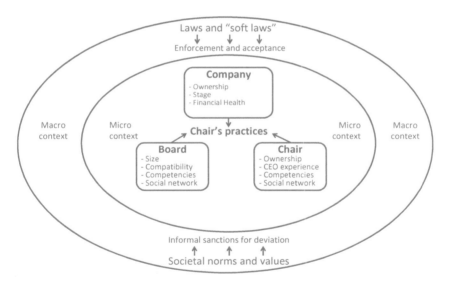

Fig. 1.1 Context for the chair's work

[6] See INFORM: Closing the Gap between Formal and Informal Institutions in the Balkans. Available from: http://www.formal-informal.eu (Accessed 3 December 2018).

and indirectly). In addition to stiffer regulations, respondents emphasized the following trends:

- More public scrutiny
- More transparency for the company, the board and the chair
- More accountability for boards and chairs
- More reporting.

Although the countries we studied have had very different systems of corporate governance in the past, today their national governance codes define the role and functions of a chair in a similar way—even if some codes such as the UK's and the Netherland's—are more elaborate on the subject. The underlining message is that the chair has to provide leadership for the board. According to UK code: "The chairman is responsible for leadership of the board and ensuring its effectiveness on all aspects of its role."[7] The major functions of a chair, as defined by the various European codes, can be summarized in the following way:

- Creating the conditions for the board's and individual directors' effectiveness
- Conducting board discussions that lead to effective collective decisions
- Organizing periodical board evaluations
- Serving as a role model for directors and executives
- Developing productive working relationships with the CEO and management
- Communicating with the company's stakeholders, including shareholders

Some country codes mention other chair functions, such as providing comprehensive board materials for directors in a timely manner, integrating new board members, setting and demonstrating corporate values, guiding the company secretary and so on. In summary, national codes define the chair as the leader of the board, leaving to the incumbents, their boards and other stakeholders, significant discretion in interpreting this definition and adapting the role to the context.

[7] Financial Reporting Council (2016). The UK Corporate Governance Code. Available from: https://www.frc.org.uk/getattachment/ca7e94c4-b9a9-49e2-a824-ad76a322873c/UK-Corporate-Governance-Code-April-2016.pdf (Accessed 3 December 2018).

The levels of **enforcement and acceptance** of corporate governance laws and regulations vary among countries. Many chairs reported that, while the developments of the last decade or two had changed the formal side of their work, many former practices remained intact. Chairs from Russia shared stories of directors with major shareholdings attending the meetings of remuneration committees and influencing the outcomes, even though they were technically barred from membership. Chairs from Denmark, Italy, Russia and Turkey reported that certain significant shareholders actively participated in setting the agendas of board meetings, proposing resolutions and even attending uninvited!

We discovered that acceptance of formal rules is strongly influenced by a number of other macro factors (see Fig. 1.1). **Societal norms and values** (national culture) serve at times as enablers and at times as constraints for the formal rules, as well as influencing the work of chairs directly. We found culturally specific practices in all countries. However, traditional norms are more dominant in those where society applies stronger **informal sanctions** for deviation. Some Russian chairs reported using the traditional practice of *razgovor po dusham* (literally "heart-to-heart")—a tough informal conversation behind closed doors—to persuade board members to come prepared or to stop misbehaving in meetings. Pulling strings through informal social networks to improve board effectiveness by changing its composition (primarily in government-linked companies) is another commonly reported practice. Some Turkish chairs shared tales of trying to balance board effectiveness with managing the relationships between directors. In chairing meetings, for example, they identify directors with higher social status and treat them accordingly. Organizing social events, such as dinners, outings and conferences for board members, is an important element of their work. Chairs may give directors specific tasks and projects not directly related to the board's work, such as paying customer a visit, helping an executive with an investment plan or taking a company banker for lunch. In Italy, where professional and personal networks tend to mix, some chairs spend holidays with directors, shareholders and executives, thus combining business with pleasure. One-to-one conversations over coffee are one of the "core" practices of Italian board leaders, while British chairs get a lot of business done over a meal in a restaurant.

The **macroeconomic situation** in a country is another factor influencing the work of a chair. According to our respondents from all countries, their work becomes more intense in times of economic crisis or slowdown: they focus boards on short-term issues, become more assertive in setting agendas, spend more time with CEOs and challenge them, and run board meetings in more authoritative ways. One chair from Russia said, "*As the economic situation worsened, I began to rely more on informal practices to lead the board and motivate management.*" In good times, the board's agenda becomes more future-oriented, directors spend more time on strategy and leadership development, and chairs adopt a more supportive leadership style.

One of the unexpected findings of this research project was that chairs see **technology**, and especially information technology, as a permanent factor impacting their work. As one UK chair put it:

> *Information technology has dramatically changed and will keep changing how I work. We have gone 100 percent digital and paperless at two boards I currently chair. I communicate with my boards and CEOs via WhatsApp chat. All directors have access to the companies' financial and operating data in real time—we don't need to listen to management reports during board meetings. We run committee meetings on WebEx. And I am available to my directors and CEOs 24 hours a day no matter where I am physically.*

Or, as a chair from Russia said, "*Technology is a great enabler for me today, but how it will play out in the future I have no idea. I may be replaced by a robot-chair in five years. I have to watch it and to adapt my work.*"

The micro context of the chair's work is largely defined by the **characteristics of the company, the composition of the board and the incumbent chair** (see Fig. 1.1).

Company characteristics include the type of ownership, size and life cycle stage (start-up, initial growth, maturity, decline or revival), and financial health. We found that company characteristics have a stronger differentiating impact on what chairs do than national or cultural differences. Both in public companies with multiple shareholders and in private companies with a small number of shareholders, the relationship with shareholders is a priority for the chair. However, the goals and supporting practices may vary. In private companies, chairs may proactively seek shareholders' views, engage them in dialogue about the business, invite them to attend some board meetings or have them meet with directors informally. One chair from Denmark has developed a questionnaire to gauge shareholders' expectations on a range of issues from dividends to company's values. He interviews shareholders annually and feeds the information back to the board. One chair from Russia created a WhatsApp group for the three shareholders and himself, and they exchange information on a daily basis. At the same time, chairs of companies with reference shareholders make special efforts "*to keep them out of the boardroom*" (as a chair from Denmark put it) and to separate "*shareholders' meetings from board meetings*" (a chair from Russia).

In public companies, chairs strive for equal treatment of shareholders and pay a lot of attention to respecting regulations. Direct proactive communication with a particular shareholder is the exception rather than the rule in all the countries we studied. However, chairs generally try to be responsive when shareholders require their attention.

In family businesses, chairs pay special attention to nurturing relationships with family members of various generations, often doing more than the book prescribes. Examples include discussing long-term business and shareholders' strategy (Denmark, Netherlands, Switzerland); fostering harmony between family, other shareholders, board and management (Netherlands); defining and selecting board members (Switzerland); advising on talent development (Denmark); and mentoring family members (Denmark, Turkey).

At companies in the earlier stages of development with relatively inexperienced senior managers, chairs usually make sure their boards are involved in developing strategy, raising funds and mitigating operational risks. One experienced director from Italy, who serves both on boards of public companies and start-ups explained: "*In a startup board all boundaries are blurred. The chair drives an agenda, but he is equal to other directors, while in a public board, the chair should have authority and stand apart.*" In large mature organizations, leaders tend to steer boards towards controlling and advisory functions. Compliance also sits high on their agendas.

Chair practices may be affected by the **financial health of a company**. Board leaders do not significantly change their board routine if decline in company's performance is gradual, but a sudden plunge or unusual event leads to an increased intensity of their involvement and interaction with directors and CEO. At the same time, effective chairs are conscious not to overshadow the CEO even at the times of crisis. As one of Russian chair put it: "*In this situation [a crisis] I supported the CEO, because I believed he could manage it—he just needed time. As chair I could take responsibility and try to fix it, but I was not sure it would be a smart decision.*" In some situations, the CEO and chair divide their responsibilities. While the CEO focuses inwards, the chair covers the "outward perimeter", talking with regulators, suppliers, creditors and the media. However, the majority of chairs try to avoid publicity. One Swiss chair describes the responsibility of chair as "*to be seen more in the office than in the newspaper*".

The poor financial health of a company leads to more intense communication with not only majority but also minority shareholders: regular calls, pre-board meetings and even brainstorming sessions help not only to calm their worries but also to solicit help and advice. As one Italian director put it: "*Some of these formal procedures can be cumbersome and time consuming, especially when your company is in crisis, but a chair must take to them like a duck to water.*"

Such **characteristics of a board** as its size and composition (presence of executive and non-executive directors, membership of shareholders or their representatives, inclusion of directors with high social status and differing skill sets of directors) also impact a chair's practices. However, we found no significant effect of such factors as presence or absence of female directors.

In companies with larger boards (more than ten members), chairs often try to shift analytical work to committees. They work thoroughly on meeting agendas, carefully monitor timing and restrict individual directors' airtime. Chairs of smaller boards allow for more freedom of expression and may tolerate—or even encourage—unstructured spontaneous discussions, sometimes adding more items to the agenda during meetings.

In the case of boards with both executive and non-executive directors, many chairs either start or finish regular board meetings with in-camera sessions for non-executives only (Netherlands, Russia, UK). Some chairs also organize informal meetings for non-executive directors only (Netherlands, Denmark, UK).

Sometimes consciously and sometimes unconsciously, chairs pay special attention to VIP board members: shareholders, their representatives or people with a special social status, such as high-ranked government officials, politicians or prominent businessmen. These "celebrities" may get more airtime. They may also be consulted before and during the board meeting, or asked to open or close a discussion. This tendency is more pronounced in cultures with high power distance, such as Italy, Russia and Turkey.

We found that certain variables—like the incumbent **chair's relationship to the company's owners**, **prior experience as a CEO**, **professional background** and **social status**—can result in somewhat different practices. These findings correlate with previous research on sources of

power and corresponding practices of board leaders.[8] Chairs with relatively high power resulting from ownership (whether their own significant
shareholding or a close relationship with major shareholders), previous
CEO experience, industry expertise or high social status tend to be more
assertive in chairing the board than those who lack such advantages. We
term these, respectively, ownership power, structural power, expert power
and prestige power.

These "powerful" chairs usually set the boards' agendas themselves,
actively interact with CEOs and other executives by mentoring and even
managing them, and communicate widely with external stakeholders. In
the boardroom they often take centre stage and do not hesitate to speak
their mind, proposing decisions and defending them robustly. Chairs
"without power" operate in a more facilitating mode. They collaborate
with CEOs and committee chairs to develop board agendas and leave
external communication to senior managers. At the same time, we noted
that effective chairs who lack all of the four traditional sources of power
develop their own form of power over time. They gain respect and fol-
lowership from directors by professionally exercising their role of a chair.
One director from Russia told us:

> In one of my boards we have three shareholders, two industry experts and two
> high-profile businessmen. They all respect and follow our chair who has no stock
> in the company, has never worked in the industry, is not a billionaire, but really
> knows how to run a board.

THE THREE MAIN ROLES OF THE CHAIR

The academic literature on chairing a board is limited. Most publications
are based on theoretical concepts and secondary sources rather than field
research. Some authors emphasize the procedural aspects of the chair's
work—setting board agendas, supplying directors with relevant information, conducting board and shareholder meetings or organizing periodical

---

[8] McNulty, T., Pettigrew, A., Jobome, G. and Morris, C. (2011). The Role, Power and
Influence of Company Chairs. *Journal of Management and Governance*, 15, pp. 91–121;
Pettigrew, A. and McNulty, T. (1995). Power and Influence In and Around Boardroom.
Human Relations, 48, pp. 845–873.

board evaluations—thus reducing the role to that of a senior moderator.[9] At the other end of the spectrum, scholars highlight the leadership responsibilities of the chair, who acts as the guardian of the values of the firm and maintains the highest standards of integrity among directors and executives.[10]

A few scholars who examine what chairs actually do (mostly in the UK) portray them as board leaders playing a number of specific roles. Earlier studies emphasize managing the CEO and senior executives; integrating, developing and supervising directors; and representing the company externally.[11] Later researchers focus on what chairs do to maximize the collective decision-making power of the board.[12] Today, there is a consensus among academics that the work of a chair is to lead the board. However, what this leadership entails remains a subject of a debate.

This situation is perhaps best summed up by one of the founding fathers of the contemporary corporate governance movement in the UK, the late Sir Adrian Cadbury. He was head of the commission that issued the famous "Cadbury Report"[13] in 1992 on best practice in corporate governance and long-term chair of Cadbury-Schweppes. His view was:

The role of a chairman is a personal one. Chairmen have to decide what they are going to do for their boards and for their board colleagues.[14]

[9] Bezemer, P., Peij, S., Maassen, G. and van Halder, H. (2010). The Changing Role of the Supervisory Board Chairman: the Case of the Netherlands (1997–2007). *Journal of Management & Governance*, 16(1), pp. 37–55; McNulty, T. and Pettigrew, A. (1999). Strategists on the Board. *Organization Studies*, 20(1), pp. 47–74.

[10] Higgs, D. (2003). Review of the Role and Effectiveness of Non-Executive Directors. Available from: http://www.ecgi.org/codes/documents/higgs.pdf (Accessed 26 March 2018); Hossack, R. (2006). Together at the Top: the Critical Relationship Between the Chairman and the CEO. *Ivey Business Journal*, Jan/Feb, pp. 1–4. Available from: https://iveybusinessjournal.com/publication/together-at-the-top-the-critical-relationship-between-thechairman-and-the-ceo/ (Accessed 3 December 2018).

[11] Stewart, R. (1991). Chairman and Chief Executive: an Exploration of their Relationship. *Journal of Management Study*, 28 (5), pp. 511–527; Garratt, B. (1999). Developing Effective Directors and Building Effective Boards. *Long Range Planning*, 32(1), pp. 28–35; Roberts, J. (2002). Building the Complementary Board. The Work of the Plc Chairman. *Long Range Planning*, 35(5), pp. 493–520.

[12] Kakabadse, N., Knyght, R. and Kakabadse, A. (2013). High-Performing Chairmen: the Older the Better. In: A. Kakabadse and L. van den Berghe, ed., *How to Make Boards Work*. London: Palgrave, pp. 342–349; Kakabadse, A. and Kakabadse, N. (2008). *Leading the Board: the Six Disciplines of World Class Chairman*. London: Palgrave.

[13] The Committee on the Financial Aspects of Corporate Governance (1992). *Report of the Committee on the Financial Aspects of Corporate Governance*. London: Gee and Co.

[14] Cadbury, A. (2002). *Corporate Governance and Chairmanship: A Personal View*. London: Oxford University Press.

As we indicated earlier, personality plays a part in how chairs go about executing their role. However, in all the countries that we studied, we found that incumbent chairs define their role in a similar way. According to them, the work of the chair consists primarily of interacting with the board, shareholders and CEO/senior management. These three groups of stakeholders take up the majority of the chair's time, energy and emotion, and to a large degree define the complexity of the job. In addition, chairs take on some auxiliary functions, such as speaking on the company's behalf; interacting with regulators, key customers or vendors; and mentoring executives or high potentials. The extent of these duties varies from chair to chair and is largely defined by the contextual factors presented in Fig. 1.1. In the remaining part of this chapter, we will concentrate on the three core roles of European chairs (Fig. 1.2).

Leading the Board

A good chair, as respondents and interviewees from all countries largely agreed, provides effective leadership not for the company but for the board, enabling it to function as the highest decision-making body in the organization. As one respondent put it: *"The chair is responsible for and represents the board, while the CEO is responsible for and is the public face of*

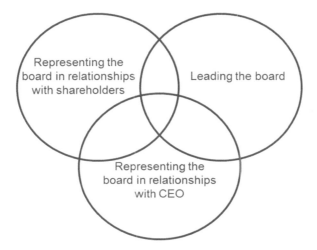

Fig. 1.2 Roles of chairs in the European context

the company." This is an important distinction, which makes being the chair a very different job from being the CEO.

Eighty-five per cent of the chairs in our survey had been CEOs at some point in their career, yet they emphasized that leading a board requires a different mindset and a distinct set of skills. CEOs thrive by setting a vision, making bold moves, appointing people, giving them specific orders, assuming responsibility and setting an example. They are the stars of the show. Chairs operate in a different context, which requires a different mode of leadership. Boards are very special social groups—their members are mature, accomplished professionals with multiple affiliations and often full-time jobs somewhere else.[15] They meet infrequently, spend little time together and yet have to make decisions that will determine the fate of the company for years to come.[16] Their leader has to maximize the return on the limited time they are able to invest in the company. And he or she must do so without having access to such traditional CEO tools as hiring and firing, offering compensation or promotion as an incentive, organizing team-building sessions, allocating investment budgets or bringing in an executive coach.

Effective chairs do not try to make their boards operate like teams, but rather master what Harvard Business School Professor Amy Edmondson calls "teaming"—effective collaboration among professionals without forming traditional teams. This implies creating the conditions for collaboration to emerge naturally whenever the group convenes. Lorsch has identified the "chairman's ability" to nurture dialogue among all board members as the key success factor.[17] We found that this ability translates into three distinct functions: engaging, enabling and encouraging. Hence our term: *3E-leadership.*

Engaging board members. In most cases board members are highly capable individuals selected for their knowledge, experience and decision-making skills. Yet they are often physically detached from the company,

---

[15] Hillman, A., Nicholson, G. and Shropshire, C. (2008). Directors' Multiple Identities, Identification, and Board Monitoring and Resource Provision. *Organization Science,* 19(3), pp. 441–456.

[16] Barroso-Castro, C., Villegas-Periñan, M. and Dominguez, M. (2017). Board Members' Contribution to Strategy: The Mediating Role of Board Internal Processes. *European Research on Management and Business Economics,* 23 (2), pp. 82–89.

[17] Lorsch, J. W. and Zelleke, A. (2005). The Chairman's Job Description. *Directors and Boards,* 30(1), pp. 28–32.

have many issues on their plates and experience multiple demands on their time. Bringing their attention to the concerns of a specific company is not an easy task, and experienced chairs recognize this well. As one respondent put it: "*You need to make sure they are physically there, they are emotionally engaged, they know what we are talking about, and they put their brains to collective work.*" Directors need to be engaged from the beginning to the end of every board meeting, but also stay connected to the company in between board meetings. As one chair explained: "*I call my directors every five to six weeks just to remind them they are on this particular board and the next meeting is coming.*" The study uncovered a multitude of specific practices used by chairs to keep directors engaged from WhatsApp messages to one-to-one dinners, which all serve as gentle reminders about their duties. Engagement within the boardroom comes from fair allocation of in air-time, personal attention to each director, dynamism in discussions and effective handling of "rogue" board members.

Enabling board members is about creating a productive working environment for board discussions, removing informational and psychological barriers, and supporting each board member and the group as the whole. It requires pre-meeting, in-meeting and post-meeting work that goes far beyond merely facilitating discussions. Effective chairs fulfil their enabling function by carefully selecting items for the board's agenda. As one respondent put it, "*It has to be strategic, material, ripe for decision and no one else in the company can decide on it.*" They must also allocate enough time for each item and keep board meetings reasonably short, as well as providing crisp, concise and readable materials in advance; framing discussion questions, facilitating productive discussions and articulating decisions; quickly providing detailed minutes after the event and ensuring effective follow-up; and informing directors about important developments at the company. One respondent summarized it this way:

> *I have enormous power without having any material resources. By controlling what goes onto the agenda, how the discussion question is framed, who gets to speak first, I can make a huge difference to the outcome. I have to use this power wisely for the benefit of the board.*

Encouraging board members involves keeping them motivated and productive by providing feedback; creating opportunities for reflection and learning; and making them feel important, impactful and appreciated. One respondent explained:

> *These people (directors) rarely get feedback—they are successful high-powered individuals, but it does not mean they don't need a slap on the back or a word of encouragement. I regularly let them know how I value their contribution and how they could make it even more valuable.*

While the functions of engaging, enabling and encouraging intertwine and reinforce each other, our research uncovered specific practices that board chairs use to perform each of them. We will present these in the next chapters.

Relationships with the CEO and Management

The CEO (along with in some cases other senior executives) is an important counterpart of the chair. In the European countries we studied, the law or corporate governance guidelines oblige board leaders to maintain productive working relationships with their chief executives, to communicate with them and to provide advice and feedback. Some countries go further: board chairs are expected to mentor the CEO.

Earlier academic studies emphasize chair-CEO complementarity, partnership and the need to draw a line between what each of them does for the company.[18] According to Higgs, the chair should not seek executive responsibility and should let the chief executive take credit for his or her achievements. The chair can be an informed, experienced and trusted partner, the source of counsel and challenge designed to support the chief executive's performance. However, the chair must not get in the way of other non-executive directors questioning the chief executive.[19] Drawing a line between the work of the chair and that of the CEO was essential in the context of the transition from combined to separate positions, which started in the UK and other European countries in the 1990s and has largely become standard practice.

---

[18] Parker, H. (1990). The Company Chairman—His Role and Responsibilities. *Long Range Planning*, 23(4), pp. 35–43; Stewart, R. (1991). Chairman and Chief Executive: an Exploration of their Relationship. *Journal of Management Study*, 28(5), pp. 511–527.

[19] Higgs, D. (2003). Review of the Role and Effectiveness of Non-Executive Directors. Available from: http://www.ecgi.org/codes/documents/higgs.pdf (Accessed 3 December 2018).

Our study found chair-CEO interaction to be intense, complex and more nuanced than is prescribed by the regulations. These relationships are shaped by contextual factors: the chair and CEO's respective relationship to ownership; their previous experience; the personalities of both individuals; and societal norms. Nevertheless, we have identified several "archetypes" of chair-CEO relationships.

Collaboration. This is a close, intense and well-structured interaction between professionals with equal status and shared goals. Chair and CEO work together on issues requiring cooperation, such as board agendas, format of board materials and communication with external stakeholders. They let the other party play his or her role independently but support, challenge and advise each other when required. Some respondents' quotes illustrate this type of relationship: *"We set every board meeting agenda together"* (Netherlands); *"We go on business trips together—it helps to build trust and have the same picture"* (Switzerland).

We found that collaboration prevails in relationships between chairs and CEOs who have no significant stake in the company, similar social status and no history of superior-subordinate interaction. "Collaborating" chairs usually have no other major commitments and have not been CEO of the company. This type of chair-CEO relationship is typical in countries with low-context and low-power-distance cultures: Denmark, the Netherlands and Switzerland.

Cohabitation. The name for this archetype comes from the French governing practice of *cohabitation*, whereby a right-wing president may co-exist with a left-wing parliamentary majority—and vice versa. In the corporate world, it implies that the chair and the CEO work independently towards goals defined by each of them separately. They interact rarely and formally, with cooperation limited to the regulatory minimum. Here are some quotes from our interviews: *"I never talk to the CEO's direct reports—it's the area of his responsibility"* (Switzerland); *"I write to all board members to solicit ideas for the annual board agenda, the CEO is one of them—I don't feel I need to do anything special for him"* (chair from Russia); *"We never have one-to-one meetings with my chair, mostly we communicate via the corporate secretary"* (CEO from Russia).

Cohabitation usually emerges when the chair and CEO have conflicting views on how the business should develop or their respective roles, yet neither has the expert, ownership or prestige power to prevail. It also arises between celebrity chairs and strong-minded CEOs who are not ready to bend to the demands of the board's boss.

Mentoring occurs when a senior professional (the chair) interacts with a junior partner (the CEO). The main goal is for the former to provide the latter with the knowledge, experience and resources to perform the CEO's functions. Sometimes the mentoring relationship is formalized, as in the following case: *"We establish developmental objectives for the CEO and we have formal mentoring sessions with him once a quarter"* (chair from Russia). More often there is an informal understanding and agreement between the parties and mentoring may take different forms—from helping to draft a strategy presentation to introducing the CEO to important people. These are just a few examples of such an approach: *"The CEO develops strategy—I listen to him and challenge his assumptions"* (Netherlands); *"It is my job to guide the CEO to be good at receiving and processing the response from the board"* (Denmark).

The mentoring archetype develops when the chair is more experienced, has been a CEO before and has the time and inclination to help the incumbent CEO. The CEOs who enter this type of interaction usually have no stake in the company, have been recently appointed and have never been a CEO before. This type is more prevalent in countries with low power distance and a culture of apprenticeship, such as Denmark and especially the Netherlands.

Commanding (or "boss"). Under this model, a superior (chair) directly manages a subordinate (CEO). The former establishes targets and objectives, conducts formal and informal performance reviews, determines compensation, provides corrective and supportive feedback and sometimes reviews or approves major decisions to be made by the latter. Here are some examples of this type of interaction: *"The CEO prepares a 'Chair Report'—monthly update of his performance for me and then I review it with him"* (Netherlands); *"I made it clear to my CEO—I need to pre-approve all deals exceeding $50 million, all social media campaigns and all hiring for the top 200 positions"* (Turkey).

The chair becomes the boss of the CEO when there is significant power distance between the two. Most commonly the power is derived from the chair's position as a significant shareholder (or representative of such a shareholder), while the CEO has no stake in the company. In the course of our research we also came across a number of cases where the power distance came from the chair's high status as a current or former member of the government. Unsurprisingly, we found more cases of commanding relationships in countries with a culture of high power distance—notably, Russia and Turkey—but they exist in other European countries as well.

Advising. This is the least common type of chair-CEO relationship, yet there were several respondents from Denmark, Switzerland and Russia who reported operating as counsellors to all-powerful CEOs. The boards they chaired acted mostly as ceremonial bodies to legitimize the CEO's decisions. In this archetype the CEO shapes the relationship, while the chair assumes the role of junior partner. As one chair from Russia explained:

> *I come to see him (the CEO) every month; we speak one-to-one, very informally. I update him on the board's work, ask his opinion on important issues. He may ask my views on anything from Obama politics to the last remuneration committee meeting. Sometimes he asks for help in specific deals. I feel that he values my advice.*

This type of relationship arises when the CEO is a significant shareholder, almost always the founder of the company, while the chair has no stake and has often had previous professional relationships with the CEO as a consultant, advisor or employee.

None of the archetypes described above exists in its pure form. In reality, chairs combine elements of different modes of interaction with CEOs, yet it is important to distinguish a typology in order to help chairs strike the right balance for a specific company, board and CEO.

In our interviews with chairs, directors and CEOs, we sensed an emerging consensus about an effective model of chair-CEO relationships for the future. This is based on the notion that the chair is the leader of the board, not an individual player. The board serves as a collective "boss" of the CEO. The task of the chair is to make sure that the board creates a dynamic framework for management action, which includes setting goals, allocating resources and establishing rules and accountability. Creating and managing this framework is an important part of the joint work of the board, which a good chair initiates, orchestrates and encourages—but never monopolizes.

As a rule, in good times, boards of directors develop a tendency to be over-supportive of the management, which may lead to some unpleasant surprises. Conversely, in bad times, directors tend to become too critical.[20] Experienced chairs are aware of these biases and nudge their boards towards an optimal balance between support and challenge. A chair from the Netherlands put it this way:

---

[20] Haleblian, J. and Rajagopalan, N. (2006). A Cognitive Model of CEO Dismissal: Understanding the Influence of Board Perceptions, Attributions and Efficacy Beliefs. *Journal of Management Studies*, 43(5), pp. 1009–1026.

> *The board should support the incumbent management and the CEO unconditionally. If they lose your support, you should fire them. So you never challenge management—only their specific ideas, projects, and plans—but do so constantly. As a chair I make sure it happens in the board room and outside of it, but I am not the "chief challenger". I organize the process.*

Usually, the chair interacts with the CEO more often than the other board members. They may discuss board agendas and plans, review board materials, finalize a company press release, follow up on board decisions or meet regulators together. Good chairs, however, always remember that, in this interaction, they represent the board rather than themselves. They also keep other directors informed about new developments and insights—and involve them whenever they can be more effective than the chair alone.

Relationships with Shareholders

If a CEO's "boss" is the board of directors, the board's "boss" is the shareholders. The relationship with the people and institutions that have entrusted the board to govern the company on their behalf is a key concern for the leader of the board. Corporate governance guidelines suggest that chairs should conduct effective communication with all shareholders, while stock market regulations impose severe restrictions on how and when this communication can take place. Chairs of public companies strive for a balance between attention to performance and compliance. They want to be available and attentive, yet independent and non-partisan. Chairs of private companies have more freedom in structuring the relationship with shareholders. However, they have to deal not merely with financial investors but also with active owners (such as entrepreneurs, families, venture capitalists and private equity investors) who have personal stakes in, passion for and strong views about the business.[21] Although the type of ownership and shareholder profile have a strong impact on chair-shareholder relationships, other factors presented in Fig. 1.1 also shape these relationships. Our research allowed us to identify those with the strongest impact, as summarized in Fig. 1.3.

---

[21] McNulty, T., Pettigrew, A., Jobome, G. and Morris, C. (2009). The Role, Power and Influence of Company Chairs. *Journal of Management & Governance*, 15(1), pp. 91–121; Huse, M. (2007). *Boards, Governance and Value Creation*. Cambridge: Cambridge University Press.

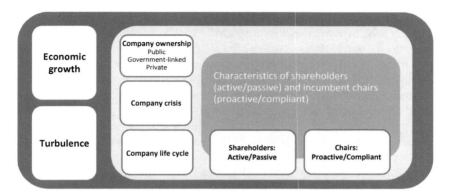

Fig. 1.3 Chair-shareholder relations: Strongest impact factors

We found that chairs take two attitudes towards relationships with shareholders.

Compliant chairs focus on what is prescribed by the existing regulations, strive to minimize the risks of non-compliance and do not show the initiative in interacting with shareholders. As one chair described her approach: "*I always write back to shareholders when they write back to me.*"

Proactive chairs venture beyond what is prescribed by the book, reach out to shareholders and often prioritize performance over compliance. One from our sample "*invites representatives of large and small shareholders to the board meetings to express their concerns*", while another gives shareholders a "*structured questionnaire*" about their expectations.

Depending on circumstance, the same person may operate in both "compliant" and "proactive" modes at different times.

Similarly, shareholders differ in their attitudes. "*Active shareholders*"[22] hold the company close to their heart because of the size of their holdings,

[22] Anderson, R.C. and Reeb, D.M. (2003). Founding-Family Ownership and Firm Performance: Evidence from the S&P 500. *Journal of Finance*, 3, pp. 1301–1328; Hillman, A. J. and Dalziel, T. (2003). Boards of Directors and Firm Performance: Integrating Agency and Resource Dependence.

Perspectives. *Academy of Management Review*, 28(3), pp. 383–396; Desender, K. (2009). The Relationship between the Ownership Structure and Board Effectiveness. *University of Illinois at Urbana-Champaign, College of Business Working Papers 09-0105*. Available from: https://ssrn.com/abstract=1440750 (Accessed 3 December 2018).

their emotional attachment to it or the organizational mission. They actively seek information, and may challenge the management, board and chair. Sometimes, they may even try to impose their own alternative ideas.

Usually private equity investors, business founders, venture capitalists, family shareholders, activist funds and governments operate in this way. "*Passive shareholders*" are content with what they are entitled to, based on corporate governance regulations and limit their engagement with the company, board and chair. Individual and institutional equity investors usually fall into this category, as do mutual and pension funds.

As we mentioned earlier, public and private companies present noticeably different contexts for chair-shareholder interactions. Companies with significant government participation or influence (we call them "government-linked" borrowing the term from Singapore) are a special case, as government representatives may consider the chair "their person" and try to impose some specific ideas on the board through its leader. More generally, when a company goes through a crisis, the intensity of chair-shareholder interaction increases, with both sides usually becoming more proactive—if not assertive. We noticed similar dynamics in start-ups and companies going through serious restructuring, while in mature, stable organizations these relationships tend to be less intense and more formal.

Two macro factors influence the nature of chair-shareholder relationships: turbulence and the general economic climate. When a new piece of corporate governance regulations comes out, a disruptive technology hits the market, terrorists stage an attack on the country's capital or the economy experiences a prolonged depression, the chair and shareholders tend to interact more, seeking collaboration and going beyond the prescribed frameworks. In stable and economically favourable macro environments, on the other hand, both parties tend to become either more assertive or less engaged, focusing on their own agendas or reducing the intensity of their interaction.

Our research revealed numerous practices that board chairs use to manage their relationships with shareholders. We will describe them in detail in Chaps. 2, 3, 4, 5, 6, 7, 8, and 9. In the meantime, we present below 11 archetypes of chair-shareholder relationships, which emerged from our conversations with chairs, shareholders, directors and CEOs. As for chair-executive relationships, none of our archetypes exists in its pure form. In practice, they overlap and interfere with each other, but they provide an effective lens through which to examine and understand the complexity of chair-shareholder relationships across European companies.

Exchanging information. This type of interaction is core to chair-shareholder relationships. As one chair put it, "*What you absolutely have to do is communicate (with shareholders). This is so important.*" Proactive and compliant chairs on one side and active and passive shareholders on the other in most cases willingly engage in a two-way exchange of information. However, this exchange takes different forms depending on other contextual factors presented in Fig. 1.3.

Compliance-driven informing. In the case of public companies with widely held shares, chairs with a compliant attitude ensure that shareholders receive the information they are entitled to. Some chairs limit their personal participation to talks and Q&A sessions at general assemblies and delegate the rest to investor or public relations departments.

Business-driven informing. As one chair from the UK explained, "*One of my top priorities is to make sure that shareholders understand what happens at the company, what the board is preoccupied with, what decisions it has made and what are the implications.*" This type of relationship is characteristic for proactive chairs leading boards at private and sometimes public companies, usually with reference shareholders, and in all of the countries we researched takes the forms of periodical written reports or memos to shareholders; personal formal and informal meetings; phone calls, e-mails and messages.

The two types of relationships described above do not assume any feedback from shareholders, putting them on the receiving side only. In the two types that follow, they are actively involved.

Seeking shareholders' expectations. Proactive chairs believe they need to understand shareholders' views on key issues for the company—and to pass this information on to the board. They not only listen attentively to shareholders but also help them to formulate their expectations. Usually this approach works with a limited number of key shareholders. Traditional practices—formal and informal meetings, shareholder conferences, breakfasts, lunches and dinners—are complemented with innovative approaches, such as invitations to speak to the full board or questionnaires.

One respondent presents shareholders with a set of questions representing key strategic dilemmas. He uses this so-called "*matrix of expectations*" as the basis of structured interviews with shareholders and the questions change depending on the context. When should in the next

1–50 years should we sell? Which do you prefer: to reinvest profits or to take dividends? What growth strategy should we pursue: organic or non-organic? What is more important: pride in ownership or rational professionalism? Some corporate governance pundits may consider this approach an invitation to shareholders to step into the shoes of directors and executives, but the Danish author of the model believes that it allows for the shareholders and the board to see eye to eye and greatly benefits the company: "*I am not promising them we will do what they want, I am promising that we will keep it in mind.*"

Engaging. This type of relationship goes beyond pure information exchange to exchanging and at times co-creating ideas with shareholders. As one chair from Switzerland advocating this approach said: "*Don't look at them (shareholders) as enemies, they are your owners and they are your partners.*" Engaging usually takes place between proactive chairs and active shareholders when the parties have a broad agreement about their respective roles and the boundaries between them. It often emerges in family businesses or start-ups and at times of strain or crisis.

Standard engaging practices include sharing board materials with shareholders and discussing them; seeking ideas on specific issues; preparing summaries of board meetings for shareholders; and inviting them for meals. Some chairs encourage continuous exchange through WhatsApp groups, and organize brainstorming sessions for all board members and shareholders. They may even hold strategic retreats for the shareholders only or invite them to visit the company and discuss their impressions. Some respondents reported asking shareholders for help in recruiting new board members and executives, and in interacting with regulators, vendors or customers.

Many chairs emphasized that engaging relationships require a significant time commitment and high level of flexibility.

As one put it: "*You just need to be available. They may have what they think is a brilliant idea and want to share it with you at the most inconvenient (for you) moment, but if you are not there they will share it with somebody else, and the whole governance system will be at risk.*" Another agreed: "*I think I spend 60 to 70 percent of my time working with shareholders. If you get it right, the rest is easy.*"

Equal-distancing. This is about avoiding the risk of giving preferential treatment to any shareholder—or even the perception of such treatment. It is about giving shareholders enough information, "*but not more than to other shareholders*", as one interviewee put it. Some chairs reported that they would not initiate consultation with a shareholder unless all others were party to the discussion, would not have a meeting with a shareholder unless similar meetings were due to take place with all other shareholders, or would copy all shareholders in answering an e-mail from one of them.

Although quite common in public companies, many compliance-conscious chairs of private companies follow the equal-distancing approach. As one experienced chair from Italy put it: "*When you have a limited number of shareholders you have to show that you treat them equally.*"

Bridging. Proactive chairs help shareholders to interact effectively among themselves, so that both the board and the company can benefit from the owners' alignment. As one private equity shareholder explained: "*Good chairs help us to manage relationships with other shareholders by listening to all sides and bringing objectivity.*" The research showed that this type of relationship mostly emerges at private companies with multiple stakeholders, where chairs use a variety of practices from organizing and facilitating regular formal or informal meetings and shuttling between shareholders to setting up WhatsApp or Telegram groups, hosting shareholder dinners and getting on the phone when required.

Resisting. This type of relationship emerges as a chair's reaction to shareholders' attempts to "cross the line" by becoming too involved with the board and the company. It also occurs when the chair and the shareholders disagree on the company's focus and strategy. One chair summarized this approach: "*The first thing I say to every shareholder is, 'I am the master in the boardroom. If you don't like it, fire the board and elect a new one.'*"

The chairs we interviewed reported on resisting: activist shareholders who wanted to change the company's strategy, its board composition or its management; active reference shareholders who tried to have the board adopt a specific resolution, invite themselves to board meetings or speak directly with senior executives; and family shareholders who sought to influence the board in decisions on CEO succession. They used such practices as: signing a non-aggression pact establishing clear limits to shareholders' involvement in exchange for constant information flow from the chair (Russia, UK); proactively setting the borders in oral conversations with shareholders (Denmark, Russia, Netherlands, UK); organizing separate regular meetings between shareholders and the chair—and sometimes other board members (Denmark, Russia, UK); threatening to resign (Denmark, Switzerland, UK); and rallying the board against intrusive shareholders (Denmark, Russia). The potential risk of shareholder intervention in the business of the board turned out to be very sensitive and important to many chairs we interviewed. As one of them stated: "*I focus on what is the best for the company and I am in charge of doing it. If shareholders hire me, they should let me do the job.*"

Accommodating. In some situations, chairs choose to yield to the shareholders rather than resist them. This type of relationship emerges in companies with government participation. It also occurs in cases of an all-powerful founder-shareholder interacting with a professional chair of the board, mostly in private companies and in countries with high power distance (such as Russia and Turkey). "Accommodating chairs" may put the interests and agenda of a specific shareholder above those of the company and the board. As one of them admitted: "*I always remember who nominated me as chair!*" They may proactively solicit shareholders' views on a specific item on the board's agenda—or indeed all of them—before the board meeting through informal consultation at lunch or dinner or formal written communication (Italy, Turkey, Russia).

When the government is a majority shareholder, a chair may become a conduit—rather than a partner—of government. One respondent commented: "*It is a highly political function. 70 percent of initiatives come from the government and only 30 percent are generated by the board.*"

Ignoring. Although most respondents emphasized the importance of relationships with shareholders, some ignored them in practice, preferring to spend their time on leading the board or interacting with the CEO. This happens mostly at large public companies with many small shareholders during relatively good times. The most common practice is to delegate this function to company officers, such as the investor relations director, public relations director, CFO or CEO (Italy, Russia, Switzerland, Turkey, UK).

Imposing. Proactive chairs use this assertive approach to deal with shareholders, when they have the power (which can come from the chair's relationship to ownership or owners, personal prestige or expertise), consider the issues to be important or have no time or willingness to use other strategies. Imposing can take the forms of a tough face-to-face conversation; a public attack on the opponent; a court case against a shareholder; or a networking activity (Italy, Denmark, Netherlands, Russia). One chair explained:

> *Government is an institution, but there is always a real man behind the institution. There are people who are responsible for the government stake in our*

company and I have good working relationships with them. Most of the time we find common ground. In rare cases when we don't agree, I speak to people in my network who are above them or can influence them.

Effective European board chairs use a variety of strategies and specific practices to manage their relationships with shareholders and their effectiveness is function of multiple contextual variables, yet there is one common thread in their approach: in these relationships, they represent the board of directors rather than themselves. This was emotionally summarized by an experienced chair from Denmark:

Who am I to deal with a significant shareholder on equal terms? A part-time board chair getting the equivalent of US$100,000 a year. Not serious. But when the whole board speaks to them, they listen. So I always remind shareholders that I am an interface between them and a board. I never speak my mind; it's the collective voice of the board of directors they are hearing.

SUMMARY

In all of the European countries we have studied, the board of directors is the highest decision-making body in an organization and the chair is its leader. The work of the chair takes place in a specific context, and macro, mezzo and micro contingencies have a noticeable impact on it. One of the major findings presented in this chapter and in this book is that cultural differences do not affect the work of board leaders as much as other variables, such as the ownership structure of a company, its financial health, board composition or the macroeconomic situation.

Chairs from all the countries we studied define their responsibilities in similar ways and strive to play three core roles: leading the board, representing the board in relationships with shareholders and managing relationships with the CEO/senior executives. They use similar high-level behaviour strategies to play all of these roles, such as the *engaging-enabling-encouraging* triad in leading the board or the 11 modes of interacting with shareholders. We also found that respondents from different countries have largely overlapping views on the personal attributes that make chairs effective and the mistakes that reduce their effectiveness (described in detail in Chap. 10).

Yet country specifics are important and worth exploring. They transpire not so much in *what* chairs do, but *how* they do it, creating an extremely rich variety of chair practices—what a psychologist might call "first-level iterative behaviours"—which board leaders use to get their jobs done. Discovering these practices and understanding the contexts in which they emerged was a very exciting journey for our research team. The findings of that journey—or rather, nine journeys through nine very different countries are presented in the next nine chapters. They constitute a very rich seam of data for practising and aspiring chairs and directors, shareholders, regulators, educators—indeed anybody who wants to understand what happens in and around the boardroom and to learn from the experiences of effective board leaders. We invite you to follow in our footsteps on this fascinating tour of Europe.

REFERENCES

Anderson, R.C. and Reeb, D.M. (2003). Founding-Family Ownership and Firm Performance: Evidence from the S&P 500. *Journal of Finance*, 58(3), pp. 1301–1328.

Barroso-Castro, C., Villegas-Periñan, M. and Dominguez, M. (2017). Board Members' Contribution to Strategy: The Mediating Role of Board Internal Processes. *European Research on Management and Business Economics*, 23 (2), pp. 82–89.

Bezemer, P., Peij, S., Maassen, G. and van Halder, H. (2010). The Changing Role of the Supervisory Board Chairman: the Case of the Netherlands (1997–2007). *Journal of Management & Governance*, 16(1), pp. 37–55.

Cadbury, A. (2002). *Corporate Governance and Chairmanship: A Personal View*. London: Oxford University Press.

Cawston, G. and Keane, A.H. (1968). *Early Chartered Companies: A.D. 1296–1858*. New York: B. Franklin, pp. 86–87.

Desender, K. (2009). The Relationship between the Ownership Structure and Board Effectiveness. *University of Illinois at Urbana-Champaign, College of Business Working Papers 09-0105*. Available from: https://ssrn.com/abstract=1440750 [Accessed 26 March 2018].

Garratt, B. (1999). Developing Effective Directors and Building Effective Boards. *Long Range Planning*, 32(1), pp. 28–35.

Gevurtz, F. (2004). The European Origins and the Spread of the Corporate Board of Directors. *Stetson Law Review*, 33, pp. 925–954.

Financial Reporting Council (2016). The UK Corporate Governance Code. Available from: https://www.frc.org.uk/getattachment/ca7e94c4-b9a9-49e2-a824-ad76a322873c/UK-Corporate-Governance-Code-April-2016.pdf [Accessed 3 December 2018].

Furr, R. and Furr, L. (2005). Is Your Chairman A Leader? *The Corporate Board*, 26(154), pp. 11–15.

Haleblian, J. and Rajagopalan, N. (2006). A Cognitive Model of CEO Dismissal: Understanding the Influence of Board Perceptions, Attributions and Efficacy Beliefs. *Journal of Management Studies*, 43(5), pp. 1009–1026.

Higgs, D. (2003). Review of the Role and Effectiveness of Non-Executive Directors. Available from: http://www.ecgi.org/codes/documents/higgs.pdf [Accessed 26 March 2018].

Hillman, A. J. and Dalziel, T. (2003). Boards of Directors and Firm Performance: Integrating Agency and Resource Dependence Perspectives. *Academy of Management Review*, 28(3), pp. 383–396.

Hillman, A., Nicholson, G. and Shropshire, C. (2008). Directors' Multiple Identities, Identification, and Board Monitoring and Resource Provision. *Organization Science*, 19(3), pp. 441–456.

Hossack, R. (2006). Together at the Top: the Critical Relationship between the Chairman and the CEO. *Ivey Business Journal*, Jan/Feb, pp. 1–4. Available from: https://iveybusinessjournal.com/publication/together-at-thetop-the-critical-relationship-between-the-chairman-and-the-ceo/ [Accessed 26 March 2018].

Huse, M. (2007). *Boards, Governance and Value Creation*. Cambridge: Cambridge University Press.

INFORM: Closing the Gap between Formal and Informal Institutions in the Balkans. Available from: http://www.formal-informal.eu [Accessed 3 December 2018].

Kakabadse, A., Kakabadse, N. and Barratt, R. (2006). Chairman and Chief Executive Officer (CEO): that Sacred and Secret Relationship. *Journal of Management Development*, 25(2), pp. 134–150.

Kakabadse, N., Knyght, R. and Kakabadse, A. (2013). High-Performing Chairmen: the Older the Better. In: A. Kakabadse and L. van den Berghe, ed., *How to Make Boards Work*. London: Palgrave, pp. 342–349.

Kakabadse, A. and Kakabadse, N. (2008). *Leading the Board: the Six Disciplines of World Class Chairman*. London: Palgrave.

Krause, R. (2016). Being the CEO's Boss: An Examination of Board Chair Orientations. *Strategic Management Journal*, 38(3), pp. 697–713.

Lekvall, P. (ed.). 2014. *The Nordic Corporate Governance Model*. Stockholm: SNS Förlag.

Levrau, A., & Van den Berghe, L. (2013). Perspectives on the decision-making style of the board chair. *International Journal of Disclosure and Governance*, 10(2), pp. 105–121.

Lorsch, J. W. and Zelleke, A. (2005). The Chairman's Job Description. *Directors and Boards*, 30(1), pp. 28–32.

McNulty, T. and Pettigrew, A. (1999). Strategists on the Board. *Organization Studies*, 20(1), pp. 47–74.

McNulty, T., Pettigrew, A., Jobome, G. and Morris, C. (2011). The Role, Power and Influence of Company Chairs. *Journal of Management and Governance*, 15, pp. 91–121.

Parker, H. (1990). The Company Chairman—His Role and Responsibilities. *Long Range Planning*, 23 (4), pp. 35–43.

Pettigrew, A. and McNulty, T. (1995). Power and Influence In and Around Boardroom. *Human Relations*, 48, pp. 845–873.

Roberts, J. (2002). Building the Complementary Board. The Work of the PLC Chairman. *Long Range Planning*, 35(5), pp. 493–520.

Roberts, J. and Stiles, P. (1999). The Relationship between Chairmen and Chief Executives: Competitive or Complementary Roles? *Long Range Planning*, 32(1), pp. 36–48.

Shekshnia, S. and Zagieva, V. (2017). The Practices of Boards across the World. *INSEAD Knowledge*. Available from: https://knowledge.insead.edu/leadership-organisations/the-practices-of-boards-across-theworld-7056 [Accessed 26 March 2018].

Stewart, R. (1991). Chairman and Chief Executive: an Exploration of their Relationship. *Journal of Management Study*, 28(5), pp. 511–527.

The Committee on the Financial Aspects of Corporate Governance. (1992). *Report of the Committee on the Financial Aspects of Corporate Governance.* London: Gee and Co.

CHAPTER 2

The United Kingdom: Indirect Leadership

Stanislav Shekshnia

THE CHAIR'S WORK IN CONTEXT

The United Kingdom of Great Britain and Northern Ireland (UK) consists of England, Scotland, Wales and Northern Ireland, each with various degrees of autonomy. The UK has a constitutional monarchy, a parliamentary system of governance and a developed economy. In 2017, gross domestic product (GDP) was US$2.6 trillion[1] (ninth largest in the world at purchasing power parity) with per capita GDP of Int$43,268.[2] Of this total, value added in the service sector represents 79% of GDP, industry 14% and agriculture 6%.[3] The UK is ranked 14th in the world on the Human Development Index.[4]

---

[1] The World Bank (2018). World Development Indicators. GDP Ranking. Available from: https://datacatalog.worldbank.org/dataset/gdp-ranking [Accessed 3 December 2018].

[2] The World Bank (2018). World Development Indicators. GDP per capita 2017, in international dollars. Available from: https://data.worldbank.org/indicator/NY.GDP.PCAP.PP.CD?year_high_desc=true [Accessed 3 December 2018].

[3] World Bank (2018). Services, Value Added. Industry, Value Added. Agriculture, Value Added. Available from: https://data.worldbank.org/indicator/NV.IND.MANF.ZS [Accessed 10 May 2018].

[4] UNDP (2018). Human Development Indices and Indicators. 2018 Statistical Update. Available from: http://hdr.undp.org/en/2018-update [Accessed 28 September 2018].

S. Shekshnia (✉)
INSEAD, Fontainebleau, France

© The Author(s) 2019
S. Shekshnia, V. Zagieva (eds.), *Leading a Board*,
https://doi.org/10.1007/978-981-13-3197-8_2

29

Almost 6 million businesses in the UK employ some 26.7 million people.[5] Privately held companies employ 83% of the labour force.[6] There are approximately 10,000 listed companies, in which financial institutions, foreign investors and private stockholders are the main shareholders. The UK is one of the most active shareholder communities in the world with a 59% voting turnout.[7]

The UK also has one of the oldest systems of corporate governance in the world, largely based on "soft law" (governance guidelines) and "comply or explain" principles, as defined in the UK Governance Code, updated in 2016.[8] There is no mandatory structure for boards, but the single-tier model with both executive and non-executive directors predominates. As the highest governing body, the board makes key executive appointments and takes decisions about the remuneration of top managers, strategy, major capital investments, risk management and disclosure.

In practice, board engagement varies greatly, as reflected in the number of meetings held per year. Boards of larger companies have a standard set of committees for audit, nomination and remuneration. Committees for strategy, environment, ethics, and health and safety may also exist. The average number of board committees for a listed UK company is 3.8[9] (EU average 3.4).[10]

UK boards are not large with 10.2 members on average for Financial Times Stock Exchange (FTSE) 150 companies (EU average 12.3). Large

[5] Rhodes, C. (2017). Business Statistics. *Briefing Paper, Number 06152.* Available from: https://researchbriefings.files.parliament.uk/documents/SN06152/SN06152.pdf [Accessed 10 May 2018].

[6] Office for National Statistics (2018). Public and Private Sector Employment. Available from: https://www.ons.gov.uk/employmentandlabourmarket/peopleinwork/employmentandemployeetypes/datasets/publicandprivatesectoremploymentemp02 [Accessed 10 May 2018].

[7] Van der Elst, C. F. (2011). Revisiting Shareholder Activism at AGMs: Voting Determinants of Large and Small Shareholders. *European Corporate Governance Institute (ECGI), Finance Working Paper,* 311.

[8] Financial Reporting Council (2016). The UK Corporate Governance Code. Available from: https://www.frc.org.uk/getattachment/ca7e94c4-b9a9-49e2-a824-ad76a322873c/UK-Corporate-Governance-Code-April-2016.pdf [Accessed 3 December 2018].

[9] Spencer Stuart (2017). UK Board Index 2017. Available from: https://www.spencerstuart.com/research-and-insight/uk-board-index-2017 [Accessed 10 May 2018].

[10] Heidrick & Struggles (2014). Towards Dynamic Governance 2014: European Corporate Governance Report. Available from: http://www.heidrick.com/Knowledge-Center/Publication/European-Corporate-Governance-Report-2014-Towards-Dynamic-Governance [Accessed 10 May 2018].

boards—more than 15 members—are virtually non-existent. The proportion of independent directors has been steadily increasing over the last two decades and has now reached more than 60% for large public companies. Women represent 25% of board members and 4.7% of chairs.[11]

The UK Governance Code recommends the separation of the CEO and chair positions, as adopted by most publicly owned companies. UK companies can have executive, non-executive, affiliated or independent chairs, and the last of these categories is on the rise. The number of full-time chairs is decreasing, making them a small minority.[12]

The Code provides detailed guidelines about the role, duties and responsibilities of the chair. As the leader of a collective body (board of directors), the chair is responsible for the following:

- Creating the conditions for the board's and individual directors' effectiveness
- Demonstrating the highest standards of integrity and probity, setting clear expectations concerning the company's culture, values and behaviour, and establishing the style and tone of board discussions
- Developing productive working relationships with the CEO and other executive directors
- Guiding the company secretary
- Communicating with external stakeholders, including shareholders. Conducting periodical board evaluations.

Existing Research

No other country from our sample can compete with the UK in terms of the number of academic articles devoted to the chair of the board. Thanks to these publications, we know a great deal about British chairs' demographics, backgrounds, roles and competencies. This knowledge contributed significantly to the design of our study. In the following sections, we present a short overview of the most relevant literature.

Earlier research in the UK focused on the chair's demographic, background, relation to the company and influence within it. Scholars examined such variables as chairs' titles, professional backgrounds, relationships

---

[11] Spencer Stuart (2017). UK Board Index 2017. Available from: https://www.spencerstuart.com/research-and-insight/uk-board-index-2017 [Accessed 10 May 2018].
[12] Ibid.

to ownership, prior ties with their companies and time spent performing the role, among other factors. Empirical studies confirmed that a chair who also holds the CEO job is likely to have more power than the individual who is only a chair.[13] Similarly, full-time chairs were found to carry more weight in a company than their part-time colleagues.[14] Chairs promoted from within the organization are likely to have stronger influence than outsiders, by building on their superior company knowledge (expert power).[15] Older chairs tend to be considered by other directors as more effective than younger board leaders.[16]

Building on the work of other researchers, McNulty, Pettigrew, Jobome and Morris developed a nine-model chair typology which predicts the type of influence a chair will have based on her status (executive vs non-executive), background (insider vs outsider) and time commitment (full vs part time). Their empirical study of 160 chairs from FTSE 500 companies established that, in addition to overall greater power, executive chairs with a full-time commitment exert greater influence in strategy and resource allocation tasks, while non-executive board leaders with a part-time commitment have more power in monitoring and controlling tasks. For their studies, the authors developed a list of tasks chairs perform on the job, taking an important step towards identifying what chairs actually do.[17]

Another stream of research is dedicated to the roles and the functions of board chairs. Often referred to as "the first among equals," UK chairs take on a number of specific roles, some of them managerial and other of a supporting nature. Kakabadse, Kakabadse and Myers built on the previous research and designed a large-scale survey-based study for a sample of FTSE 350 companies. The authors identified such core functions as delineating chair and CEO roles, leading the board, managing directors' and

---

[13] Finkelstein, S. (1992). Power in Top Management Teams: Dimensions, Measurement, and Validation. *Academy of Management Journal*, 35(3), pp. 505–538; Udueni, H. (1999). Power Dimensions in the Board and Outside Director Independence: Evidence from Large Industrial UK Firms. *Corporate Governance: An International Review*, 7(1), pp. 62–72.

[14] Pettigrew, A. and McNulty, T. (1995). Power and Influence In and Around the Boardroom. *Human Relations*, 48(8), pp. 845–873.

[15] Finkelstein, S. (1992). Power in Top Management Teams: Dimensions, Measurement, and Validation. *Academy of Management Journal*, 35(3), pp. 505–538.

[16] Kakabadse, N., Knyght, R. and Kakabadse, A. (2013). High-Performing Chairmen: the Older the Better. In: A. Kakabadse and L. van den Berghe, ed., *How to Make Boards Work*. London: Palgrave, pp. 342–349.

[17] McNulty, T., Pettigrew, A., Jobome, G. and Morris, C. (2011). The Role, Power and Influence of Company Chairs. *Journal of Management and Governance*, 15, pp. 91–121.

executives' succession and contributing to strategic decision-making.[18] Executive chairs are active both inside and outside the boardroom. They set their boards' agendas, frequently communicate with the CEOs and senior executives and interact with institutional shareholders. Non-executives are less active in external relations and let CEOs have a bigger say in setting boards' agendas.[19] Some researchers emphasize the uniqueness of each chair's role and the need for each board leader to find individual ways of dealing with specific challenges.[20]

Chair-CEO relations have been the subject of a number of studies. The main recurring theme is the need to define the responsibilities of these two key people in the company and then stick to them.[21] On the basis of interviews with chairs and CEOs in the National Health Service organizations, Stewart suggested that the two roles should form a dynamic partnership and complement each other. This idea resonated with other scholars and was supported in later publications.[22] Yet other researchers emphasize the chair's role as a counterweight to the influence of the CEO and suggest that the chair should lead the process of appointing, evaluating and, if necessary, dismissing the CEO.[23]

---

[18] Kakabadse, A., Kakabadse, N. and Myers, A. (2008). *Chairman and the Board: A Study of the Role, Contribution and Performance of UK Board Directors.* Cranfield School of Management and Manchester Square Partners.

[19] McNulty, T., Pettigrew, A., Jobome, G. and Morris, C. (2011). The Role, Power and Influence of Company Chairs. *Journal of Management and Governance*, 15, pp. 91–121.

[20] Kakabadse, N., Knyght, R. and Kakabadse, A. (2013). High-Performing Chairmen: the Older the Better. In: A. Kakabadse and L. van den Berghe, ed., *How to Make Boards Work.* London: Palgrave, pp. 342–349.

[21] Kakabadse, A. P., Kakabadse, N. K., and Knyght, R. (2010). The Chemistry Factor in the Chairman/CEO Relationship. *European Management Journal*, 28(4), pp. 285–296.

[22] Stewart, R. (1991). Chairmen and Chief Executives: An Exploration of their Relationship. *Journal of Management Studies*, 28(5), pp. 511–528; Kakabadse, N., Knyght, R. and Kakabadse, A. (2013). High-Performing Chairmen: the Older the Better. In: A. Kakabadse and L. van den Berghe, ed., *How to Make Boards Work.* London: Palgrave, pp. 342–349.

[23] Roberts, J. (2002). Building the Complementary Board. The Work of the PLC Chairman. *Long Range Planning*, 35(5), pp. 493–520; Hossack, R. (2006). Together at the Top: the Critical Relationship between the Chairman and the CEO. *Ivey Business Journal*, Jan/Feb, pp. 1–4. Available from: https://iveybusinessjournal.com/publication/together-at-the-top-the-critical-relationship-between-the-chairman-and-the-ceo/ [Accessed 26 March 2018]; Kakabadse, A., Ward, K., Korac-Kakabadse, N., and Bowman, C. (2001). Role and Contribution of Non-Executive Directors. *Corporate Governance: The International Journal of Business in Society*, 1(1), pp. 4–8.

A few studies have focused on the personal attributes and professional competencies associated with effective board chairing. On the basis of interviews with chairs, CEOs and independent directors from FTSE 100 companies, Kakabadse, Ward, Kakabadse and Bowman identified such qualities as maturity, relational skills, meeting skills, political and social competence, and coaching capabilities.[24] Roberts interviewed 35 chairs, CEOs and non-executive directors and found that lack of ambition for executive power, complementarity to the CEO and ability to preside over meetings and create trust among directors are critical for effective chairing of a board.[25] In the above-mentioned study of directors, Kakabadse et al. identified wisdom, sensitivity and resilience as important chair qualities.[26]

We could not find a study devoted specifically to describing and analysing the practices of chairs, as understood in this book. However, some scholars provide interesting insights into the subject while focusing their attention on other research questions. Pettigrew and McNulty identified the chair's attention to what happens outside the boardroom and the ability to conduct an informal dialogue with other directors and executives as vital practices for ensuring effective board process.[27] Lee-Davies, Kakabadse and Kakabadse wrote about "deliberative practice", which implies asking good questions, and gathering and sharing useful information to support decision-making, without taking and defending a position, as a foundation for effective chairing of the board.[28]

UK CULTURE MAP

UK culture is described as relatively "low context", medium on the "dimensions" of deciding and disagreeing, medium-low on trusting and scheduling, and high on applications-first (as opposed to principles-first)

---

[24] Kakabadse, A. P., Kakabadse, N. K., and Knyght, R. (2010). The Chemistry Factor in the Chairman/CEO Relationship. *European Management Journal*, 28(4), pp. 285–296.

[25] Roberts, J. (2002). Building the Complementary Board. The Work of the PLC Chairman. *Long Range Planning*, 35(5), pp. 493–520.

[26] Kakabadse, A., Kakabadse, N. and Myers, A. (2008). *Chairman and the Board: A Study of the Role, Contribution and Performance of UK Board Directors*. Cranfield School of Management and Manchester Square Partners.

[27] Pettigrew, A. and McNulty, T. (1995). Power and Influence In and Around the Boardroom. *Human Relations*, 48(8), pp. 845–873.

[28] Lee-Davies, L., Kakabadse, N. K., and Kakabadse, A. (2007). Shared Leadership: Leading through Polylogue. *Business Strategy Series*, 8(4), pp. 246–253.

reasoning (see Appendix A for a full explanation). On the basis of this assessment, we hypothesize that UK chairs provide the board with low-profile but firm leadership and tend to focus on effectiveness. They communicate in a clear and concise manner, but not without metaphors and humour. They demonstrate discipline and demand it from other people, but they prefer to deal with disciplinary problems behind closed doors rather than in the boardroom. British chairs respect deadlines and other commitments, but they are pragmatic about prolonging a board meeting or giving a director extra time to speak. They work on building consensus, but they can put gentle pressure on dissident directors. They are very respectful in their interactions with board members, executives and shareholders, but they have a high respect for the chair's role and defend its autonomy and authority. They do not like surprises and pay particular attention to avoiding them (Fig. 2.1).

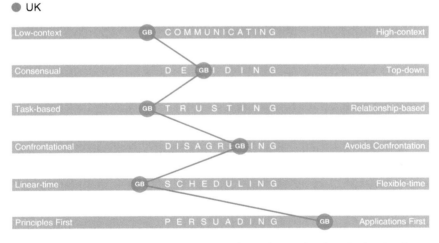

Fig. 2.1 UK Culture Map. Source: Based on the work of INSEAD Professor Erin Meyer, and her *The Culture Map* book (Meyer, E. (2014). *The Culture Map: Breaking Through the Invisible Boundaries of Global Business*. New York: PublicAffairs)

DATA

Two INSEAD-sponsored studies—the INSEAD Global Chair Survey 2015[29] and the INSEAD Global Chairs Research Project 2016[30]—primarily provide the data for this chapter. Within the framework of the former, we received 36 questionnaires from the UK chairs. The following profile emerged:

- Aged just under 60
- Educated to Master's level (only one PhD)
- Chairs two boards
- Sits on another two or three boards as an independent director
- Very experienced as a board member
- Has worked as a CEO or senior business executive (or more rarely as an academic or civil servant)
- Receives around US$78,000 a year per chair position

For the Global Chairs Research Project, we conducted semi-structured interviews with eight experienced chairs—three women and five men, aged from 54 to 72—who at the time of the encounters chaired a total of 15 boards of directors, including 7 boards of publicly listed corporations, 7 privately held companies, 2 charities and a government agency. None of them held a significant stake in the companies they chaired or was engaged in any private business or full-time employment. The business boards they chaired consisted of 5–11 directors, meeting between 5 and 12 times per year. Board composition varied in terms of the gender, age and professional backgrounds of members, but all included executive, non-executive, independent and affiliated directors. All boards had nomination, remuneration and audit committees (sometimes audit and risk management or audit and control). Some boards had committees for strategy, ethics and health/environment/safety.

---

[29] Shekshnia, S. and Zagieva, V. (2016). Chair Survey 2015. Available from: https://www.insead.edu/sites/default/files/assets/dept/centres/icgc/docs/chair-survey-2015.pdf [Accessed 3 December 2018].

[30] Shekshnia, S. and Zagieva, V. (2017). Board Chairs' Practices across Countries – Commonalities, Differences and Future Trends. Available from: https://www.insead.edu/sites/default/files/assets/dept/centres/icgc/docs/board-chairs-practices-across-countries.pdf [Accessed 3 December March 2018].

The people we interviewed for the more qualitative research project are somewhat more senior and more experienced, as both directors and chairs, than the survey participants. In general, they come from a variety of industries and companies, and are well paid. They have an executive background and later became full-time board chairs and directors—a path that seems to be almost universal in the UK. Although most are independent and non-executive, they spend a lot of time at their companies—between four and ten days per month.

In addition to the chairs, we interviewed three professional CEOs, three experienced independent directors and three representatives of shareholders to form a 360-degree picture of the chair's work (we refer to them collectively as "observers"). The CEOs (one woman and two men) had 32 years of combined chief executive experience at two private and two publicly listed companies and worked with eight chairs. The directors (one woman and two men) had, over the course of their careers, been members of 25 boards of directors, at both private and public companies and had worked in this capacity with 37 board chairs. The shareholders (three men) represented an investment fund, a venture capital company and a family holding, each of them having worked with dozens of board chairs.

UK CHAIRS: PRINCIPAL CHALLENGES AND PRACTICES

The INSEAD Global Chair Survey 2015[31] identified the following main challenges for the chairs of British companies in descending order of importance:

- Managing difficult board members (special cases)
- Relationships with controlling or large shareholders
- Relationships with minority shareholders
- Level of collaboration and team work among board members (board dynamics)

All the chairs we interviewed agreed that relationships with shareholders and collaboration among board members were top priorities. All

---

[31] Shekshnia, S. and Zagieva, V. (2016). Chair Survey 2015. Available from: https://www.insead.edu/sites/default/files/assets/dept/centres/icgc/docs/chair-survey-2015.pdf [Accessed 3 December 2018].

observers confirmed this view and added a further challenge: not getting buried under the ever-growing regulatory mountain and keeping the strategic focus of the board. The observer-directors emphasized the importance of containing "rogue" directors for effective functioning of the board. The observer-CEOs put chair-CEO relationships among the top three priorities. The following discussion explains both general strategies that UK chairs use to deal with these challenges and specific tools that they use to implement their strategies.

Relationships with Shareholders

In dealing with shareholders, UK chairs strive for a balance between pro-activity and equality. They want to be seen as available, listening and attentive but independent and non-partisan at the same time. They seek to put the interests of the company before those of individual shareholders, no matter how big or important the latter may be.

Several respondents emphasized that they do not distinguish between majority and minority shareholders. They are careful not to give preferential treatment to any shareholder group or even the impression of such treatment, especially in publicly listed companies. Some will not initiate consultation with a particular shareholder unless others are party to the discussion. In the words of one chair, they *"give them enough information, but not more than to other shareholders"*.

The chairs in our sample agreed that, for public companies, executive compensation is the number one topic in their interaction with shareholders. One formally consults with the top 25 largest shareholders on remuneration and personally supervises the preparation of the annual remuneration report. They are aware of activist shareholders but have limited interaction with them. Overall, respondents regard interaction with shareholders of public companies as a time-consuming, sensitive activity that does not always add value to the business but has to be undertaken to avoid conflict.

For chairs of private companies, the independence and equal treatment of all shareholders are important, although the smaller number of shareholders and less strict governance rules than in public companies allow for more intense interaction. One chair of a private company with three shareholders sends a board book and speaks to a representative of each of them a few days before the board meeting, walking her counterpart through the agenda. She does not look for *"input or guidelines, but makes sure the shareholders are aware of what is on the next agenda"*. Ideas from each shareholder are shared with her at meetings specially convened twice a year. Another chair writes to the largest shareholders to enquire whether they would like a private meeting; about half take up the invitation. One chair of a public company invites the five largest shareholders and independent directors for a working dinner once a year to discuss business within permitted boundaries.

For observer-shareholders, effective chairs serve as the most important interface between themselves and the company. Good chairs are attentive to the shareholders' concerns, understand them and effectively translate their ideas for the board and the management. They are proactive in sharing information and seeking shareholders' positions. One respondent from a private equity company shared that: "*Good chairs help us to manage relationships with other shareholders by listening to all sides and bringing objectivity.*"

Effective chairs at private companies write to shareholders, periodically (from one to three times a year) meet with them in person, speak on the phone and communicate via e-mail and messaging apps. They make sure that shareholders understand what is happening at the company, what the board is preoccupied with, what decisions it has made and the implications of all of these. In public companies, chairs ensure that shareholders are treated equally and fairly, organize shareholder assemblies in a transparent way and are available for communication.

As we originally hypothesized, good chairs in the UK maintain a constructive dialogue with shareholders for the benefit of the company, but not in the boardroom. They emphasize the importance of protecting the independence of the board and their authority over its workings. As one put it: "*We operate under the two meeting principles: one is for directors (the board), another for shareholders. If you happen to be both, learn to behave yourself.*" Another respondent shared his experience of threatening to put an unexpected proposal from a large shareholder to an immediate vote, so that it would be outvoted by independent directors. We came across examples of legally binding written agreements between large shareholders and companies, as well as informal agreements between shareholders and chairs.

Managing Difficult Board Members

According to the INSEAD Chair Global Survey 2015, "managing difficult board members" was the number one challenge for chairs in the UK. Director-observers confirmed this, although chair-respondents seemed to take the challenge in their stride. As one said, "*You have to work with what you've got—you are not a CEO selecting your team.*" Generally, "challenging directors" fall into two categories: first, those who do not listen but speak a lot, and second, those who say little or do not speak at all. A common strategy for dealing with directors with "verbal diarrhoea" is containment, and for the silent type engagement.

A number of tactics for containing vocal board members were cited: having a private word in their ear, offering to help (sometimes calling it "coaching"), suggesting professional support or making a formal performance evaluation. Perhaps the simplest step of all was direct but polite confrontation in the boardroom: "Bill, you are talking too much"; "Margaret, I will have to ask you to stay quiet for the next quarter of an hour"; "James, thank you. Now we need to hear from other board members." If nothing worked, our respondents resorted to recommending that the individual should not stand for re-election. There was general agreement that, if the chair was firm and consistent, most cases could be remedied.

Effective chairs pay a lot of attention to engaging otherwise silent members and ensuring that even those not inclined to speak at meetings contribute to the collective work of the board. One commented: "*My major task is to make silent directors speak—they are my major underutilized asset.*" Rather than calling on them in the boardroom, he solicits their opinions before the meeting and then presents their views to the board, acknowledging the source. Some ask for written opinions to ensure that everybody participates. Others adopt the format of asking every director to state his or her opinion. One observer-director recalled how a chair personally coached "timid board members" and their involvement visibly increased.

In summary, "special cases" are dealt with in a tactful but firm way. UK chairs do not hesitate to challenge directors since this contributes to the main focus identified by respondents: the board's effectiveness.

Board Dynamics

Helping the board to reach good collective decisions is a top priority. Aware of the multiple identities and commitments of directors, chairs are modest in their team-building ambitions: "*I don't think the board needs to become a team,*" or "*Perhaps it is a very special team.*" Observers tend to support this approach. One experienced independent director said: "*The good chairs in my life were quite careful not to make attempts to convert a board into their 'executive team': they respected the autonomy and indepen-dence of directors."*

However, good chairs deploy specific strategies to make this diverse group of people, which meets only a few times a year, work productively. These fall into pre-meeting, in-meeting and post-meeting categories, as summarized in Table 2.1.

Table 2.1 UK chairs' strategies and practices

Stage	Strategies	Practices
Pre-meeting	Set expectations	Induction interview with a director
	Reach out to every director	Induction programme for a newcomer to the company
	Consult every director	Phone call before the board meeting
	Avoid surprises	Consulting about the agenda
	Provide necessary data	Pre-board dinner for non-executive directors
		Pre-board dinner for the whole board
		Pre-board dinner for non-executive directors and CEO
		Defining format of board materials
		Checking board materials before they are sent to directors
		Digital board book
		Encouraging directors to spend time at the company, including customer visits
		Convening board meetings in different company locations
		Deep dives
Leading the meeting	Get the right agenda	Consulting with CEO
	Focus on discussion, not presentation	Consulting with board members
	Create an atmosphere of trust	30 (presentations):70 (discussion) per cent rule
	Apply equal treatment	Starting a board meeting with a short in-camera session for non-executive directors
	Focus on taking a specific, actionable decision	Closing with an in-camera session for non-executive directors
	Facilitate	Framing a discussion question
	Exercise self-restraint	No voting
		Asking every director to state their position
		Writing proposed resolutions on a flip-chart
		Speaking last
		Not indicating one's personal position
		Conducting an "express evaluation" at the end of the meeting

(*continued*)

Table 2.1 (continued)

Stage	Strategies	Practices
Post-meeting	Involve the whole board in finding ways to improve	Conducting formal 360-degree board evaluation
	Learn from formal evaluations and informal feedback	Off-site meetings for the whole board
	Stay connected with every board member	Open-agenda one-to-one meetings
		Annual evaluation meetings with every director
		Personal call every month with every director
		Annual lunch with every director
		Skype meeting with every director

Pre-meeting

All respondents agreed that the pre-meeting stage is critically important, and invest time and energy in preparation, the ultimate goal being to ensure that they have motivated, well prepared directors in the boardroom. They therefore conduct induction interviews with new members, at which expectations are set. One observer-director recalled her experience:

> *When I joined my first board I had a two-hour conversation with the chair, who in a very concise manner explained: the mission and the rules of the board; the roles of the chair, committees and corporate secretary; how the relationship with the executives worked; what was expected of me in terms of time commitment, preparation, and participation, etc. It was like attending a business school course!*

The induction programmes also include meetings with executives, site visits, product introductions and so on. As one chair explained: "*We organize induction programmes for all new directors—they visit key units and functions, and spend time with the risk department.*"

Chairs reach out to directors before each board meeting to re-engage. Some consult with other members about the agenda. One said: "*I ring every director before approving next meeting's agenda to ask what they want to see on it.*" While members rarely come up with drastic alterations, such conversations help to concentrate their minds on the upcoming meeting. To observer-shareholders good chairs table agenda items that are essential for the company and its stakeholders, ensure the strategic focus of the meetings and do not let their boards discuss issues they have not prepared for.

Pre-board dinners are another way to engage directors, review the agenda and ensure that everybody is on the same page. Most chairs limit these to non-executive directors; others extend it to executives. One noted: "*A board dinner is a good way to make sure we have no ugly surprises in the boardroom next morning.*"

The quality of materials is critically important for effective board work. Respondents cited the need for clarity, limited volume and enough time to study the board book in advance. Some chairs set the format of board materials; others co-define it with the CEO. Some check the materials before they are sent to directors, but most trust the management to produce a quality board book: "*I don't check materials before they go to the board members—it's too controlling and interfering. The company secretary has the power to turn them down.*" A number of boards chaired by respondents have gone 100% digital (electronic communications rather than print).

To improve directors' knowledge of the company and its business, some chairs facilitate site visits and meetings with employees, customers and so on. The chair of a hospital board introduced a routine whereby "*every non-exec spends one day with patients.*" Another described how "*we conduct board meetings in different geographies and always visit operations and meet with customers.*"

Leading the Meeting

The success of a board meeting is a function of three variables: the right agenda, the preparedness and motivation of the participants—and the right process. Items on the agenda should be, in the words of one of the chairs, "*strategic*", "*ripe for a decision*", "*material*" and such that "*no else in the company could make a quality decision*" about them. Another chair insists that there should be no less than four and no more than six items on the agenda for one meeting. In most cases, the chairs we interviewed partner with the CEO to set the agenda. Others invite all directors to review the agenda and pitch their ideas.

Respondents believed the board should spend most of its time on discussions rather than listening to management or committee presentations. One imposes a 30:70 ratio—30% of time for presentations and questions, 70% for discussion and making decisions. Others use similar but less strict approaches.

For a discussion to be productive, it has to be candid and involve all board members. The chair's task is to create an appropriate atmosphere. When asked how they approached this task, our respondents spoke about "*trust, respect, and personal attention*". The most common strategies to achieve this were equal treatment for all, facilitation of discussions and self-restraint. As one chair explained:

> *I have two rules—every director has to have roughly the same amount of air-time, and we should reach consensus. Sometimes one board member is more knowledgeable than another on the subject matter and wants to have more time, but I say: "You are an expert—you should be able to make your point quicker." Usually people smile and accept it.*

Another affirmed: "*You build trust by demonstrating respect, and you show respect by valuing everybody's opinion and acknowledging everyone's contribution … I always thank every director who put forward an idea after the decision has been made, even if that particular idea was rejected.*" Another strategy was to ask each board member to state his or her personal position on the subject matter before concluding the discussion.

Restraining their own participation in the discussion is another tactic used by chairs to promote trust and engagement. As one put it: "*I try to take as little room as possible. My task is to help others to speak their minds.*" Another added: "*I always try to avoid indicating personal views and preferences. If I have to speak, I speak last.*"

The task of facilitating a discussion includes stating the facts; framing the question, providing every director with an opportunity to speak; summarizing; formulating a resolution; and making sure that every director understands and supports it. One respondent explained:

> *As a novice chair, I underestimated the degree to which people participating in the same discussion and listening to the same proposed decision may have different ideas about what it actually means. As a result we would have some unpleasant conversations. Later on I learned the lesson and now always take time to make sure everybody understands the proposed resolution the same way.*

Another chair writes the proposed resolution on a flip-chart and walks the board through it.

The independent directors interviewed for our project emphasized fairness in allocating time and organizing discussions as essential elements of effective board chairing. According to them, good chairs energize the board (without over-exciting it), focus directors on a task and facilitate interaction. They do so by opening board meetings with energetic constructive statements, formulating clear discussion questions, concentrating on the discussion process (rather than the potential decision), engaging silent directors and containing talkative ones. Effective chairs use body language to communicate with the board. As one of the respondents put it: "*Chair A animates the board, he does not say much, but the way he says it and what he does without saying a word makes directors motivated and concentrated.*"

Many chairs conduct some sort of evaluation at the end of each board meeting. This reinforces respect for each director, builds trust and helps the board to learn and improve. One respondent said: "*At the end of the meeting I ask every director to comment on how we did as a team and how I did as a chairperson.*" Another puts three questions to the non-executive directors at the end of the meeting: "*What worked well? What did not work? What should we do differently next time?*"—and implements their recommendations at the next session.

Post-meeting
Formal board evaluation is a well-established practice in the UK. Board assessments are conducted every 12–24 months, sometimes with the help of external consultants, sometimes via an anonymous survey of board members (and, in some cases, senior executives). One respondent explained: "*We do 360 digital evaluation every year and every three years we invite an independent consultant to conduct a thorough assessment with the help of semi-structured interviews with all directors and key managers.*" According to a 2016 Spencer Stuart study, 56% of FTSE 150 boards conducted an internal evaluation and 43% used external help, while three companies did not have board evaluations at all.[32]

Some chairs arrange off-site meetings to discuss how collective decision-making could be improved: "*Once every year, we go to an off-site dedicated to improving board dynamics. With the help of a facilitator we brainstorm how to improve and try out new approaches.*" Others combine gatherings like these with strategic discussions. Overall, loosely structured off-site

---

[32] Spencer Stuart (2017). UK Board Index 2017. Available from: https://www.spencer-stuart.com/research-and-insight/uk-board-index-2017 [Accessed 10 May 2018].

sessions are seen as an important tool to improve a board's cohesiveness and performance.

Working with the board as the whole is complemented by one-to-one interactions. One chair rings *"each director every month to keep them concentrated on the company."* Another invites every board member for lunch once a year. Yet another has a Skype conversation every six weeks. One commented: *"They [the directors] should feel that you are available, you care about them and their views, but you are not intrusive."* Observer-directors back this view. For them, effective chairs reach out to directors between meetings, share news from the company and consult about upcoming meetings. They also pay individual attention to each board member, providing advice and coaching if requested. Good chairs establish two-way communication with directors via phone, e-mail and messaging apps—and promptly reply to them.

Relationships with the CEO and Management

Maintaining a good relationship with the CEO is high on the chair's agenda. Interaction is usually more intense, complex and nuanced than "I run the board—you run the company," and goes beyond the supervisory or mentoring functions prescribed by the Code. Although our respondents asserted that *"CEO development is one of my annual objectives"* and *"I question and challenge the CEO both privately and in the board room,"* the notion of cooperation, partnership and support emerged as more important practices. A very experienced chair put it this way: *"I am helping him to deal with loneliness, almost acting like a shrink,"*—and they have an open-agenda meeting or a phone conversation every two weeks. Another considers herself *"a sounding board for the CEO"*. In this particular case, they meet every two weeks and talk about both current business issues and the personal challenges of the CEO, who defines the content of their conversations. One respondent, who holds multiple chairs and has solid experience in executive development, lets the respective CEOs define the format of their interactions: *"At the global food company we always have a one-to-one meeting a couple of days before the board meeting, he sends me a lot of SMS and I answer. At another company, we have regular Skype meetings. At the third organization, we exchange e-mails almost daily."*

One respondent described how he negotiated a *"non-aggression pact"* with the CEO: *"You never bump a board with an important decision without sufficient time to analyze it—I make sure they know about all important con-cerns before the board meeting, rather than at the meeting."*

There was consensus among respondents that developing strategy is the CEO's business, which the board should "endorse" (unless there is a crisis, in which case it should take over temporarily as a collective chief executive). The chair's role is to help by listening, asking questions, challenging assumptions, connecting the CEO with experts and sharing personal experiences of being a CEO. Some respondents performed other services at the CEO's request such as meeting with customers, regulators, suppliers and the media. In general, however, respondents believed that chairs should not interact with third parties except shareholders. The only time they should intervene is in a crisis.

For observer-CEOs, effective chairs are first and foremost available yet non-intrusive. One CEO recalled with horror her experience of working with a chair who would send her 400 e-mails a day! Another chair she worked with was the opposite—no e-mails, rare and minimal interaction, but always negative feedback. A third chair, whom she considered to be effective, took time to listen, asked a lot of questions, said comparatively little, provided comprehensive feedback once a year and offered specific advice after important events. Observer-CEOs agree that effective chairs play a number of important roles vis-à-vis the chief executive, namely partner, mentor, adviser and occasionally provider of services or resources. In their view, good chairs partner with CEOs in defining the board's agenda, in managing communication with shareholders and in planning and preparing CEO succession. The former serve as mentors to the latter helping them run the company and/or develop specific skills.

In contrast to the chairs in our sample, the CEOs believe that industry knowledge is essential for good chairs, who must advise their chief executives on such issues as business strategy, regulatory issues, senior appointments and capital investments. They also help CEOs to fulfil their duties by occasionally speaking on behalf of the company to external stakeholders and the media, engaging with regulators and meeting with key customers and suppliers. Some observer-CEOs also mentioned that their chairs introduced them to important people in business and government, thus sharing their social networks with the chief executive.

Observer-shareholders emphasized the critical importance of a healthy relationship between the chair and the CEO, with some adding the CFO into the equation. For them, effective chairs use a variety of practices: they know the company's business inside out (by maintaining intense communication with CEO, CFO and internal and external auditors); they attract the chief executive's attention to potential problems and opportunities; they provide feedback on a regular basis; and they mentor the CEO or have another board member play this role. One private equity investor shared his perspective:

> *In the companies we invest in we have very effective chairs. They sit down with their CEOs every month for an hour or two. This conversation always includes feedback to the CEO, business updates, and discussion of upcoming events. They also translate our expectations to the CEO. And they disrupt the CEO and management team by asking difficult questions.*

We found a noticeable difference between institutional shareholders, on the one hand, and private equity investors on the other hand, with regard to the chair's role in CEO evaluation and succession. The former believe it is responsibility of the board, while the latter consider it the business of the chair.

OTHER CHALLENGES AND PRACTICES

In the UK, unlike other countries, **informational asymmetry with the CEO and management** is not seen as a major challenge to the work of the chair. Most are philosophical about it. In the words of one: "*You should acknowledge it and live with it. You will never know as much as the CEO does, but you have to trust him/her. If trust is not there, you should change him/her.*" Some chairs resort to asking the CEO to write monthly one-pagers, holding meetings with the chief executive's direct reports, having lunches with high potentials and convening company conferences to improve their feel for what is going on in the organization. One chair insists that "*other executives, at least the CFO, should be on the board*". Another describes the chair-CEO-CFO triangle as a "*critical factor for the business's success*".

Respondents acknowledged that multiple identities and a **lack of commitment from directors** can become a real issue if not properly managed: "*This is a huge challenge. No matter how much you say upfront, people will fail you.*" To deal with it, they make their expectations clear at the outset. One respondent told us: "*I say at the recruitment stage—'You need to commit 40 days a year to this board, are you ready?'*" Another went further: "*I set a rule at the induction interview: three missed meetings and you're out.*"

Enforcing the rules is critical, although it may be enough to remind the board of them from time to time. Some respondents are more candid in confronting directors who come unprepared or unfocused: "*I say, 'It was obvious you did not read the materials. Is something special going on or did you lose interest?' or 'I need your voice in the boardroom!'*" Such conversations take place behind closed doors rather than in the boardroom.

On the enabling side, respondents emphasized the importance of: thorough and long-term planning ("*Planning is critical -we set all board and committee meetings dates for two years, and I do everything to stick to them*"); the quality of materials ("*People prepare when materials are crisp, concise and have good visuals*"); and availability of resources ("*I make sure directors when necessary have access to company and external experts*"). Setting an example to other board members is paramount: "*Although I try not to reveal my position, I always make sure directors see that I have done my homework.*"

Chair Succession

The corporate governance guidelines say little about the role of the incumbent in the process of identifying and preparing a successor. Some academic scholars advocate active participation of the existing chair in planning and preparing for his or her succession.[33] Attitudes among respondents differed remarkably—from "*I have been thinking about it from the day I became a chair*" to "*I should not mess with it; a senior independent director will organize the process when the time comes.*" One fascinating story of succession deserves to be reproduced here in full:

> When I had to go through that for the first time I looked at the Code and found nothing there. I spoke to other chairs and executive search consultants. There was no clear formula so I invented my own. First, I wrote a memo to all directors indicating my intention to step down and asking if they were interested in the position. Two said "yes". In the memo I made it clear I should have no say in choosing my successor, but I would organize the process. I put together a committee of two independent directors (those who did not want to be considered) and the CEO to oversee the process. They developed a profile (and ran it by me) and hired an executive search firm. Together with the headhunters they assessed three external and two internal candidates, and picked one from within. We sat down with him few times before I left and it worked very well.

[33] Wertheimer, M. (2008). *The Board Chair Handbook*. Washington, DC: BoardSource.

Observer-shareholders expressed strong views on the subject of chair succession. One private equity investor evaluates all the chairs of the companies his business has invested in and proactively helps to choose a candidate for succession. He is also constantly scouting for potential chairs. Similarly, a representative of a family business explained that family "owns" chair's succession in its companies and only involves the incumbents when necessary.

"Regulatory Mountains" and Strategic Focus

A number of directors and CEOs (although none of the chairs we interviewed) pointed to a final challenge and described some practices for dealing with it. As one of the observers-CEOs put it:

> *Corporate governance regulation is constantly evolving and has become increasingly complex and detailed. There is a real risk of boards becoming box-ticking machines. Good chairs see this risk and find the right balance between what is prescribed and what is important for the company.*

Effective chairs manage this challenge by familiarizing themselves with the relevant laws and Code requirements. They actively collaborate with the corporate secretary, delegate what can be delegated, deal with technical matters in an efficient manner and systematically put on the board's agenda such items as: macro and industry dynamics; company strategy; organizational reputation; risk management; and leadership talent development and succession.

SUMMARY: PROFILE OF THE CHAIR IN THE UK

In the UK, chairs have two circles of interaction, both fairly small. The inner circle consists of a dozen or so board members, including the CEO, CFO and sometimes one or two other executives, and the company secretary. The outer circle includes large shareholders, company managers, and in some cases important customers or vendors, representatives of regulators, the media and professional associations. The chair interacts with the members of the inner circle relatively frequently, meeting face to face every one to two months and remaining in regular communication in between. Meetings with the members of the outer circle happen a few times a year.

An unexpected finding of this research was that one of the most popular ways in which UK chairs accomplish their business is… to share a **good meal**! They eat out with board members, executives, shareholders and other stakeholders, at business breakfasts, tête-à-tête lunches, afternoon tea or group dinners. This may have something to do with London's recently acquired reputation as a global culinary destination, but we believe that it reflects the importance of personal relationships for the job of the chair and the British tradition of fostering them through a shared meal.

In the UK context, effective chairs are important figures, but they stay out of the public eye. The chair is responsible for and represents the board, while the CEO is responsible for and is the public face of the company. Chairs are accomplished professionals with strong views, but they lead without taking up much space and avoid the limelight. They lead board members and executives by: engaging them in a collective effort; creating an environment for effective collaboration; and encouraging productive behaviour, by providing feedback and opportunities for collective and individual learning and development. They do not give orders or issue directives. Instead, they steer or nudge followers by setting agendas, framing discussion items, soliciting opinions and seeking and providing feedback. They set clear expectations and establish rules, but the latter serve as guidelines rather than laws set in stone. Chairs provide exemplary leadership by consistently displaying the attitudes and behaviour they expect others to adopt. **"Indirect"** is probably the most accurate term to describe their leadership style.

Yet when required—in times of crisis—they step forwards, assume responsibility and demonstrate hands-on leadership. As one observer-director recalled: "*When a competitor launched an unexpected hostile take-over bid, the chair of our board moved into the company offices for three weeks and worked with the CEO and other directors day and night to defend the company. His dedication energized everybody else and became one of the key success factors.*" According to our respondents, understanding that such situations may occur and being mentally ready to take an active role is integral to the effective British chair's mindset. While not seeking the limelight, they are passionate about the companies they chair and ready to go the extra mile to serve them.

This chapter describes effective board leaders, but our research also demonstrates that there are many chairs of British companies who do not fall into this category. They lead dysfunctional boards that provide management with poor oversight and guidance or have strained relationships with shareholders and other stakeholders. We have identified four factors that reduce the effectiveness of these board leaders, who in most cases have similar personal and professional backgrounds to those of high-performing chairs.

The first factor is time devoted to the role. According to the observers, chairs who spend fewer than 30 full days a year doing their job during "normal times" or who cannot fully dedicate themselves to it during times of crisis just cannot get it right. Time commitment is one of the reasons why celebrity chairs (defined as people chairing more than three boards) are becoming extinct in the UK. The second factor is personal ego and the inability to manage it. As one director explained:

> *Unfortunately, I was a member of several boards chaired by larger-than-life characters. These leaders turned board meetings into a one-man vanity fair, alienated directors and undermined collective decision making. Some of them were very bright, but they presided over weak boards that were unable to collaborate effectively.*

The third factor is the chair's mental model about the board, its role and modus operandi. Our observers had participated in "managing" boards that dived deep into operational issues, "ceremonial" boards that were content to rubber-stamp management decisions, "confrontational" boards that were constantly undermining executives and other dysfunctional models, most of which stemmed from their chair's misguided ideas about what a good board looks like.

The last—but far from least—reason for inadequate board performance revealed by our research is the chair's lack of the skills and competencies required to use the productive practices that we have described throughout this chapter.

Corporate governance—where rapid change is not always welcome, and tradition plays an important role—will continue to evolve in the UK. Looking ten years ahead, we expect to see the following trends with regard to board chairs:

- They will concentrate even more on the board and stay out of the limelight.
- They will put in more hours and have fewer directorships, although there will be very few executive or full-time chairs.

- The relationship with the CEO will remain a top priority. It will be more intense, and evolve towards partnership, mutual mentoring and collaborative work.
- UK boards will appoint more foreigners to the chair, but the majority will remain UK citizens.
- Board leaders will become somewhat younger.
- Around 20% of chairs will be filled by women.
- Most chairs will continue to come up through the CEO school, but more of them will have backgrounds in consulting, academia and technology.
- They will have strong personalities, highly developed social skills, systemic thinking, a global mindset, advanced listening skills and strong ambitions, but enough humility to channel these into the collective work of the board.
- They will lead indirectly: engaging, enabling and encouraging directors through nudging, creating an environment of mutual respect and trust, and "walking the talk".
- Boards will take chair succession more seriously. The UK code will formulate comprehensive guidelines, and incumbents will have more ownership of the process.
- Technology will slowly but steadily conquer the boardroom. In the next decade, all UK boards will go digital, and many board meetings will become virtual.
- Much informal one-to-one communication will move online. By 2027, technology will become what sharing a good meal is today—a stable platform for leadership.

REFERENCES

Financial Reporting Council (2017). Developments in Corporate Governance and Stewardship 2016. Available from: https://www.frc.org.uk/getattachment/ca1d9909-7e32-4894-b2a7-b971b4406130/Developments-in-Corporate-Governance-and-Stewardship-2016.pdf [Accessed 10 May 2018].

Financial Reporting Council (2011). Guidance on Board Effectiveness. Available from: https://www.frc.org.uk/getattachment/11f9659a-686e-48f0-bd83-36adab5fe930/Guidance-on-board-effectiveness-2011.pdf [Accessed 10 May 2018].

Financial Reporting Council (2016). The UK Corporate Governance Code. Available from: https://www.frc.org.uk/getattachment/ca7e94c4-b9a9-49e2-a824-ad76a322873c/UK-Corporate-Governance-Code-April-2016.pdf [Accessed 3 December 2018].

Finkelstein, S. (1992). Power in Top Management Teams: Dimensions, Measurement, and Validation. *Academy of Management Journal*, 35(3), pp. 505–538.

Gov.uk (2013). Number of private sector businesses surpasses last year's record high. Available from: https://www.gov.uk/government/news/number-of-private-sector-businesses-surpasses-last-years-record-high [Accessed 10 May 2018].

Heidrick & Struggles (2014). Towards Dynamic Governance 2014: European Corporate Governance Report. Available from: http://www.heidrick.com/Knowledge-Center/Publication/European-Corporate-Governance-Report-2014-Towards-Dynamic-Governance [Accessed 10 May 2018].

Hossack, R. (2006). Together at the Top: the Critical Relationship between the Chairman and the CEO. *Ivey Business Journal*, Jan/Feb, pp. 1–4. Available from: https://iveybusinessjournal.com/publication/together-at-the-top-the-critical-relationship-between-the-chairman-and-the-ceo/ [Accessed 26 March 2018].

Kakabadse, A. P., Kakabadse, N. K., and Knyght, R. (2010). The Chemistry Factor in the Chairman/CEO Relationship. *European Management Journal*, 28(4), pp. 285–296.

Kakabadse, A., Kakabadse, N. and Myers, A. (2008). *Chairman and the Board: A Study of the Role, Contribution and Performance of UK Board Directors*. Cranfield School of Management and Manchester Square Partners.

Kakabadse, A., Ward, K., Korac-Kakabadse, N., and Bowman, C. (2001). Role and Contribution of Non-Executive Directors. *Corporate Governance: The International Journal of Business in Society*, 1(1), pp. 4–8.

Kakabadse, N., Knyght, R. and Kakabadse, A. (2013). High-Performing Chairmen: the Older the Better. In: A. Kakabadse and L. van den Berghe, ed., *How to Make Boards Work*. London: Palgrave, pp. 342–349.

Lee-Davies, L., Kakabadse, N. K., and Kakabadse, A. (2007). Shared Leadership: Leading through Polylogue. *Business Strategy Series*, 8(4), pp. 246–253.

Meyer, E. (2014). *The Culture Map: Breaking Through the Invisible Boundaries of Global Business*. New York: PublicAffairs.

McNulty, T., Pettigrew, A., Jobome, G. and Morris, C. (2011). The Role, Power and Influence of Company Chairs. *Journal of Management and Governance*, 15, pp. 91–121.

Office for National Statistics (2018). Public and Private Sector Employment. Available from: https://www.ons.gov.uk/employmentandlabourmarket/peopleinwork/employmentandemployeetypes/datasets/publicandprivatesectoremploymentemp02 [Accessed 10 May 2018].

Pettigrew, A. and McNulty, T. (1995). Power and Influence in and Around the Boardroom. *Human Relations*, 48(8), pp. 845–873.

Rhodes, C. (2017). Business Statistics. Briefing Paper, Number 06152. Available from: https://researchbriefings.files.parliament.uk/documents/SN06152/SN06152.pdf [Accessed 10 May 2018].

Roberts, J. (2002). Building the Complementary Board. The Work of the PLC Chairman. *Long Range Planning*, 35(5), pp. 493–520.

Shekshnia, S. and Zagieva, V. (2017). Board Chairs' Practices across Countries – Commonalities, Differences and Future Trends. Available from: https://www.insead.edu/sites/default/files/assets/dept/centres/icgc/docs/board-chairs-practices-across-countries.pdf [Accessed 3 December 2018].

Shekshnia, S. and Zagieva, V. (2016). Chair Survey 2015. Available from: https://www.insead.edu/sites/default/files/assets/dept/centres/icgc/docs/chair-survey-2015.pdf [Accessed 3 December 2018].

Spencer Stuart (2017). UK Board Index 2017. Available from: https://www.spencerstuart.com/research-and-insight/uk-board-index-2017 [Accessed 10 May 2018].

Stewart, R. (1991). Chairmen and Chief Executives: An Exploration of their Relationship. *Journal of Management Studies*, 28(5), pp. 511–528.

The World Bank (2018a). World Development Indicators. GDP per capita 2017, in international dollars. Available from: https://data.worldbank.org/indicator/NY.GDP.PCAP.PP.CD?year_high_desc=true [Accessed 3 December 2018].

The World Bank (2018b). World Development Indicators. GDP Ranking. Available from: https://datacatalog.worldbank.org/dataset/gdp-ranking [Accessed 3 December 2018].

The World Bank (2018c). Services, Value Added. Industry, Value Added. Agriculture, Value Added. Available from: https://data.worldbank.org/indicator/NV.IND.MANF.ZS [Accessed 10 May 2018].

Udueni, H. (1999). Power Dimensions in the Board and Outside Director Independence: Evidence from Large Industrial UK Firms. *Corporate Governance: An International Review*, 7(1), pp. 62–72.

UNDP (2018). Human Development Indices and Indicators. 2018 Statistical Update. Available from: http://hdr.undp.org/en/2018-update [Accessed 28 September 2018].

Van der Elst, C. F. (2011). Revisiting Shareholder Activism at AGMs: Voting Determinants of Large and Small Shareholders. *European Corporate Governance Institute (ECGI), Finance Working Paper*, 311.

Wertheimer, M. (2008). *The Board Chair Handbook*. Washington, DC: BoardSource.

CHAPTER 3

The Netherlands: High Engagement in Building Institutions

Mik van den Noort

THE CHAIR'S WORK IN CONTEXT

The Kingdom of the Netherlands, often referred to as Holland, has been a constitutional monarchy since 1815. It has over 17 million inhabitants and a population density of 507 people per km².[1] A fifth of its surface area is water and a large part of the country lies below sea level. It is a parliamentary democracy and a founding member of the European Union, NATO and the World Trade Organization.

In spite of its small size, the Netherlands is the fifth largest economy in the Eurozone (with a GDP of US$826 billion in 2017),[2] the 16th

---

[1] Statistics Netherlands (CBS) (2018). Population: Key Figures. Available from: https://opendata.cbs.nl/statline/#/CBS/en/dataset/37296eng/table?ts=1528360684635 [Accessed 10 May 2018].

[2] The World Bank (2018). World Development Indicators. GDP Ranking. Available from: https://datacatalog.worldbank.org/dataset/gdp-ranking [Accessed 10 May 2018].

M. van den Noort (✉)
INSEAD, Fontainebleau, France

Kets de Vries Institute, London, UK

ESMT, Berlin, Germany
e-mail: mik@mikvandennoort.nl

© The Author(s) 2019
S. Shekshnia, V. Zagieva (eds.), *Leading a Board*,
https://doi.org/10.1007/978-981-13-3197-8_3

economy in the world by GDP per capita[3] and in tenth place on the Human Development Index.[4] The economy is made up of a highly developed agriculture sector, a sophisticated services sector and significant international trade.

About 1.1 million businesses in the Netherlands employ more than 5.5 million people.[5] Large organizations (of over 250 people) account for 2300 of these firms.[6] Family-owned companies play an important role in the Dutch economy—there are approximately 277,000 of them, employing 2.1 million people and generating 27% of all enterprise turnover.[7] A system of workers' representation (*ondernemingsraad* or works council) is obligatory in any company with more than 50 employees.

Public and private limited liability companies in the Netherlands can choose a two-tier corporate governance structure, with separate management and supervisory boards, or a single board composed of both non-executive and executive directors. The one-tier board structure—traditionally viewed as an Anglo-Saxon phenomenon—was formally introduced by Dutch law on 1 January 2013, along with certain mandatory rules. However, a very small number of Dutch companies had a one-tier structure before 2013, based on specific clauses in their articles.

The Dutch Corporate Governance Code was established in 2003 by the Tabaksblat Commission, and it was revised in 2008 by the Commission Frijns. The Code was further revised by the Van Manen Committee in 2016, and the current version entered into force on 1 January 2017. Based on "comply or explain" principles, companies have to report on observance of the Code in their annual reports.

Board structures in the Netherlands are complex and highly regulated, although the Code lists no specific responsibilities for the chair. Directors are both individually and collectively liable if the board acts in an improper

---

[3] The World Bank (2018). World Development Indicators. GDP per capita, in international dollars. Available from: https://data.worldbank.org/indicator/NY.GDP.PCAP. PP.CD?year_high_desc=true [Accessed 10 May 2018].

[4] UNDP (2018). Human Development Indices and Indicators. 2018 Statistical Update. Available from: http://hdr.undp.org/en/2018-update [Accessed 28 September 2018].

[5] European Commission (2017). SBA Fact Sheet. Netherlands. Available from: https://ec.europa.eu/docsroom/documents/29489 [Accessed 16 May 2018].

[6] Statistics Netherlands (CBS) (2017). Family Business in the Netherlands. Available from: http://www.europeanfamilybusinesses.eu/uploads/Modules/Publications/netherlands-fam-bus.pdf [Accessed 10 May 2018].

[7] Ibid.

or illegal manner. The composition of a supervisory board is required to be such that all members can be critical and act independently of one another, of the management board and of any personal interests. The two pillars on which good corporate governance is founded and which traditionally form the basis of the Code are:

- good entrepreneurship, which implies integrity and transparency on the part of the management board and
- effective supervision of the management board's actions, which demands expertise on the part of the supervisory board.

These factors are regarded as essential for stakeholder confidence in both executive and non-executive directors.[8]

In the Netherlands, the average number of directors on a board is 9.2, and the trend is downwards. The percentage of women directors is slowly increasing: currently, 25.1% on Amsterdam Exchange Index (AEX) and 19.6% on Amsterdam Midkap Index (AMX) boards. However, 96% of companies do not yet satisfy the requirement for 30% of directors to be female. Only 2% of board chair positions are held by women. The average age of Dutch chairs is 66.1 years, and the average age of all directors is 59.4, but both are falling. The average number of independent board members is 5.6.[9] In 2% of boards, the chair is also the CEO.

Larger companies—defined as any entity with more than €16 million in charter capital, at least 100 employees and a works council—must adhere to the *structuurregeling* (structure regime). This gives the works council strong rights of recommendation in the appointment of one-third of supervisory board members. Furthermore, for Dutch companies with a majority of employees in the Netherlands, the supervisory board appoints and dismisses senior managers, and approves major management decisions.

While this significant—if indirect—representation of employees at board level may explain why there are relatively few large companies in the

[8]Corporate Governance Code Monitoring Committee (2016). The Revised Dutch Corporate Governance Code. Available from: https://www.mccg.nl/?page=3779 [Accessed 10 May 2018].

[9]Spencer Stuart (2016). The Netherlands Board Index 2016. Available from: https://www.spencerstuart.com/research-and-insight/netherlands-board-index-2016 [Accessed 10 May 2018].

Netherlands, the system makes for a highly skilled, highly motivated workforce that is largely aligned with company goals and targets. The Dutch productivity rate is surpassed only by the Japanese and the Swiss.

EXISTING RESEARCH

A study of the impact made by the introduction of the Dutch Corporate Governance Code on the role of the board chair reveals that chairs have become increasingly involved in both their control and service duties. While the demographics (e.g. age, tenure, gender and nationality) of chairs have changed very little, chairs are spending considerably more time on boards and committees, have reduced the number of board interlocks and have become more active in the wider discussion of corporate governance.[10]

Data on corporate governance at the top 100 listed companies in the Netherlands between 1997 and 2005 show that the emphasis has shifted from external service to internal service, that is, the task of providing advice and counselling to executive directors is growing in importance. This shift in responsibilities also affects the process for selecting non-executive directors—instead of selecting non-executives mainly on the basis of their external board networks, other qualifications may be more important.[11]

Information asymmetries and dysfunctional working relationships between non-executive and executive directors, as well as the difficulty in scrutinizing the performance of executive directors, are among the greatest challenges indicated by non-executive directors on Dutch supervisory boards.[12]

---

[10] Bezemer, P. J., Peij, S. C., Maassen, G. F., and van Halder, H. (2012). The Changing Role of the Supervisory Board Chairman: The Case of the Netherlands (1997–2007). *Journal of Management & Governance*, 16(1), pp. 37–55.

[11] Bezemer, P. J., Maassen, G. F., Van den Bosch, F. A., and Volberda, H. W. (2007). Investigating the Development of the Internal and External Service Tasks of Non-executive Directors: the case of the Netherlands (1997–2005). *Corporate Governance: An International Review*, 15(6), pp. 1119–1129.

[12] Peij, S. C., Bezemer, P. J., and Maassen, G. F. (2012). The Effectiveness of Supervisory Boards: an Exploratory Study of Challenges in Dutch Boardrooms. *International Journal of Business Governance and Ethics*, 7(3), pp. 191–208.

THE NETHERLANDS CULTURE MAP

The Dutch supposedly practise "applications-first" reasoning (deriving rules from real-world observations) as opposed to "principles-first" reasoning (deriving conclusions from general principles). However, Dutch directors and other respondents in our research seem to place great value on the chair setting formal rules and keeping meeting schedules on time.

The Dutch tend to be highly consensual, which means that chairs prefer to ensure unanimous decisions. One way of achieving this is to consult every board member during pre-meetings (in person or by phone). However, the Netherlands is also known for its "low-context" style of communication: precise, simple, clear and direct. In Dutch culture, messages are expressed and understood at face value, and open confrontation does not negatively impact relationships. On the basis of this assessment, we hypothesized that during meetings Dutch chairs would not hesitate to confront directors openly if a positive effect on the team was expected. Yet most chairs admitted that they would prefer to have a critical conversation with a board member outside the boardroom.

In the Netherlands' task-based culture, chairs and those who work with them value a strong focus on taking actionable decisions. It is comparatively easy to replace underperforming executives and directors, based on the practicality of the situation. However, Dutch boards are rigid in other respects: chairs stick to scheduled timings, plan board meetings years in advance and have a strict agenda, all of which is highly appreciated by those around them (see also Appendix A) (Fig. 3.1).

DATA

The INSEAD Global Chairs Research Project 2016[13] was the main source of data for this chapter. Within its framework, we interviewed five experienced Dutch chairs, one woman and four men, aged between 54 and 74. Together they have chaired the boards of 18 organizations, including a listed multinational consumer goods company, a listed airline, an international business school, a provincial water company, a national federation of employers, a transport holding, a national safety

---

[13] Shekshnia, S. and Zagieva, V. (2017). Board Chairs' Practices across Countries—Commonalities, Differences and Future Trends. Available from: https://www.insead.edu/sites/default/files/assets/dept/centres/icgc/docs/board-chairs-practices-across-countries.pdf [Accessed 3 December 2018].

● Netherlands

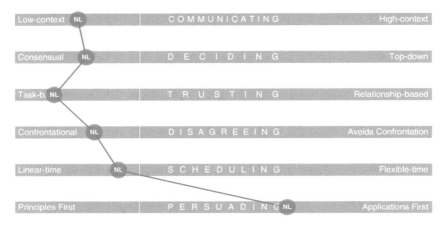

Fig. 3.1 The Netherlands Culture Map. Source: Based on the work of INSEAD Professor Erin Meyer, and her *The Culture Map* book (Meyer, E. (2014). *The Culture Map: Breaking Through the Invisible Boundaries of Global Business.* New York: PublicAffairs)

academy, a small confectionary company and a regional waste transport organization.

Currently, the interviewees chair the boards of seven companies, varying in revenues between €60 million and over €1 billion—and all with two-tier governance structures. One chair is a high-ranking government official. One is the owner of a holding company with three subsidiaries in retail and property. One combines membership of a holding board with chairing a subsidiary and the CEO position of another subsidiary. Another combines his role as chair with the post of CEO in a different and entirely unrelated company. The most senior of them recently retired from most of his board positions and now chairs one family board only.

On average, the respondents have served in their current chair positions for four years, the maximum being ten years and the minimum one year. The boards they chair consist of three to five directors of varied gender, age and professional backgrounds—the average in the Netherlands is 9.2 but is decreasing—and they meet four to twelve times per year. Only one board covered by the study has formal nomination, remuneration and audit committees.

In addition to the chairs, we interviewed three CEOs, three experienced independent directors and three representatives of shareholders, in order to gain a 360-degree perspective on the work of a chair in the Netherlands (together, we will refer to them as observers). The CEOs (three men) had 14 years of combined chief executive experience at, respectively, one publicly listed company, one private and two semi-governmental companies. The directors (one woman and two men) had been members of a total of 8 boards and worked with 11 chairs over the course of their careers. The shareholders (three men) represented an investment fund, a family holding and a venture capital company, all having worked with a number of chairs.

PRIORITIES FOR DUTCH CHAIRS

It is striking that four of the five chairs interviewed stated that "*taking the organization to the next level*" was their top priority. This may be a reflection of the Dutch entrepreneurial spirit and the level of the chairs' involvement in the success of the company. From the interviews, it appears that all the chairs have close working relationships with executives, in terms of setting the strategy, determining the organization/structure of the company, achieving the right composition of the board and fostering links with shareholders and board members. Nurturing the relationship with shareholders (with regular personal contact) and collaboration among board members was seen as an absolutely indispensable task for chairs. In dealing with shareholders, all respondents said that they strived for a balance between involvement, fairness and independence. All sought to be seen as proactive in their contacts with shareholders, as well as receptive, nonpartisan and always looking out for the interests of the organization. The less strict governance rules for the family-owned companies covered by the survey allowed for even more frequent interaction between the chair and shareholders.

One independent chair of a family company sees one of his top tasks as mentoring the second generation of owners—with their full support. He is currently working with five people, keeping them informed about the business and grooming them for the future: "*I have given the family a long-term commitment to take the company to the next level.*" Another says: "*My most important task is to assure that board members and the executive team (most of them are family) get along harmoniously.*"

Relationships with Shareholders

Dialogue between the board and investors is an established practice in many countries, including the Netherlands. It is legal and legitimate, in both the one-tier and the two-tier systems, but it has three main drawbacks: the possibility of insider trading and market abuse; the creation of company secrets, for example, about developments that may make investors unnecessarily nervous; and the difficulty of treating all shareholders equally. While investor relations are primarily the responsibility of the CEO, the chair of the supervisory board is also expected to be available—within reason—to discuss board-related issues with investors. In the Netherlands, this dialogue is not restricted to the overall chair of the board, but extends to committee chairs, senior independent directors and sometimes all directors.

The observer-shareholders in our survey unanimously agreed that effective chairs put the interests of the company first. For the observer-shareholder of a venture capital company, this is all the more important because different shareholders may have different interests and/or agendas. In practice, Dutch chairs balance the various interests of each type of shareholder—and make it apparent that this is what they are doing. They also create a general culture *and* specific opportunities for every board member/shareholder to voice an opinion.

It is also important, according to the observers, that the chair is actively involved in discussions about how and where to raise new funds for the company. One notable practice in the Netherlands is that the chair not only steers this process but is also actively involved in shaping the content of the discussion, while remaining neutral.

Most important in the eyes of one family shareholder interviewed is that the chair shows an ability to weigh the different (and sometimes competing) interests of the company and the family. This means having a relatively long-time horizon: the chair needs to anticipate themes that may play out in the next 15 years and schedule these on the board agenda. The chair in a family-owned company also needs to show that he/she has an eye for both rational (company) matters and emotional (family) matters, that are sometimes "undiscussed"—all the more so when a family is large and globally dispersed.

Similarly, one Dutch investor in a non-family company compared the chair's role to that of a "diplomat": being able to navigate the maze of different shareholders' interests and reach (or sometimes "force") a decision. In short, the effective chair is neutral and stands above the different parties.

Relationships with the CEO and Management

Investing in the relationship with the CEO is important for all chairs, and those of the Netherlands are no exception. Their interaction with the CEO is frequent: all the chairs we surveyed have an open-agenda meeting or a phone conversation every two to three weeks. One calls himself "*a sparring partner*" for the CEO: they meet every four weeks and talk about current business issues. Another has weekly Skype meetings with the CEO. All said that mentoring should come naturally rather than being forced, and thus it could never become an official duty for the Dutch chair. One respondent summed up the situation in the Netherlands:

> *For me it is important to have regular conversations with the CEO, who can then ventilate his topics or his concerns. I can then see whether the relationship between the CEO and his team in the organization is healthy... I have also made it a habit to talk to each of the executive team members once annually in a one-on-one conversation.*

All the chairs we spoke to said that developing company strategy is the CEO's business: the board should simply "endorse it". However, they were also willing to help by listening and challenging assumptions. When necessary, they connected the CEO with experts and, in some cases, shared their own personal experiences.

In the eyes of one observer-CEO, one of the most important qualities of the chair is: "*asking inspiring questions that help me sharpen, deepen and broaden my thoughts about the company today and about its future.*" All the observer-CEOs in the study appreciated informal meetings over coffee with the chair. Some also asked for informal feedback. The relationship can in most cases be characterized as a "learning relationship": the chair can be the coach, sparring partner and sounding board for the CEO, but there are clear boundaries between this role and the more formal function of being the CEO's boss.

All the observer-CEOs we interviewed believed that it was important not to limit their relationships with the chair to "business issues" only.

One gave the example that he had forgotten to invite the board on a whole-company outing to the beach. He informed the board on the morning of the event, apologizing for this late invitation. It was a sunny day and the chair turned up with his wife, both on bicycles, to join the party.

In general, Dutch CEOs seem to appreciate the involvement of chairs and the genuine interest that they show in the company, as well as the specific knowledge and experience that they bring to the table. One CEO was particularly grateful for the fact that the chair has an extensive business network and actively connects him to members who might be of business value. Another said that he regularly invited his chair to talk to the members of the management team because *"it strengthens the connection between the chair and the company and gives additional information on both sides."*

Ensuring Good Relationships Between Board Members

"The role of a chair is to be a chair," were the opening words of one interviewee, followed by:

> It is a disaster to have a weak chairperson. It is hopeless when discussion remains vague—which can happen when there is lack of meeting technique or lack of courage. The chair's task is to prepare and "conclude" and come to decisions. This means making a clear meeting schedule, having all relevant papers ready in time, distinguishing between subjects that need discussion and subjects that need a decision, and sticking to the agreed time/duration of the meetings.

The observers unanimously said that the chair's ability to prepare and plan a meeting, to lead the discussion about "touchy" subjects, and to connect, listen and create space for a meaningful dialogue, are essential for a well-functioning board. These are also essential elements of Dutch culture.

Our chairs considered the quality of their fellow board members to be high, although in some cases it had taken time and effort to reach this level. One had been given the specific task of "*shaking up*" an old-fashioned board, and was working on replacing a certain member in a dignified way, giving him "*limited time to speak*" at board meetings yet handling the situation respectfully.

In dealing with members who are "special cases", Dutch chairs appear to act tactfully but firmly, "challenging" them until the end of their term and setting clear boundaries during meetings to preserve the quality of discussions. One respondent, who is a former chair of a multinational listed company, explained: "*My board members were extremely busy people. As chair I felt I had to ensure that coming to the Netherlands was seamless for them: it made it more attractive to come to our board meetings.*"

One of the observer-directors stated that for him it was important for the chair to have his or her own "*peer network*" in order to exchange knowledge and experience regularly, but also to address personal doubts about his or her own mental agility and judgement. He believed that having a sounding board outside the boardroom had a positive influence on the dynamics inside the boardroom.

Making Good Collective Decisions

Our respondents use similar strategies or tools to be effective in the pre-meeting, meeting and post-meeting phases of chairing a board (as listed in Table 3.1).

Pre-meeting

All the chairs we interviewed invested time and energy at the pre-meeting stage to ensure that directors were motivated and well prepared. Some had informal telephone contact with their directors before each board meeting; others started the board meeting with 30 minutes of informal discussion. As one respondent put it: "*I want to know what's on their minds and what their current concerns are. It is a way for all of us to clear our hearts and minds before the official meeting starts, without the executives present.*"

All the chairs emphasize the importance of exchanging information with their fellow board members before the board meeting, for the benefit of the dialogue in the boardroom. Preparatory phone calls can last one hour per member, when complex or difficult decisions need to be taken. As one says: "*It is important that the board comes to the table in unison. We need a good dialogue; we do not fight in the boardroom or stick to our individual opinions.*" Another says: "*Opinions may differ, but showing dysfunctional behaviour during the meeting is not the done thing: we need to show a consistent image towards the executive board members.*" She added: "*Sometimes we need a short talk afterwards in order to smooth things over.*"

Chairs also reach out to board members before the meeting in order to "re-engage them" and help them concentrate on the upcoming board

Table 3.1   Dutch chairs' strategies and practices

Stage	Chairs' strategies	Chairs' practices
Pre-meeting	Prepare topics and themes with the CEO	Phone calls before the board meeting to consult about and/or clarify the agenda
	Consult every board member	Pre-board lunch for the whole board
	Avoid surprises	Defining format for board materials
	Provide necessary data	Checking board materials before it is sent
	Involve executives	Arranging for board members to spend time at the company
		Board meetings in different company locations
		Making sure that executives are invited to board meetings for specific subjects
		Organizing informal annual dinner for board and CEO/management
Leading the meeting	Write agenda	Consulting with the CEO
	Focus on dialogue, not individual opinions	Dialogue/discussion with board members
	Create atmosphere of working trust	Starting a board meeting with a short session for executives
		Closing a board meeting with
	Treat all board members equally. Focus on taking actionable decisions	a session for executives
		Framing a discussion question
		No voting
	Facilitate discussion and decision-making	Asking every board member to state their position
	Involve executives	Speaking last
	Practise self-restraint	Summarizing the discussion
		Conducting an "express" evaluation at the end of the meeting
		Using humour when things get too serious or tense
Post-meeting	Involve the whole board in finding ways to improve	Conducting formal 360-degree board evaluation
		Off-site meetings for the whole board
	Learn from formal evaluation and informal feedback	Open-agenda one-to-one meetings
		Annual evaluation meeting with every director
	Stay connected with every director	Personal call every month with every director

meeting. Pre-board lunches are used to review the agenda and ensure that everyone is on the same page. Most favour lunch with non-executive members only; others extend it to executives.

The quality of materials is seen as critical for effective board work in the Netherlands. Our chairs strive for limited volume, clarity of information and sufficient time to study materials. Some of them define the format; some co-define it with the CEO. All of the chairs we interviewed check the materials before they are sent to other board members.

To improve directors' knowledge of the company and its business, some chairs encourage and facilitate company visits. These can include meetings with employees and customers.

LEADING THE MEETING

"*Some subjects need only the stroke of a hammer, others need longer discussion,*" in the words of one chair—who added that items on the agenda should be "*relevant to our task*" and "*ripe for decision*". All of the respondents said they partnered with their respective CEOs to set the agenda. In some cases, they invited other directors to review the agenda and pitch ideas.

There is general agreement in the Netherlands that for the board discussion to be fruitful, it has to involve all board members. The chair's task is to create an atmosphere for productive exchanges. As one put it:

> *The fine art of the role is to be the performance director (regisseur). I need to think very clearly about who talks first and who talks last about the specific topics. Who is irritated by whom or what? Who is brooding about what? I need to be very alert in recognizing body language.*

Commonly used strategies to achieve a productive dialogue include equal treatment, discussion facilitation and self-restraint. All the chairs in our study allocate the same amount of airtime to each board member. The typical Dutch cultural element of reaching consensus (*polderen*) is the norm. One chair commented: "*Sometimes it is better to postpone a decision when things are too complex; a bit more reflection on the topic often helps.*"

To engage the more "silent" board members, Dutch chairs solicit their opinions before the meeting and present them on their behalf, acknowledging the source. Asking each director to state his or her opinion is another way to ensure diverse opinions in the dialogue.

When conflict or disagreement threatens to emerge, chairs consider it their responsibility to take avoiding action: "*The board is there to take decisions, not to dwell for a long time on possible disagreement. That's not what we are here for.*" Or from the perspective of one observer-director: "*It usually helps, when there are conflicts between directors, that the chair talks with the ones involved before or after the board meeting, painting the bigger picture. Usually conflicts don't last long after being addressed.*"

Withholding their own opinions is another way chairs promote trust and make room for all participants' points of view. All the chairs surveyed said that they "speak the very last". One says: "*My task, but also my pleasure, is to distil from numerous statements and opinions one clear line, in which everyone recognizes him/herself.*"

POST-MEETING

All chairs conduct some sort of evaluation at the end of each board meeting (in the absence of the executive board), believing that it reinforces mutual respect, builds trust and helps members to learn and improve. Among the questions they ask directors are: "*What did you notice? What will you take home to reflect about?*"

One respondent makes a point of informing the CEO (in general or specific terms) about what has been said during this evaluation: "*The evaluation never takes longer than 30 minutes. Time boundaries are important here, because I don't want the CEO to think that we are discussing 'important' issues in his absence.*"

Work with the whole board is complemented by one-to-one chair-director interactions. One chair invites every board member for lunch once a year. Another has Skype conversations every six weeks. As one respondent points out: "*They should feel that you are available and you care about their contribution.*"

None of the chairs considers informational asymmetry with the CEO and management to be a significant challenge. The working relationship with the CEO is open and effective. One described how "*quite important in my relationship with the CEO, who is also a majority shareholder, is to help him keep his two roles separate. This leads to heated discussions sometimes.*"

Other methods include "*asking the CEO to write a monthly one-pager for me*", "*meetings with the CEO's direct reports*" and "*company conferences*" to improve directors' feel for what is going on in the company.

The time commitment demanded of board members was a non-issue for the chairs in our study: a specific number of days is a "part of the deal". One said: "*I promote a healthy work-life balance with my fellow board members but also with the CEO and his team. Some need to be pushed away on vacation and sometimes I have to push them to look broader than just the organization.*" If board members have a tendency to assume that the chair "will take care of everything", this attitude is discussed in the annual evaluation.

Conducting board evaluations is officially part of the rules and regulations. The Dutch Code recommends the use of external specialists to conduct annual evaluations, but as one respondent noted: "*I prefer to do the evaluation myself because I think it makes us stronger both professionally and in our interactions as board. Besides, I enjoy getting a lot of additional information, with is valuable input for my role.*" This chair uses his own format with the opening question, "*How do you consider that we have worked as a board in the past year: what went well and what did not go so well?*" and lets each member speak his/her mind. The next questions are: "*What could I do more of or do better next year in my role as chair?*" and "*What do you want to do more of or do better next year?*"

One chair chooses a very different way of dealing with the annual evaluation: "*I leave the room and let the vice-chair lead the evaluation. I like it this way, but I know that some of my colleagues don't do it this way.*"

Chair succession is a critical issue in the family-owned companies chaired by our respondents. A lot of time, money and effort is spent on grooming the next incumbent for the task, including sending possible successors on national or international courses on governance. Only one of the five chairs interviewed for this project had recently been "actively" involved in finding a successor for his position. Another, who is an experienced independent chair, has never participated in her own succession: "*I do not want to rule over my grave.*"

The procedure for chair succession in the venture capital company included in our study forms part of the written "shareholders' agreement": shareholders have nomination rights for any new chair.

In general, there appears to be a difference between family-owned companies and other Dutch organizations in terms of the time served by the chair. In the latter, two terms of four years are considered long enough, whereas in the former it takes more time to build knowledge about family relationships and sensitivities, and to gain respect. Here, a term of between 8 and 12 years is considered "the norm".

What Else Do Chairs Do?

At times of crisis or other unusual events, the intensity of Dutch chairs' involvement and interaction with the board increases. As one of them says: "*It helps enormously to fit in 15-minute phone updates as often as possible. It contributes to trust and commitment among the board members.*" Building relationships with external stakeholders, such as clients, suppliers or government, is not seen as the responsibility of the chair, although some exceptions to this rule might be agreed with the CEO. For example, the chair of the hospital in our study is specifically tasked with interacting with the media on a regular basis: "*The chair is the public spokesperson of the organization and needs to be capable of reacting publicly in a responsible way.*"

Similarly, the former chair of a multinational public company was invited by the majority shareholder to deliver an official speech after the Christmas dinner for the top 150 executives of the company: "*It felt a bit like stepping out of my role, but I also felt honored and we ended up having a great evening.*"

Diversity in the Boardroom

All the chairs we interviewed saw the need for diversity on the board, in terms of both gender and knowledge/experience. One commented:

> It is vital for me as chair to be able to have and to use all available experience and professionalism that we need in our board, not just for the quality of our decision making, but also out of respect for the qualities, capabilities and experience of my fellow board members.

None of the chairs or observers interviewed for this chapter objected to "older" chairs (70+), "*as long as they have a sound mind*". Nor are there any objections to "younger" chairs (50–), "*as long as they have enough time available for the position*".

Trends and Predictions

Considerable efforts have been made to achieve gender diversity in the Netherlands, although the effects are not yet fully visible in the boardroom. Since January 2013, there has been a statutory requirement for at least 30% of directors to be women. This percentage was reached for the first time in 2017. However, this does not mean that all boards have hit the 30% mark. Companies that do not are expected to explain why in their annual reports, but few comply. There are 32 women in the 2018 edition of the Management Scope Top 100 rankings of board members, and approximately half of them are chairs.

It appeared that young people were less interested in board jobs than their seniors. In the 2018 edition of the Management Scope Top 100 rankings, there were no new names.[14] Although there appears to be a tendency to nominate younger chairs, no data is available.

The so-called celebrity chair is a rare phenomenon in the Netherlands. However, some chairs are former politicians or public figures and maintain their old networks. As one interviewee explained: "It is professionalism, expertise and network that counts, not the fact that somebody is well-known." Therefore, the main career path to the chair position will continue to go via general management.

National directors' associations have long provided specialized education for board roles in the Netherlands. Degree-level education, whether at Dutch universities or international business schools, is increasingly the norm. The growing importance of the Dutch Corporate Governance Code and further globalization of Dutch companies is an important driver for this development.

SUMMARY

Our most striking finding in the Netherlands is the near-unanimous emphasis placed by the chairs we surveyed on "bringing the organization to the next level". In other words, Dutch chairs clearly have an appetite for entrepreneurship—and even feel a duty to be entrepreneurial. As the number of smaller companies in the Netherlands is growing, it is likely that chairs will become even more entrepreneurial in future, sharing the dynamic spirit of executives and challenging their assumptions about business growth, as well as connecting their CEOs with experts throughout the world.

The use of humour that we noted among Dutch chairs is connected to the individual rather than to the role—some use it, others do not—but all share the conviction that "doing what is necessary" to keep a positive

[14] Management Scope (2018). Top-100 Commissarissen 2018. Available from: https://managementscope.nl/top/machtigste-commissarissen [Accessed 16 May 2018].

atmosphere during board meetings goes with the job. The comparison with a performance director in the theatre is apt. Chairs choreograph moves in the boardroom by choosing who will speak first and last. Reading the body language of the directors and figuring out who is brooding about what to say or who is irritated by what is also clearly an important part of the role.

One practice appears to be particularly characteristic of the Netherlands: ensuring consensus (*polderen*). In this country where consensus and equality are the norm, the chair allows each board member the same amount of airtime and ensures that the discussion takes as long as is needed for a joint decision (or compromise) to be reached. This practice is engrained in the Dutch boardroom, just as it is in the Dutch way of life.

REFERENCES

Bezemer, P. J., Maassen, G. F., Van den Bosch, F. A., and Volberda, H. W. (2007). Investigating the Development of the Internal and External Service Tasks of Non-executive Directors: the case of the Netherlands (1997–2005). *Corporate Governance: An International Review*, 15(6), pp. 1119–1129.

Bezemer, P. J., Peij, S. C., Maassen, G. F., and van Halder, H. (2012). The Changing Role of the Supervisory Board Chairman: The Case of the Netherlands (1997–2007). *Journal of Management & Governance*, 16(1), pp. 37–55.

Corporate Governance Code Monitoring Committee (2016). The Revised Dutch Corporate Governance Code. Available from: https://www.mccg.nl/?page=3779 [Accessed 10 May 2018].

European Commission (2017). SBA Fact Sheet. Netherlands. Available from: https://ec.europa.eu/docsroom/documents/29489 [Accessed 16 May 2018].

Hooghiemstra, R., and Van Manen, J. (2004). The Independence Paradox: (im) possibilities facing non-executive directors in The Netherlands. *Corporate Governance: an international review*, 12(3), pp. 314–324.

Hopt, K. J. (2017). The Dialogue between the Chairman of the Board and Investors: The Practice in the UK, the Netherlands and Germany and the Future of the German Corporate Governance Code under the New Chairman. *Revue Trimestrielle de Droit Financier*, (3), pp. 97–104.

Management Scope (2018). Top-100 Commissarissen 2018. Available from: https://managementscope.nl/top/machtigste-commissarissen [Accessed 16 May 2018].

Meyer, E. (2014). *The Culture Map: Breaking Through the Invisible Boundaries of Global Business*. New York: PublicAffairs.

Peij, S. C., Bezemer, P. J., and Maassen, G. F. (2012). The Effectiveness of Supervisory Boards: an Exploratory Study of Challenges in Dutch Boardrooms. *International Journal of Business Governance and Ethics*, 7(3), pp. 191–208.

Shekshnia, S. and Zagieva, V. (2017). Board Chairs' Practices across Countries – Commonalities, Differences and Future Trends. Available from: https://www.insead.edu/sites/default/files/assets/dept/centres/icgc/docs/board-chairs-practices-across-countries.pdf [Accessed 3 December 2018].

Spencer Stuart (2016). The Netherlands Board Index 2016. Available from: https://www.spencerstuart.com/research-and-insight/netherlands-board-index-2016 [Accessed 10 May 2018].

Statistics Netherlands (CBS) (2017). Family Business in the Netherlands. Available from: http://www.europeanfamilybusinesses.eu/uploads/Modules/Publications/netherlands-fam-bus.pdf [Accessed 10 May 2018].

Statistics Netherlands (CBS) (2018). Population: Key Figures. Available from: https://opendata.cbs.nl/statline/#/CBS/en/dataset/37296eng/table?ts=1528360684635 [Accessed 10 May 2018].

The World Bank (2018a). World Development Indicators. GDP per capita, in international dollars. Available from: https://data.worldbank.org/indicator/NY.GDP.PCAP.PP.CD?year_high_desc=true [Accessed 10 May 2018].

The World Bank (2018b). World Development Indicators. GDP Ranking. Available from: https://datacatalog.worldbank.org/dataset/gdp-ranking [Accessed 10 May 2018].

UNDP (2018). Human Development Indices and Indicators. 2018 Statistical Update. Available from: http://hdr.undp.org/en/2018-update [Accessed 28 September 2018].

CHAPTER 4

Switzerland: Diversity and Diplomacy

Rolf Frey

THE CHAIR'S WORK IN CONTEXT

Switzerland began as a loose association of cantons, which became a federal state with its own constitution in 1848. The Swiss confederation has four official languages (German, French, Italian and Romansh) and a system of direct democracy. Swiss citizens elect representatives at the levels of confederation, canton and commune. In 2017 GDP was US$679 billion and population 8.4 million[1,2] with per capita GDP of Int$65,000,[3] the ninth highest in the world. Switzerland has a highly developed economy but no significant natural resources. The agricultural sector accounts for a mere 0.6% of GDP, industry for 25% and services for almost three-quarters

---

[1] The World Bank (2018). Population. Available from: https://data.worldbank.org/indicator/SP.POP.TOTL [Accessed 13 August 2018].

[2] The World Bank (2018). World Development Indicators. GDP Ranking. Available from: https://datacatalog.worldbank.org/dataset/gdp-ranking [Accessed 13 August 2018].

[3] The World Bank (2018). World Development Indicators. GDP per capita, in international dollars. Available from: https://data.worldbank.org/indicator/NY.GDP.PCAP.PP.CD?year_high_desc=true [Accessed 13 August 2018].

R. Frey (✉)
DOMINÉ & PARTNERS, Zurich, Switzerland
e-mail: rolf.frey@domine.com

© The Author(s) 2019
S. Shekshnia, V. Zagieva (eds.), *Leading a Board*,
https://doi.org/10.1007/978-981-13-3197-8_4

(70%).[4] Switzerland is ranked second in the world on the Human Development Index.[5]

Although a member of the European Free Trade Association, Switzerland is not part of the European Union. In recent decades, the country has become an attractive domicile for international businesses thanks to its politically stable environment, a favourable macroeconomic context, a highly skilled workforce, easy access to financial markets, low corporate taxes, modern infrastructure and a business-friendly regulatory environment.

Switzerland has approximately **600,000** companies.[6] Despite an impressive number of prominent global corporations such as UBS, Nestlé, Novartis, ABB and Swatch Group, **99.8%** of the total is made up of companies with fewer than **250** employees.[7] These small and medium enterprises (SMEs) are the backbone of the economy, employing over two-thirds of the workforce[8] and accounting for 60% of GDP.[9] Exports constitute 65% of GDP.[10] Key markets are neighbours, Germany, Italy and France, as well as the UK and the US. In 2018, Switzerland topped the Global Innovation Index—an annual research report published by Cornell University, INSEAD and the World Intellectual Property Organization (WIPO)[11]—with 3.4% of GDP spent on research and development.

The principal rules of corporate governance in Switzerland are enshrined in company law and provisions are set out in the Swiss Code of Obligations.[12] As in the US (following the Enron scandal), corporate

[4] The World Bank (2018). Services, Value Added. Industry, Value Added. Agriculture, Value Added. Available from: https://data.worldbank.org/indicator/NV.IND.TOTL.ZS [Accessed 10 May 2018].

[5] UNDP (2018). Human Development Indices and Indicators. 2018 Statistical Update. Available from: http://hdr.undp.org/en/2018-update [Accessed 28 September 2018].

[6] FSO (2018). Statistical Data on Switzerland 2018. Available from: https://www.bfs.admin.ch/bfs/en/home/statistics/catalogues-databases/publications/overviews/statistical-yearbook-switzerland.html [Accessed 13 August 2018].

[7] Ibid.

[8] Ibid.

[9] Ibid.

[10] The World Bank (2018). Exports of Goods and Services (in % of GDP). Available from: https://data.worldbank.org/indicator/NE.EXP.GNFS.ZS [Accessed 13 August 2018].

[11] Cornell University, INSEAD, and WIPO (2018). Global Innovation Index 2018: Energizing the World with Innovation. Available from: https://www.globalinnovationindex.org/gii-2018-report [Accessed 13 August 2018].

[12] The Federal Assembly of the Swiss Confederation (1907). Swiss Civil Code. Available from: https://www.admin.ch/opc/en/classified-compilation/19070042/index.html [Accessed 13 August 2018].

catastrophes in Switzerland—such as the liquidity problems of ABB and the collapse of SAirGroup (parent of former Swissair) in 2002—prompted the Swiss government to review and adapt the legal framework to meet international standards.

In addition, two major codes have entered into force:

- A directive on Corporate Governance, released by the Swiss Exchange in 2002 and updated in 2018 (binding)[13]
- The Swiss Code of Best Practice (SCBP) for Corporate Governance, published by the Swiss Business Federation in 2002 (non-binding).[14]

Switzerland has a one-tier board system. The shareholders elect members of the board, its chair and members of the committees annually. According to the Swiss Code of Obligations, the board of directors has the non-transferable and inalienable duties of overall management of the company through applying the company's organizational and financial controls, and appointing, dismissing and supervising executives.

The SCBP describes best practice and makes recommendations that go above and beyond what is required by law. Since its inception, it has had a strong impact on corporate governance in Switzerland. Applying the principle of "comply or explain", it has been effective in encouraging boards to regulate themselves. According to the SCBP, the board of directors should:

- determine strategic goals, general ways and means to achieve them, and the persons responsible for conducting the company's business;
- shape the company's corporate governance and put it into practice;
- ensure in its planning the fundamental harmonization of strategy, risks and finances;
- be guided by the goal of sustainable corporate development.

Although corporate governance law in Switzerland is in many ways similar to that in other European countries, boards of directors operate

---

[13] SWX Swiss Exchange (2018). Directive on Information relating to Corporate Governance. Available from: https://www.six-exchange-regulation.com/dam/downloads/regulation/admission-manual/directives/06_16-DCG_en.pdf [Accessed 13 August 2018].

[14] Economiesuisse (2002). Swiss Code of Best Practice for Corporate Governance. Available from: https://www.economiesuisse.ch/sites/default/files/publications/economiesuisse_swisscode_e_web_2.pdf [Accessed 13 August 2018].

there in a specific context of high public engagement and scrutiny. In 2013 a majority of Swiss voters accepted the "Minder Initiative", aimed at preventing excessive executive remuneration at listed companies. A year later, the Federal Council brought into force the "Ordinance Against Excessive Remuneration at Listed Stock Corporations", which requires that boards of public companies seek shareholders' approval for the top executives' compensation through a binding vote at the annual general assembly. The boards have to ensure that the remuneration of senior executives provides optimal incentives for them and is in tune with the interests of shareholders.

In a country with four official languages, board diversity is another theme that attracts the attention of both the public and the regulators. On the one hand, boards of Swiss companies are among the most internationally diverse in Europe—and this diversity is increasing. At Swiss Market Index (SMI) companies (the top 20 Swiss companies in terms of market capitalization), the percentage of foreigners on boards has increased from 10% 25 years ago to 59% in 2017. On the other hand, only 22% of SMI board seats were held by women and only one SMI board chaired by a woman.

Swiss boards are among the most professional in Europe and have a very high proportion of independent directors: 84% for SMI companies in 2017. Furthermore, the number of SMI companies that conducted an externally facilitated board evaluation has increased from 5% in 2015 to 15% in 2016.[15]

Swiss law does not require a separation of the functions of the chair and CEO (except in banks). However, in such cases the Code recommends that the board appoint a senior independent director. In practice, almost all large companies have separate chair and CEO (no company at SMI list has a combined appointment).[16]

The Swiss Code defines the chair's responsibilities as follows:

- To ensure execution of shareholders' rights
- To organize and conduct effective annual shareholders' meetings

[15] Spencer Stuart (2017). Switzerland Board Index 2017. Available from: https://www.spencerstuart.com/research-and-insight/switzerland-board-index-2017 [Accessed 13 August 2018].

[16] Schmid, M. and Zimmermann, H. (2008). Should Chairman and CEO Be Separated? Leadership Structure and Firm Performance in Switzerland. *Schmalenbach Business Review* (SBR), *LMU Munich School of Management*, 60(2), pp. 182–204.

- To prepare and conduct board meetings ("ensure that procedures relating to preparatory work, deliberation, passing resolutions and implementation of decisions are carried out properly")[17]
- To provide appropriate information to board members

The Code also explicitly stipulates that the chair is entrusted with running the board of directors "in the company's interests".

SWITZERLAND CULTURE MAP

Before looking into the specific practices of chairs of Swiss companies, it is relevant to define Swiss culture. Describing Swiss culture in a uniform way would not do justice to the cultural diversity of a country with four linguistic regions: German, French, Italian and, to a lesser extent, Romansh. The three key Swiss regions each border and share a language with large countries possessing rich cultures: Germany and Austria to the north and east, respectively, France to the west and Italy to the south. The people of each Swiss region are influenced by the culture of the neighbours they share a language with, from the books they read at school to the media they consume as adults.

At the same time, there are some values which transcend linguistic and regional differences, and that have become associated with Switzerland. Such values include respect for cultural diversity, a consensus-oriented approach to governing, pragmatism, quality and punctuality.[18] These common values have been engrained not only through shared experience, but also through the education system, military service and regular language-learning exchanges between people of different regions.

What does this imply for the work of a chair of a Swiss company board? We would hypothesize that the timeliness, quality and reliability associated with the craftsmanship of Swiss watchmaking would also be expected from and by the chairs. We would also expect them to lead in a consensus-seeking, non-hierarchical way. Where neighbouring countries generally

---

[17] Economiesuisse (2002). *Swiss Code of Best Practice for Corporate Governance.* Available from: https://www.economiesuisse.ch/sites/default/files/publications/economiesuisse_swisscode_e_web_2.pdf [Accessed 13 August 2018].

[18] Oertig-Davidson, M. (2011). *Beyond Chocolate: Understanding Swiss Culture.* Basel: Bergli Books; Hofstede Insights: Country Comparison: Switzerland. Available from: https://www.hofstede-insights.com/country-comparison/switzerland/ [Accessed 13 August 2018].

● Switzerland

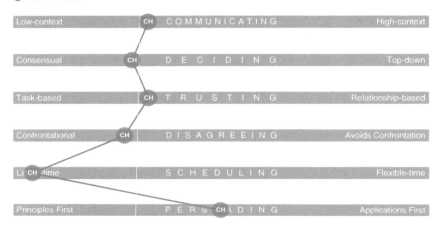

Fig. 4.1 Switzerland Culture Map. Source: Based on the work of INSEAD Professor Erin Meyer, and her *The Culture Map* book (Meyer, E. (2014). *The Culture Map: Breaking Through the Invisible Boundaries of Global Business.* New York: PublicAffairs)

put "principles first", Swiss pragmatism strikes a balance between honouring principles and recognizing "application needs". On this basis, chairs will constantly keep their eye on the outcomes and will steer their boards to making actionable decisions. In addition, they will value diversity and will be proficient in managing boards comprising people with different backgrounds (see also Appendix A) (Fig. 4.1).

Existing Research

While several empirical studies have been conducted on corporate governance in Switzerland, only a few focus specifically on the role of the chair.

One study measures the impact of the age of board chairs on company performance.[19] The authors analyse survey results from over 1500 chairs of private Swiss companies. They show a negative correlation between the age of a board chair and company performance after the former exceeds

[19] Wälchli, U. and Zeller, J. (2013). Old Captains at the Helm: Chairman Age and Firm Performance. *Journal of Banking and Finance*, 37, pp. 1612–1628.

50 years. These results are specific to the chairs of private companies: in listed Swiss firms, the age of the board chair and profitability appear unconnected. The study claims that this difference between the chairs of listed and unlisted Swiss firms is likely due to weaker corporate governance standards in unlisted firms. This study is consistent with other research, showing that board chairs are "among the most prominent players in a corporation".

Another study suggests that there is a direct correlation between a chair not renewing his or her mandate and the transition of the CEO to the chair role.[20] In a research paper[21] for which the chairs of international Swiss companies were interviewed, the direct impact of the chair on the culture of the board, and ultimately the company culture, is highlighted. The chairs interviewed as part of the research shared the view that they have a considerable influence on board culture. Open communication, a critical yet constructive discussion culture and an inclusive decision-making process are critical to ensure active and engaged contributions from all members of the board. Through their participation in board meetings, members of the executive committee are also influenced by the board culture. This has a cascading effect on their management and the company culture at large.

Data

We interviewed nine chairs of companies headquartered in Switzerland. Of these organizations, four are part of the SMI, three are part of the Swiss Performance Index (SPI), one is listed abroad, one is state owned and one is family owned. In four of the listed companies, significant stakes are still held by the founding families with various degrees of voting power. The sectors of the ten companies include financial services, pharmaceuticals, consumer goods, manufacturing, retail and transportation. All but two are significantly involved in international activities, and the majority do most of their business outside Switzerland.

[20] Wälchli, U. (2008). *Corporate Governance von Schweizer Verwaltungsräten.* Available from; http://biblio.unibe.ch/download/eldiss/08waelchli_u.pdf [Accessed 13 August 2018].
[21] Lorenz Koller, B.M. (2010). *The Role of the Chairperson of the Board of International Swiss Companies Listed on the Swiss Stock Exchange in Consideration of Board Systems.* Available from: https://www1.unisg.ch/www/edis.nsf/SysLkpByIdentifier/3862/$FILE/dis3862.pdf [Accessed 13 August 2018].

The ages of the chairs interviewed range from 56 to 72. Nationalities include Swiss (seven), Austrian (one), German (one) and British (one), and their educational backgrounds include a mix of economics, business administration and engineering degrees. Only one is a woman. All of the chairs held CEO positions prior to joining boards, and they currently hold an average of 3.8 board mandates. The time dedicated to the chair's role ranges from 30% to 40% to full time.

In order to get a broader view, we also interviewed three CEOs, three experienced directors and three shareholders. The shareholders (one woman, two men) represented a controlling family, an investment fund and a government-linked company. All non-chair interviewees have served on various boards and worked with several chairs.

Challenges and Practices

The INSEAD Global Chair Survey 2015 identified the main challenges for the chairs of international companies, and our interviews were structured accordingly.

Relationships with Shareholders

Although our chair-respondents repeated that they owed their duty to the company rather than to shareholders, they devote considerable time and attention to their relationships with the latter. One chair said that he ultimately views the relationship between the board and large shareholders as collaborative: "*Don't look at them as enemies,*" he said, "*they are your owners and they are your partners.*"

When the company they chair has a controlling or anchor shareholder, respondents invested a lot of time in meeting its key representatives—often founders or family members. As one chair put it, "*What you absolutely have to do is communicate. This is so important.*" Regular meetings ensure that the chair and the influential shareholders stay aligned in terms of company strategy and connected at a personal level. The chairs arrange meetings mindfully and proactively, and acknowledge that they are appreciated by the shareholders, since they give them a sense of control over the strategic direction and ultimately the future of the company.

When a large stake is held by institutional investors, some chairs nurture personal relationships and organize annual roadshows to meet with their representatives and engage them in discussion—often about the governance of the company. While institutional investors do not receive any substantial information outside the formal notifications sent to all shareholders, they do have the opportunity to engage directly with key company representatives. In the case of a state-owned company, the range of stakeholders increases—from political to union representatives—as does the complexity of stakeholder management. One chair of the state-owned company we spoke to takes a proactive communication approach by organizing regular formal and informal meetings.

Contrary to their relationships with majority shareholders, respondents seldom had personal connections with minority shareholders beyond the annual shareholder meeting. While they took the concerns of minority shareholders seriously and provided investors and the press with written updates, communication with shareholders was handled by the investor relations team or at times the CFO.

For the shareholder-respondent representing a controlling interest in a family business, the long-term view of the chair was of utmost importance. At the same time, he believes that an effective chair meets with shareholders' representatives on a regular basis to keep them informed about key developments. "*The inclusion of an anchor shareholder allows us to focus on long-term value creation rather than react to short-term financial market pressure*," shared one of board members. The same long-term view was also a priority for the representative of the shareholder of a government-controlled financial institution with a public service mandate.

Recruiting Board Members

Contrary to many other European countries, board chairs in Switzerland are quite active in recruiting new board members. Our respondents emphasized the importance of vetting directors before putting them forward for election to ensure effective functioning of the board. They invest a lot of time in assessing personality, character, communication skills and cultural fit of future directors, which helps to avoid problems later on.

Collaboration is one of the core national values in Switzerland and it translates directly into chair practices, starting with the selection and induction of new board members. Several chair-respondents mentioned collaboration and openness as key values they expected to see in directors. "Know-it-all" or "know-better" types do not get to join boards. One chair said that an absolute "no go" for him was someone with an overinflated ego. While they sought members who were knowledgeable and experienced, they also wanted directors who would constructively contribute to the work of the board and "play as a team".

In some instances, "courting" a future director took up to three years, during which time the chair assessed the fit with the company and the board. The values of potential directors are scrutinized to ensure alignment with those of the company. Respondents often mentioned integrity as a key attribute. One said, *"We need board members that are team players,"* while acknowledging that individual voices had to be heard. He conceded that handling inquisitive and critical board members could be challenging, but still wanted board members to be engaged and speak their mind: *"It just needs to happen within certain rules of conduct."*

Facilitating Effective Board Discussions

All of the respondents ensure that board members receive material in a timely manner before meetings. They expect board members to come prepared, having already formed a point of view, and ready to ask questions or raise concerns. Chair-respondents see their role as effective management of the meeting, balancing the tension between sticking to the agenda and keeping within time limits, and giving everyone a chance to speak. Framing the agenda items and staying on topic were essential, yet, as one put it, *"One should not be a slave to the agenda."*

The respondents stressed the need to stay humble and refrain at times from intervening, while also making sure all voices are heard: *"I listen. I also decide when it is time to decide, but everyone can express himself without fear."* Most share their own views last. Asking questions in a Socratic way, even when one knows the answer, is a good way to solicit other points of view. As one of the directors put it: *"I expect the chair to make sure that the opinions of all board members are heard before he/she comes to a conclusion or the board votes on a topic."*

Although consensus-orientation is strong in Swiss boardrooms, voting is not completely absent; some chairs use it as a last resort to make a decision.

All the board members interviewed expect the chair to ensure that relevant challenges are discussed by the board (*"For me it is the chair's responsibility to make sure that the right topics are discussed in the board meetings"*—in the words of one director). They see the chair as responsible for setting the regular board agenda and for putting an emphasis on addressing the long-term strategy of the company. They also find it important that the chair help the board reach a consensus in cases of dispute. Two board members believe that chairs increase board effectiveness by assigning different board members "special missions", that is, projects outside of the regular board committee responsibilities.

Chair-respondents indicated that they rarely had to deal with uncooperative or dissident directors. In such cases, they arranged one-on-one meetings to address the issue head on or even asked nonconformist directors to step down from the board.

Board evaluation is not mandatory in Switzerland, but most chair-respondents consider it an effective practice to improve a board's cohesiveness and productivity, highlight competency gaps and identify directors with the potential to become committee and eventually board chairs. Evaluation generally takes place once a year. Some chairs use external consultants; some prefer to conduct the process privately. Non-chair-respondents emphasized that the ability to conduct a board evaluation is indispensable for chairs and the effective ones make sure every director is engaged and feels free to speak his or her mind.

Beyond board meetings, some board members join field or company visits, which, depending on the location, can be a two-to-three-day trip. These visits are unique opportunities for board members to spend quality time together and get to know each other better, which foster a collaborative spirit.

Insignificant Time Commitment from Board Members

Lack of time commitment was not generally identified as a concern by any of our Swiss respondents. In one instance, where a committee chair was clearly struggling to invest the time necessary to perform the additional duties, the respondent recommended changes in the committee's composition. One mentioned that in a previous role he had asked someone who was not pulling his weight to leave the board (and affirmed that he would do so again if faced with a similar situation). Another evoked the "one chance and you're out" rule, which he had enforced in the past by asking a board member to step down.

Diversity in Board Members' Backgrounds

Besides the skills and experience that bring complementarity into the board, gender diversity and—particularly for companies operating internationally—cultural diversity are actively sought. The chair of an SME mentioned that his board members actively try to recruit women, but they had so far been unsuccessful because the women approached already had other offers. Clearly, although the pool of experienced female directors in Switzerland is increasing, it is still small compared to that of men. Hence, the competition for talent is intense.

Several of chairs of multinational companies see diversity primarily through the lens of global operations. In such cases, board composition ideally takes account of the ethnic diversity of the company. At the same time, for companies with a strong Swiss culture, ensuring that the chair and some members of the board are Swiss nationals is seen as critical.

Informational Asymmetry with the CEO and Management

There is obviously informational asymmetry between the chair and the CEO, given that the latter is closer to day-to-day operations. Furthermore, an almost full-time chair inevitably has more information than other directors, whose participation is limited to attendance at board or committee meetings. One respondent said, "*When you just come in six times a year, the knowledge you have is limited compared to the chairman.*" In both instances, there is a need for trust and for regular updates. In addition to regular written bulletins from the CEO or the board briefing—sometimes as long as 25 pages—a pre-board-meeting dinner offers a way to mitigate any potential disconnect. This explains why some chairs have moved away from PowerPoint presentations and like to articulate their points of view more personally, leaving less room for interpretation (see also the next section).

Relationships with the CEO and Management

Several chairs mentioned mutual respect between the chair and the CEO as a sine qua non of effective leadership. One respondent said that board and management needed to be viewed as "*one team*": executives and non-executives have their own roles, but "*the aim of what we are doing has to be the same.*" All chair-respondents invested a significant amount of time supporting their CEOs, for whom they served as mentors, supporters or sparring partners. All had been in the role of CEO, mostly in other companies, and thus knew how lonely it can feel at the top. One chair of a large company insisted that in order to be a truly effective chair, you need to know what it is to be in the CEO's seat but no longer want to sit there. One director mentioned that he expects the chair to be able to develop a challenging yet constructive relationship with the CEO and foster an open dialogue within the board.

Two chairs had held the CEO post in the company that they were currently chairing. They mentioned that they had to adjust to their new role, particularly the respondent who had formerly combined both positions (CEO and chair). In this dual role, he had to balance a tendency to make decisions with the facilitating and consultative approach required of the chair—not an easy transition, although he felt it was clearly the right way to go. Another went as far as referring to the "unit" formed with his CEO—which he wants people to see—and was confident that this proximity would not blur his judgement. The pair undertakes many international trips together in order to meet staff, potential hires and clients jointly. One chair, who is based in a different country from the CEO, calls the CEO almost every Sunday to touch base.

Trust between the chair and the CEO is put to the test in tough times and crises. One respondent's number one rule is "no surprises". He has made a pact with the CEO that any troubling development within the company will be reported to him at once; success stories can wait. Another chair said simply, "*I care for him as a CEO but also as a person, and I believe it is mutual.*" When asked about their relationships with others in the management team, some said they made a point of meeting with every key executive on a one-to-one basis from time to time. Others did not, preferring to avoid what could be seen as interference in the CEO's area of responsibility.

On the part of the CEOs interviewed, mutual trust with the chair is important and the foundation of successful cooperation. They expect the chair to be a sparring partner from whom they can get feedback on their ideas. As one of the CEOs put it: "*The relationship with the chair has to be a true partnership in the best interest of the company: supporting, inspiring, controlling.*" For CEOs, it is also important to have a competent board, which can help him or her, and according to our respondents, it is the chair's responsibility—and not that of the nomination committee—to ensure that the board is professional, complete and comprised of members with complementary skills and backgrounds.

Relationships with External Stakeholders

Most Swiss chairs try to stay away from engaging with external stakeholders beyond the shareholders. However, in situations of crisis or if the CEO is not available, they have more exposure. In some instances, they do this on purpose to deflect attention from the CEO. One chair is the *"face of the company"* in its dealings with NGOs, governmental agencies and the public on the specific topic of environment and climate change. However, he insisted that it was important that the chair not step on the CEO's toes; there needs to be a clear separation of duties. Another was more inwardly focused, preferring *"to be seen more in the office than in the newspaper"*. The board members interviewed also expect the chair to build good relationships with the various key stakeholders (shareholders, politicians, regulators, etc.).

Chair Succession

In Switzerland, the chair, board members and committee chairs are elected directly by the shareholders at the annual meeting. In theory, the nomination committee is responsible for succession planning for the post of chair. In practice, the approach varies depending on the incumbent's personality, the shareholding structure and other factors. Some of our respondents reported that they had both emergency and long-term succession plans. In an emergency, the vice-chair or a senior independent director takes over until a permanent solution is found. For a long-term solution, some chairs work closely with their nomination committees and even engage external consultants, while others stay away from the process.

Onboarding is an important part of chair succession in Switzerland. It usually takes several months, and the incumbent is very much involved. The induction may include one to ones with the outgoing chair, directors and key executives; company and customer visits; and even coaching sessions with professional providers.

SUMMARY

When asked how they would describe the essence of their role, chair-respondents used such terms as "first among equals", "shepherd", "conductor", "trusted advisor", "link between the board and the CEO", "servant leader" and "an owner responsible for the well-being of the company". The discourse they use in describing their work and the practices they espouse emphasize the enabling aspect of their role. Chairs in Switzerland are very diligent with regard to compliance and such technical aspects of board work as frequency and length of meetings, or timely provision of board materials and their quality. They also pay a lot of attention to board composition, actively selecting and preparing new board members. Other observers seconded this view.

At the same time, personality and previous experience leave their mark on the style of board leaders in Switzerland. Some are more directive than others in managing a board; some focus more on business strategy and others on relationships with the CEO and so on. We found some divergence in our respondents' views on the need for chairs to have industry expertise. Some felt that it was indispensable, especially in highly regulated sectors, such as finance, where there was a risk of an expert CEO having too strong an influence on the chair and, by extension, the board. However, some of our interviewees were not sector experts and functioned in a very effective manner, by ensuring that specialist knowledge was properly represented on the board.

In the next decade, we predict that the number of CEO-chairs in Switzerland will decrease, but they will not disappear altogether. Most chairs will preside over only one board, committing many hours to it. We also foresee that the diversity in chairs' backgrounds will increase in terms of gender, age, nationality and professional qualifications. We believe there will be a significantly higher number of female chairs, as currently more than 30% of newly appointed directors in Switzerland are women. Foreigners will continue to represent a significant proportion of chairs in the country, but Swiss nationals will remain a majority. There will be more younger chairs, but the average age will not decrease significantly. The "profession" will continue to require maturity and experience.

In addition, digital and communication technologies will make their presence felt on the boards of Swiss companies, enabling directors to stay connected and reducing information gaps. Chairs will move away from paper to digital board books, while committee meetings will be held via Zoom, Skype and similar technologies. As a result, boards will spend less time discussing historical numbers and more on matters of substance.

We expect that in the next decade board chairs in Switzerland will focus more on the "soft" aspects of their work—board dynamics, quality of discussions and interactions outside the boardroom. Regular board evaluations will become standard practice, not only for listed but also for private companies, and discussions about improving board effectiveness will become routine for directors.

Further specific predictions include the following: board chairs will continue to interact proactively with shareholders, perhaps paying more attention to equal treatment and other regulatory aspects. Shareholder activism will be on the rise. Delisting will become an increasingly prevalent option for corporate boards.

More generally, corporate governance regulations are likely to tighten, which will require more of the chair's attention. However, true to its own traditions, Switzerland will remain a country with an emphasis on soft rather than hard regulation.

REFERENCES

Cornell University, INSEAD, and WIPO (2018). Global Innovation Index 2018: Energizing the World with Innovation. Available from: https://www.globalinnovationindex.org/gii-2018-report [Accessed 13 August 2018].

Economiesuisse (2002). Swiss Code of Best Practice for Corporate Governance. Available from: https://www.economiesuisse.ch/sites/default/files/publications/economiesuisse_swisscode_e_web_2.pdf [Accessed 13 August 2018].

FSO (2018). Statistical Data on Switzerland 2018. Available from: https://www.bfs.admin.ch/bfs/en/home/statistics/catalogues-databases/publications/overviews/statistical-yearbook-switzerland.html [Accessed 13 August 2018].

Gehrig, B. (2018). Die fünf Prioritäten für Verwaltungsräte. *Neue Zürcher Zeitung.* Available from: https://www.nzz.ch/wirtschaft/die-fuenf-prioritaeten-fuer-verwaltungsraete-ld.1348257 [Accessed 3 December 2018].

Hofstede Insights: Country Comparison: Switzerland. Available from: https://www.hofstede-insights.com/country-comparison/switzerland/ [Accessed 13 August 2018].

Lorenz Koller, B.M. (2010). *The Role of the Chairperson of the Board of International Swiss Companies Listed on the Swiss Stock Exchange in Consideration of Board Systems.* Available from: https://www1.unisg.ch/www/edis.nsf/SysLkpByIdentifier/3862/$FILE/dis3862.pdf [Accessed 13 August 2018].

Meyer, E. (2014). *The Culture Map: Breaking Through the Invisible Boundaries of Global Business.* New York: PublicAffairs.

Montagnon, P. (2018). Sika/Saint-Gobain Pact is High Point in Shareholder Collaboration. *Financial Times.* Available from: https://www.ft.com/content/a5d1bfdc-6894-11e8-b6eb-4acfcfb08c11 [Accessed 13 August 2018].

Oertig-Davidson, M. (2011). *Beyond Chocolate: Understanding Swiss Culture.* Basel: Bergli Books.

Schilling, G. (2017). Transparency at The Top. The Management Boards of Switzerland's Private and Public Sectors. Available from: https://www.schillingreport.ch/upload/5/4173/schillingreport2017_E.pdf [Accessed 13 August 2018].

Schmid, M. and Zimmermann, H. (2008). Should Chairman and CEO be Separated? Leadership Structure and Firm Performance in Switzerland. *Schmalenbach Business Review* (sbr), *LMU Munich School of Management*, 60(2), pp. 182–204.

Spencer Stuart (2017). Switzerland Board Index 2017. Available from: https://www.spencerstuart.com/research-and-insight/switzerland-board-index-2017 [Accessed 13 August 2018].

SWX Swiss Exchange (2018). Directive on Information relating to Corporate Governance. Available from: https://www.six-exchange-regulation.com/dam/downloads/regulation/admission-manual/directives/06_16-DCG_en.pdf [Accessed 13 August 2018].

The Federal Assembly of the Swiss Confederation (1907). Swiss Civil Code. Available from: https://www.admin.ch/opc/en/classified-compilation/19070042/index.html [Accessed 13 August 2018].

The Swiss Federal Council (2013). Ordinance against Excessive Remuneration at Listed Stock Corporations. Available from: https://www.nkf.ch/wAssets-nkf2/docs/informationen/Minder-Ordinance_Translation_2013-11.pdf [Accessed 13 August 2018].

The World Bank (2018a). Exports of Goods and Services (in percent of GDP). Available from: https://data.worldbank.org/indicator/NE.EXP.GNFS.ZS [Accessed 13 August 2018].

The World Bank (2018b). Population. Available from: https://data.worldbank.org/indicator/SP.POP.TOTL [Accessed 13 August 2018].

The World Bank (2018c). World Development Indicators. GDP Ranking. Available from: https://datacatalog.worldbank.org/dataset/gdp-ranking [Accessed 13 August 2018].

The World Bank (2018d). World Development Indicators. GDP per capita, in international dollars. Available from: https://data.worldbank.org/indicator/NY.GDP.PCAP.PP.CD?year_high_desc=true [Accessed 13 August 2018].

The World Bank (2018e). Services, Value Added. Industry, Value Added. Agriculture, Value Added. Available from: https://data.worldbank.org/indicator/NV.IND.TOTL.ZS [Accessed 10 May 2018].

UNDP (2018). Human Development Indices and Indicators. 2018 Statistical Update. Available from: http://hdr.undp.org/en/2018-update [Accessed 28 September 2018].

Volonté, C. (2016). Mehr Wissen im Verwaltungsrat. *Finanz und Wirtschaft*. Available from: https://www.fuw.ch/article/mehr-wissen-im-verwaltungsrat/ [Accessed 3 December 2018].

Wälchli, U. (2008). *Corporate Governance von Schweizer Verwaltungsräten*. Available from: http://biblio.unibe.ch/download/eldiss/08waelchli_u.pdf [Accessed 13 August 2018].

Wälchli, U. and Zeller, J. (2013). Old Captains at the Helm: Chairman Age and Firm Performance. *Journal of Banking and Finance*, 37, pp. 1612–1628.

CHAPTER 5

Denmark: Attentive Master of the Boardroom

Steen Buchreitz Jensen and Stanislav Shekshnia

THE CHAIR'S WORK IN CONTEXT

Denmark is one of the world's oldest monarchies, with a history stretching back to the Viking Age (eighth to eleventh centuries).

The country has a population of 5.6 million people. It is classified as a high-income economy, with GDP of US$325 billion and per capita GDP of US$51,364.[1] The Constitution of 1849 is the foundation of the current political system. Denmark has a number of political parties, none of which commands a majority in parliament. Since 1909 the country has been ruled by coalition governments, making collaboration and consensus-seeking a hallmark of the political landscape.

Denmark is often cited as one of the best countries to live in. It ranked top of the "World Happiness Report" in 2013 and 2016, based on

---

[1] The World Bank (2018). World Development Indicators. GDP Ranking. Available from: https://datacatalog.worldbank.org/dataset/gdp-ranking [Accessed 28 September 2018].

S. B. Jensen (✉)
Scandinavian Executive Institute, Kolding, Denmark
e-mail: sbj@se-institute.dk

S. Shekshnia
INSEAD, Fontainebleau, France

© The Author(s) 2019
S. Shekshnia, V. Zagieva (eds.), *Leading a Board*,
https://doi.org/10.1007/978-981-13-3197-8_5

variables such as per capita GDP, social support, healthy life expectancy, freedom to make life choices, generosity, freedom from corruption and positive and negative affects (emotions). Denmark was placed sixth in Forbes' annual list of "Best countries for business 2016".

The most common forms of enterprise in Denmark are:

- public companies (*aktieselskaber* or *A/S*);
- private limited liability companies (*anpartsselskaber* or *ApS*) Foundations (*fonde*);
- agricultural cooperatives (*andelsselskaber* or *Amba*); and
- partnerships (*interessentskaber*).

The vast majority of Danish companies are limited liability companies (around **200,000**), although some, including several listed companies, such as Novo Nordisk and Carlsberg, are ultimately owned or controlled by foundations. Denmark has one of the highest levels of ownership concentration in Europe—62% of 50 largest public companies have a significant shareholder and most smaller Danish enterprises are family owned or controlled.[2] The high ownership concentration translates into specific governance regulations, ensuring a high level of owners' control and impacts boards' and chairs' practices.

Both public companies (most of them are not listed, but chose that form of organization, roughly **42,000** in Denmark) and limited liability companies are regulated by the Companies Act (*Selskabsloven*) of **2009**, which lays down the fundamental principles, most of them in line with OECD guidelines on corporate governance, for example, equal treatment of all shareholders, protection of minority shareholders' rights, protection of creditors, election of governing bodies, transparency and disclosure. These also specify decision-making mechanisms and reporting requirements. The Danish Business Authority (*Erhvervsstyrelsen*) oversees compliance with the Act, and any changes in articles of association, composition of the board or management must be registered with it. The first Corporate Governance Code based on "explain or comply" principle was adopted in **2005**; adherence to it is monitored by a private Danish Corporate Governance Committee (DCGC).[3]

---

[2] Hansen, J. L and Lønfeldt, C. (2014). Corporate Governance in Denmark. In: P. Lekvall, ed., *The Nordic Corporate Governance Model*. Stockholm: SNS Förlag, p. 118.

[3] Ibid., pp. 118–120.

In addition to the Companies Act, listed companies are subject to the Capital Markets Act (as of 1 January 2017) and to EU regulations concerning disclosure requirements and market abuse. They are also subject to the Recommendations for Corporate Governance issued by the Danish Committee on Corporate Governance on a "comply or explain" basis. The Recommendations, which are not legally binding, cover the following:

- Communication and interaction with investors and other stakeholders
- Tasks and responsibilities of the board of directors
- Composition and organization of the board of directors
- Remuneration of management
- Financial reporting, risk management and audit

The so-called Nordic model, whereby shareholders have significant powers and exercise them via an annual or extraordinary general meeting and statutory auditors reporting to them, is the dominant governance structure for Danish corporations. In theory, general meeting can decide on practically any issues and intervene into the management of the company. In practice, they limit themselves to board appointment, dividends, distribution and major transactions.[4] Extraordinary general meetings for transacting specified business can be called by the board, an auditor or at the request of a shareholder representing at least 5% of the share capital. Public companies must have a board of directors separate from executive management, whereas private companies can opt to have a board or not depending on the legal structure they have chosen. The dominant legal structure of established limited liability companies is *aktieselskaber* (*A/S*), which requires a board. While, in theory, double mandates are allowed, in practice only non-executive directors sit on the board while the CEO is invited to attend board meetings on a permanent basis except for some items.

Unlike in some other European countries, in Denmark there is clear subordination and division of authority between governing bodies. Shareholders elect the board of directors (*tilsynsråd*) and statutory auditors for one year and set their compensation. Both the board and the auditors report to the general shareholders meeting and could be dismissed by it at any time. The board of directors plays the roles similar to that in other European countries—appointment of management, approval of strategy

---

[4] Ibid., p. 129.

and major transactions, risk management, communication of major events to stakeholders and so on. Executive management—either CEO or a management board (*direktion*) reports to the board and could be dismissed by it at any time.[5]

The important distinguishing feature of the Nordic model is employee representation on the board. In Denmark, employees have the right to elect their representatives as fully fledged board members with the same rights and responsibilities as directors elected by shareholders, provided the company has employed at least 35 people for the last three years. The number of employee representatives equals half the number of other members. If the number of regular members is uneven, the number of employee representatives is rounded up. So if the board has three regular members, the maximum number of employee representatives is two. The employees have to elect their representatives before the general shareholders' assembly, which confirms their directorship.[6]

Danish boards are usually small in size (5.3 for listed companies in 2014),[7] but among the most open and diverse in Europe, especially at large companies. At top 25 public companies in the country, independent directors represent 77%, foreign directors—42% and female directors—28%. Around 28% of chairs are foreign nationals, and there is no one chairwoman. On average, a chair is 61.7 years old and chairs 2.3 boards.[8]

The Companies Act specifies that the chair organizes the board meetings, is not allowed to occupy an executive position and may have a decisive vote. The Code recommends that the chair maintains good relationships with shareholders, manages the board and improves its effectiveness through self-evaluations and continuous improvement.[9]

DENMARK CULTURE MAP

According to *The Culture Map* by INSEAD Professor Erin Meyer, Denmark is a "low-context", "consensual", mostly "applications-first" and "task-based" culture with a "linear-time" scheduling style (see Appendix 1 for a

---

[5] Ibid.

[6] Thomsen, S., Rose, C., and Kronborg, D. (2016). Employee Representation and Board Size in the Nordic Countries. *European Journal of Law and Economics*, 42(3), pp. 471–490.

[7] Ibid., p. 146.

[8] Spencer Stuart (2017). Nordic Board Index 2017. Available from: https://www.spencerstuart.com/research-and-insight/nordic-board-index-2017 [Accessed 30 November 2018].

[9] Hansen, J. L and Lønfeldt, C. (2014). Corporate Governance in Denmark. In: P. Lekvall, ed., *The Nordic Corporate Governance Model*. Stockholm: SNS Förlag, p. 152.

full explanation). For boards of directors, this implies consensus-based decision-making, candid informal communication between directors, pragmatic discussions and respect for deadlines.

The low power distance and consensual element of the culture make Danish leaders democratic enablers. They not only permit but encourage followers to speak up, thus creating considerable freedom for new ideas to flow across an organization, regardless of the status of the person who made the initial suggestion.[10] Every idea—even if it was a leader's—can be challenged. Leaders are not afraid of seeking inputs from employees and admitting mistakes. Danish leadership style is often described as network based, empowering and motivating.[11] Teams are perceived as an instrument to facilitate effective leadership.[12] Harmonious interpersonal relations are highly valued, so leaders invest their time and efforts in maintaining a healthy atmosphere at their companies. Organizational structures tend to be flat with few hierarchical levels. Denmark is one of the most egalitarian countries in terms of gender in Europe (Fig. 5.1).

Danish business culture and governance practices have been strongly influenced by a powerful cooperative movement and the "folk" high school system designed and actively promoted by the nineteenth-century philosopher and educator Nikolaj Grundtvig, who advocated experience-based education, and emphasized equality and collaboration.[13] Similar values guided the pioneers of the cooperative movement, many of whom had graduated from Folk schools. By the late nineteenth century the cooperative became the dominant ownership structure in such key industries in Denmark as agriculture and retail. Cooperatives are governed according to the "one member, one vote" principle under which every member has the same say in the decision-making process, no matter what his or her stake.

---

[10] Simons, T., Pelled, L. H., and Smith, K. A. (1999). Making Use of Difference: Diversity, Debate, and Decision Comprehensiveness in Top Management Teams. *Academy of Management Journal*, 42(6), pp. 662–673.

[11] Schramm-Nielsen, J., Lawrence, P., and Sivesind, K. H. (2004). *Management in Scandinavia: Culture, Context and Change*. Cheltenham: Edward Elgar.

[12] Brodbeck, F.C., Frese, M., and el. (1998). *Leader Perceptions in Europe: A 21 Nations Study Based on the GLOBE Project*. Paper presented at the 14th EGOS colloquium. Maastricht, The Netherlands.

[13] See Danish folk high schools website: http://www.danishfolkhighschools.com [Accessed 3 December 2018].

● Denmark

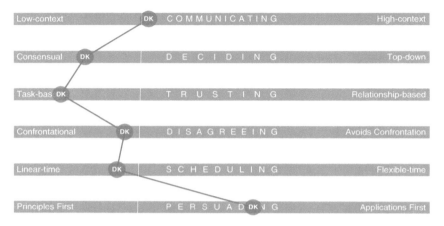

Fig. 5.1 Denmark Culture Map. Source: Based on the work of INSEAD Professor, Erin Meyer, and her *The Culture Map* book (Meyer, E. (2014). *The Culture Map: Breaking Through the Invisible Boundaries of Global Business.* New York: PublicAffairs.)

Existing Research and Hypotheses

The existing research demonstrates that chairs in Denmark, like those in other Scandinavian countries, generally try to lead their boards towards consensus and rarely resort to voting. The chair organizes a discussion, helps each director to come up with a position and, if consensus cannot be reached, postpones the decision. Chairs of Danish companies usually pay particular attention to leading the induction process for new board members and actively represent the company in the external world.[14]

Some studies have tried to establish correlations between a chair's characteristics and such independent variables as board composition, CEO turnover and company performance. Surprisingly, the size of the chair's board network seems to have no impact on the diversity of his or her board, although it is widely assumed that networks play a major role in the recruitment of directors.[15] The researchers who reached these conclusions

[14] Christensen, S., and Westenholz, A. (1999). Boards of Directors as Strategists in an Enacted World – the Danish Case. *Journal of Management and Governance*, 3(3), pp. 261–286.

[15] Randøy, T., Thomsen, S., and Oxelheim, L. (2006). A Nordic Perspective on Corporate Board Diversity. Available from: http://www.nordicinnovation.org/Global/_Publications/

assume that the power of the so-called old-boy network is being eroded, "which in turn will manifest itself in a growing inclination on the part of the board to emphasize truth and frankness in serving their shareholders". As in other countries, Danish companies where the chair of the board is an insider have a higher CEO turnover than companies with an external chair.[16] Another study of Nordic countries found a negative correlation between the number of boards the chair sits on and the company's financial performance.[17]

On the basis of existing literature on Danish culture, the Danish leadership tradition and board chairs' work in the Danish context, we have formulated a number of hypotheses about chairs' strategies vis-à-vis their main stakeholders and major challenges.

Chairs and boards. In the Danish context, board leaders operate as facilitators, striving for harmony and consensus, ready to sacrifice efficiency for relationships, yet never forgetting about effectiveness. They do not "take much space in the boardroom", encourage directors to speak their minds, communicate in a straightforward but polite manner, pay serious attention to the quality of materials and plan board agendas for months ahead.

Chairs and shareholders. Board chairs listen actively to shareholders' concerns, and they regularly update the latter on company developments. The communication with shareholders is candid and often informal.

Chairs and management. Chairs establish partnering relationships with the CEOs of their companies. The dialogue is regular, cordial, two-way and often informal, yet the chairs never forget that they are speaking with the CEOs on behalf of their boards.

Chair succession. Incumbent chairs do not participate in the selection of their successors, leaving this business to nomination committees and shareholders, yet they readily transfer their know-how to the successors once the latter have been identified.

Reports/2006/The%20performance%20effects%20of%20board%20diversity%20in%20 Nordic%20Firms.pdf [Accessed 3 December 2018].

[16] Lausten, M. (2002). CEO Turnover, Firm Performance and Corporate Governance: Empirical Evidence on Danish Firms. *International Journal of Industrial Organization*, 20(3), pp. 391–414.

[17] Randøy, T., Thomsen, S., and Oxelheim, L. (2006). A Nordic Perspective on Corporate Board Diversity. Available from: http://www.nordicinnovation.org/Global/_Publications/ Reports/2006/The%20performance%20effects%20of%20board%20diversity%20in%20 Nordic%20Firms.pdf [Accessed 3 December 2018].

We started our research journey with these hypotheses in mind and, as always, the reality turned out to be far more complex and nuanced. Among other things, we found the description of Denmark's culture as low-context, consensual, applications-first and task-based overly simplistic for understanding the work of chairs. In reality, many chair practices are ambivalent, for example, they may combine powerful leadership with strong group orientation or a focus on results with consensual decision-making, yet are perfectly legitimate from a cultural point of view. We discovered that a tension between two elements of Danish culture—strong group orientation (the informal practice of *Jantoloven*,[18] which makes people put the interests of the group above their own and strive for group cohesiveness) and strong freedom orientation—had a profound impact on many aspects of chairs' work and manifested itself in a number of distinctive practices. Unsurprisingly, while interviewing our respondents, we heard constant references to "alignment".

DATA

For this project, we interviewed nine board chairs, one woman and eight men, aged 50–70. Eight of them currently chair boards of limited liability companies, five of them publicly listed, while one heads a private foundation. Each has a minimum of ten years' experience serving on professional boards, as well as several years' experience as a chair. Of the nine chairs, eight have many years of experience as CEOs of large Danish companies.

In addition, we interviewed four CEOs, two independent directors and four shareholders. The CEOs were between 50 and 60 years old. Two of them were also major shareholders or represented the interests of major shareholders. Two others were professional executives who did not own any of the company's stock. The two independent directors each had more than ten years of experience as board members and had previously held CEO as well as chair positions. Among the four shareholders, three were related to the founders, and still represented family interests. One headed a private equity fund.

[18] Jakobsen, M. (2018). Janteloven/Jantelagen (Scandinavia). In: A. Ledeneva, ed., *The Global Encyclopedia of Informality*. London: UCL Press, pp. 254–259.

The Work of a Chair: The Incumbent's View

Before we describe the specific working practices of chairs of Danish companies, we would like to summarize the views of our respondents on the role of a board chair and how it should be executed.

In their opinion, two roles are essential: *the link and the enabler.* First, a good chair joins the dots between the board, the shareholders, the management and other important stakeholders. He or she actively listens and makes relevant information available to this entire network and its individual members. Creating the network and keeping it alive is perceived as the key function of a board leader.

The second crucial role is to enable the board to perform as a group of professionals and make quality decisions. This is also what the corporate governance regulations prescribe, yet our respondents felt strongly and passionately about the enabling aspect in a way that went beyond compliance. As one of them said: *"I strive for a situation where the chair is a tool—to get the best out of the board."* Both the result—good and timely decisions—and the process—fair and collective work—are important and neither is dispensable. This view resonates with the "integrating, developing and supervising directors'" role identified by Stewart (1991).[19]

Non-chair respondents generally agreed with this view of the chair's roles. As one of them put it: *"A good chair helps me focus my energy on that board in a way where I can best contribute."* They also emphasized that trust in the chair and the board in general makes this easier.

As for the question of *how* the role of chair should be executed, our answer is: "as a master who listens". We have borrowed this metaphor from one of the participants, who described his relationships with shareholders in the following way: *"I actively interact with you—listen, inform, ask—but I am the master in the boardroom."* Other respondents stressed the importance of fairness and respect for being an effective board leader in Denmark. As one of the directors put it: *"If there is mutual respect in the boardroom you don't need to spend much energy on issues related to this, and can focus the energy in other directions which create more value."*

[19] Stewart, R. (1991). Chairman and Chief Executive: an Exploration of their Relationship. *Journal of Management Study*, 28 (5), pp. 511–527.

We will present the main findings of our research, based on the three main challenges chairs face:

- Relationships with shareholders
- Leading the board
- Relationships with the CEO and management

We will also touch on the issue of succession.

Relationships with Shareholders

Denmark represents a somewhat unique and interesting context for examining chair-shareholder relationships. On the one hand, the country has one of the highest proportions of privately or family-owned/controlled companies in Europe. As one of the respondents said: "*In Denmark you find a real person behind every company's façade, no matter what its shareholders' ledger says.*" This implies that in most cases chairs have to work with "active shareholders" (see Chap. 1), who are passionate about the company, possess knowledge about it, actively seek information and may have their own strong views on its development. One respondent-owner explained it this way:

> *I am trying to be an active owner—engaged, but not interfering, supporting management and board and challenging them at the same time for the benefit of the company. I deliberately don't have an office in the company, but I visit it frequently and I am on the phone with the chair and the CEO on a weekly basis.*

On the other hand, Danish business culture (pragmatic, informal, straight-talking), the corporate governance guidelines and the high importance of autonomy for incumbent board leaders make the country's chairs "proactive" rather than "compliant" (see Chap. 1). In other words, they actively engage with shareholders, often beyond formal requirements, care about the long-term success of the business and prioritize performance over compliance. Yet they are very sensitive about their authority over the board and are ready to fight off shareholders' attempts to challenge it. As one of them put it: "*If the owner makes a suggestion which contradicts the overall direction we have agreed on I have no problem telling him: 'That is a good idea, but we won't implement it.' I expect them to respect my decision.*"

These features create a somewhat unique dynamic in chair-shareholder relationships, which we call **engaging-asserting**. Board leaders proactively seek shareholders' views, help them to form opinions, present these opinions to the board, consult them on important matters and inform them about board agendas, decisions and the rationale behind them. At the same time, chairs assert their board's independence and their own authority in running their boards the way they see fit—as the earlier quote about being "a master in the boardroom" suggests. The relationship is by no means fixed. At times it moves towards more engagement and then fluctuates towards assertiveness. One of the chair-respondents compared it to a ship always adjusting its course in the ocean to make the journey as efficient and safe as possible.

Before we present specific practices supporting the engaging-asserting model (see Table 5.1), we would like to make two caveats. First, chairs of Danish companies do care about "passive shareholders" (see Chap. 1), mostly financial individual and institutional investors, and make sure the

Table 5.1 Chairs' practices for interacting with active shareholders

Engaging practices	*Asserting practices*
Inquiring about shareholders' interests, needs and values	Articulating personal expectations and setting boundaries between the board and the shareholders
Sharing personal world view, interests and values	Articulating rules of engagement to shareholders
Seeking shareholders' expectations with regard to the company	Writing down rules of engagement and sharing them with shareholders
Sharing board materials with shareholders and discussing them before the meeting	Nudging shareholders to get to know corporate governance regulations
Seeking shareholders' inputs on specific issues	through reading or attending specialized courses
Preparing summaries of board meetings for shareholders	Putting the board's weight into the game
Conducting follow-up meetings with shareholders after board sessions	Preventing shareholders from reaching out to management and directors without the chair's participation
Initiating regular meetings or phone calls with shareholders	Breaking board meetings to have separate conversations with director-shareholders
Organizing informal meetings between shareholders	Rallying the board against intrusive shareholders
Calling and chairing formal shareholders' meetings	Threatening to resign
Using shareholders' networks for recruitment, information gathering or lobbying	Resigning

latter get from the company what the corporate governance regulations prescribe. Yet most chairs are less preoccupied with passive investors than their colleagues in the UK or the Netherlands, largely leaving this task to the CEO and management. The governance framework encourages them to do so; it allows to "relate confidential information to dominant shareholders where this is necessary for them in their role as the ultimate decision makers in respect of the company's governance."[20]

Second, the relationships between chairs and shareholders at some family companies go beyond the **engaging-asserting** dynamic. The chairs may take on some additional roles without formalizing them or receiving any extra compensation. For example, they may assess the leadership potential of younger-generation family members and mentor them, or they may provide strategic and investment advice. The respondents felt it was a part of building mutual trust and constructive relationships with the key shareholder of the company: "*In family-owned companies I am involved in some projects that would normally be handled by management. In addition to the board's formal duties, these owners see the board as a resource for inspiration, learning and development.*"

Enquiring about shareholders' interests, needs and values—and sharing their own. Many respondents emphasized the importance of investing time and emotional capital in understanding shareholders as human beings rather than just business people and building relationships with them, especially at an early stage. This is achieved through personal meetings without a formal agenda, where the chair takes a lead in questioning shareholders, but also proactively shares what is important for him or her. The goal is not to build friendship but to create mutual awareness as a foundation for constructive cooperation in the future. As one chair put it:

> *Alignment with a controlling owner is one of my main priorities. I invest a lot of time before entering a new board in order to make sure that I understand and support the owners' priorities. If the owner is not a board member I continue this dialogue by aligning major decisions before board meetings.*

Seeking shareholders' expectations with regard to the company. According to our respondents—both chairs and shareholders—this practice is essential for effective relationships. All the chairs we interviewed

[20] Hansen, J. L and Lønfeldt, C. (2014). Corporate Governance in Denmark. In: P. Lekvall, ed., *The Nordic Corporate Governance Model*. Stockholm: SNS Förlag, p. 145.

reported spending significant time before and immediately after taking the job on conversations with shareholders to understand their expectations as investors, owners, founders, or relatives of the founders and so on. Some board leaders achieved this through a series of informal meetings, while three respondents reported more structured approach. The latter had interviewed shareholders, asking them a set of questions, writing down the answers and returning the information to them in the form of a memo. The process is repeated on an annual basis.

One of the chairs has developed a questionnaire around key strategic dilemmas to make shareholders' expectations more explicit. He calls it a "matrix of expectations" and uses it in annual structured interviews with his three shareholders to gauge and map their expectations. The chair then summarizes the results and presents them back to the owners and the board. The set of questions has evolved year on year to reflect the changing business context. According to the chair, the approach has helped the shareholders to formulate their positions and the board to understand the constraints on its work. As he stated, it has been "*an eye-opener for the shareholders*", who insisted they were completely aligned before they went through the exercise, only to discover significant disagreements. The matrix of expectations asks the shareholders to position themselves on "dimensions", including the following:

- *Selling the business now versus 50 years from now*
- *Profits versus growth*
- *Dividends versus acquisitions*
- *Conservation versus evolution versus revolution*
- *Growth strategy: organic versus acquisitions*
- *Focus: low-hanging fruit versus long-term development*
- *Ownership pride versus professional rationalism*

Putting the board's weight into the game. The following quote from one of the respondents requires no further explanation:

Who am I to deal with a significant shareholder on equal terms? A part-time board chair getting the equivalent of US$100,000 a year. Not serious. But when the whole board speaks to them, they listen. So I always remind shareholders that I am an interface between them and the board. I never speak my mind; it's the collective voice of the board of directors they are hearing.

Threatening to resign and resigning. Chair-respondents considered resignation or the threat of resignation a legitimate way to assert their authority. As one put it: "*I tell my shareholders: I listen to you, yet I have my own way; if you don't respect it, I will resign.*" Some chairs take it even further. They suggest that in cases of disagreement, shareholders fire the whole board and elect a new one. Although such situations are rare, some respondents reported going through them and even eventually stepping down.

Leading the Board

We found that, to a large extent, the practices of Danish chairs stem from their view of their role as that of an enabler and connector, who actively engages all board members and at the same time asserts authority over them. Chair-respondents did not consider a board of directors a cohesive team but saw it as a group of professionals capable of collaborating to make collective decisions. The underlying assumption is that such people respect each other as professionals rather than developing mutual trust through team-building activities organized by their leader.

The chairs recognized and valued the diversity of directors' agendas and opinions, and worked proactively to bring them to the table as a rich foundation for decision-making. One of the respondents shared her story of chairing the board of a large family fund. The board consisted of family and non-family members with very different backgrounds. She defined her main task as aligning directors' interests and began by proactively seeking to understand—and then integrate—individual directors' expectations into the board's agenda. She would call all the directors before board meetings to find out if they wanted to add any items to the agenda or had any particular concerns about the proposed resolutions. She also phoned all of them after meetings to find out if they felt their concerns had been adequately addressed. As the chair, she wanted not only to avoid problems, but also to create a reflective and learning environment for the board.

We found that, unlike their counterparts in some other European countries such as Germany or Russia, board leaders in Denmark could be quite idealistic, often using concepts like "purpose" and "values" to manage their boards. One respondent would always have his directors, many of them international high-profile professionals, meet with company employees who had done something extraordinary, listen to their stories and talk about company values the day before the actual board meeting. He felt it *"would remind the board about the importance of our work, and therefore they were more focused and motivated to contribute"*. Another chair believed that explicitly articulated values help boards, especially large ones, to align, and that the board leader should make sure the values are articulated and adhered to. Some respondents said that their boards developed sets of corporate values which had been cascaded down through the organiza-tion, while others lifted the existing corporate values up to the board level.

We will describe some specific practices chairs in Denmark use to man-age their boards by looking at pre-meeting, in-meeting and post-meeting activities, as well as some specific aspects of their work, such as managing a difficult board member and working with employee-elected directors.

Pre-meeting

Before every board meeting, an effective Danish chair reaches out to key stakeholders—shareholders, board members, key executives—to discover their expectations, positions and concerns. This allows them to engage directors and to avoid surprises in the boardroom—something many respondents felt strongly about. Non-chair respondents particularly appre-ciated this practice regardless of the form it took—a phone call, a meeting or an e-mail.

All respondents reported spending significant time preparing for each board meeting. They felt the quality of materials played an important role in ensuring their boards' effectiveness. Most chairs had intense discussions with their CEOs during the preparation phase. Others believed that man-agement should have more autonomy to express their position. This dual-ity also applied to management presentations: one respondent checked all presentations before they went to the board members; the others trusted management to prepare materials. The former did a lot of homework to avoid surprises; the latter believed that spontaneity would improve the final decision.

Danish chairs shorten board-meeting agendas by dealing with technical and less important issues off line and delegating work to board commit-tees. Committees serve as task forces for looking more deeply into impor-tant issues, conducting analytical work and preparing recommendations for the board. Their small size allows for in-depth discussions and quality decisions. As one of the respondents put it: *"At the end of the day, facts should create the foundation for effective board decisions. The committees help to create this foundation."*

The timing for sending materials varied from one to two weeks before the meeting, the shared philosophy being "neither too late, nor too early", since board members have multiple commitments and a limited attention span. Some chairs defined the format and content of the board materials down to the last detail. Many included a summary of the last meeting's materials in the board book, as well as additional materials that had arisen since the previous meeting.

Digital platforms to handle the exchange of all board information are becoming more common in Denmark. All respondents—chairs, board members and executives—appreciated this trend. However, several of them mentioned that it is important to keep the platform as simple as possible. Directors who serve on several boards expressed confusion when they were exposed to several different platforms, each with its own logic. Security is often more complicated than when material is distributed by mail, and this makes accessing it less flexible. One director noted: "*The structure of the online platform should be simple. We should not spend our time handling the platform but should focus on essential board issues. Sometimes using a cloud filesharing service with good security like Google Drive or Dropbox may be the most effective way.*"

Some chairs in Denmark are personally involved in integrating new directors by setting expectations, answering questions, making introductions to key stakeholders and conducting mentoring and coaching sessions, while others leave such activities to the management and the corporate secretary.

In-meeting

Danish chairs vary in the way they deal with management participation in board meetings. Half of the respondents invite only the CEOs; others call in the CEOs (and their direct reports) from time to time. Interestingly, this variation does not depend on the size or complexity of the business. In most cases, executives participate in discussions of only some items. The most common practice for our respondents was to update directors on recent events and on interactions with management since the previous meeting.

Most chairs conduct in-camera sessions (without executives present) at the beginning or end of the board meeting. Executive-respondents believed that the board uses this time to evaluate the management. However, several chairs pointed to another purpose—to discuss disagreements without executives present and to demonstrate unity to them, which seems very important for Danish chairs.

Some chairs pointed out that there is a big difference if these in-camera sessions are held before or after the board meeting. Before the meeting, the chair sets the scene and ensures that directors have aligned expectation about the agenda, timing and so on. After the meeting, sessions often become a review of follow-up actions.

Danish chairs strive to enable collaboration between directors and refrain from domineering and taking too much space in the boardroom. They pay special attention to fairness and equality among all board members, encourage productive discussion and minimize passive listening time. We discovered a number of practices designed to support highly collaborative meetings.

Establishing rules for board discussions and ensuring adherence to them is one of them. Indeed, one chair had drawn up a list of guidelines, as follows:

Guidance for Chairing Board Meetings

- *Provide enough time for preparation, discussion and decision making*
- *Prioritize important topics in advance*
- *Ambiance is important, encourage everyone to contribute*
- *Avoid dominance or partiality*
- *Treat all directors equally*
- *Acknowledge the specific knowledge of each member*
- *Never forget silent directors*
- *Plan in great detail*

Managing time allocation is another key practice that supports collaboration. It combines such specific strategies as forbidding or limiting management presentations during board meetings, placing agenda items that require significant time and mental effort earlier and before lunch, and allocating equal time for comments to each board member. One chair shared that he limits his meetings to three or a maximum of four hours. This puts productive pressure on the board and on executives to be prepared and to work hard.

Guiding the flow of discussion in real time is a significant challenge. Respondents reported responding with such practices as giving the floor to the most knowledgeable director first, to set the tone; going round the table asking every member to state their opinion either at the beginning or at the end of the discussion; openly encouraging directors to speak, while reminding them of the need for brevity and specificity; calling on a specific director to contribute; and cutting directors short when they take too much airtime or make irrelevant comments. Chairs in Denmark pay special attention to equal allocation of airtime and participation by every director. One chair-respondent shared that he personally coached employee representatives to help them gain the confidence to speak up in meetings. For him "*a meeting where everyone contributes is a much better meeting*".

Conflict management is always part of a chair's job. As discussions in Denmark tend to be frank, directors are not afraid to state their positions openly and to challenge the opinions of others. Chairs encourage debates yet keep them under control. As one respondent put it: "*I am not afraid of disagreement. You need a good deal of it for a healthy board. But I don't allow aggression or disrespect in the boardroom.*" In Denmark, chairs deal with a conflict directly in the boardroom and often get the whole board involved. One common practice is to give each of the conflicting parties the floor, so that they can formulate their position, and then to involve the whole board in resolving the conflict. This practice reflects the cultural norms of open disagreement and direct negative feedback. Non-chair respondents in particular believe that the ability to handle disagreements in the boardroom is very important for effective chairing. If a disagreement is the result of limited data about an issue, the chair will postpone the discussion to a later meeting and organize a committee to provide solid data for the discussion.

Action-oriented minutes are an important outcome of a good board meeting, and Danish chairs pay special attention to preparing and distributing them. The level of detail varies from one board to another, but in all cases they are more than dry resolutions and cover expressed views and positions. According to one chair: "*Such a style prevents the board from forgetting, ignoring or resurfacing key positions of the board members.*"

Post-meeting
Between meetings, Danish chairs try to create and maintain a single information space for all directors. One chair said that, whenever he gets a question from one board member, he sends it with his answer to the entire board. Some board leaders create chats for all directors, some write short updating memos and others have the CEO to send monthly updates to directors.

Many respondents hold one-to-one discussions with directors immediately or sometimes after the board meeting as a way to preserve freshness of impressions and reinforce their engagement. One phones each board member after the meeting and asks them how he performed, if anything went wrong and what could be improved next time.

Board evaluation is a common practice in Denmark, and chairs use it as a method to build a shared understanding of what the board does well, where the gaps are and how they can be plugged. From our sample seven out of nine chairs conduct board evaluations every year. Three use external consultants, while the other four are thinking about experimenting with them in the future. The size and the complexity of the business are not the determining factors here—the choice is driven by the chair's preferences. One respondent described a very sophisticated evaluation process in cooperation with an external consultant. It involves 360-degree and individual interviews with board members and executives, plus consultants attending board meetings as observers. The assessment covers such areas as:

Core foundations

- *Business challenges and priorities*
- *Clarity and alignment of roles and responsibilities*
- *Board composition and capabilities*
- *Board information and understanding*

Operational feedback

- *Board processes (rhythm, style etc.)*
- *Board time allocation and focus*
- *Committee effectiveness*
- *Supporting business processes*

Behavioral enablers

- *Chairman's role and relationships*
- *NED/Executive relationships*
- *Nature of Board dynamics*
- *Individual contributions*

The chair orchestrates this work, listens to the initial findings and facilitates the discussion of the consultants' report at the next board meeting.

In particular, the respondent makes sure that the board agrees on specific actions to improve its effectiveness and follows up on their implementation.

Chairs who do not use professional consultants for board evaluation emphasize the importance of dialogue and group discussions. As one of them said: "*Board evaluation is not a test. It is a tool which should stimulate dialogue and reflection. This requires careful design of the survey depending on the board's composition and current challenges.*" Another respondent said that he was not interested in the individual competencies of directors, but in the collective ability of the board. Each year, the board defines an evolving set of collective competencies, and at the end of the year every director evaluates the board along these dimensions. Then the whole board discusses the outcomes of the evaluation and plans specific actions to improve its own effectiveness.

Whether they use external consultants or not, all chair-respondents believe in board evaluation as a tool that creates value rather than a formal procedure. As one of them put it: "*The evaluation allows us to have a dialogue about issues that do not surface in the daily board work.*" In Denmark, shareholders do not participate in the board evaluation process (unless they happen to be board members), but some chairs reported sharing the evaluation results with important shareholders to keep them in the loop on such important issues as board performance and composition.

A number of chair-respondents were active in shaping the composition of their boards. As one said: "*If involving directors is too difficult because the board is too large, its size should be reduced. Effective boards are relatively small.*" This respondent described a critical situation where he had chaired a very large board. After a few meetings, he realized that it was extremely hard to make any decision. The chair approached the shareholders and they agreed to halve the board's size. As a result, the speed of decision-making and quality of collaboration with management increased. Other respondents reported asking shareholders to remove underperforming directors from their boards, as described in the next section.

Managing Difficult Board Members

Chairs in Denmark value all directors and try to enable them to make a productive contribution. At the same time, they believe, as one respondent put it: "*The board needs to signal unity towards management. If we cannot, we need to address it.*"

Danish board leaders recognize that there are different types of non-conforming directors and their non-cooperative actions may be driven by different motives, some of them unconscious. The first strategy is therefore to analyse and understand what is behind the deviant behaviour. As one respondent put it: "*When you deal with a quiet director you should ask yourself: does the person keep silent, because she agrees with our decisions, or because she disagrees? If the latter, we cannot move on—it will backfire in the future.*" Most respondents reported organizing personal meetings with non-conforming directors to acknowledge their importance to the board, listen to their concerns, ask clarifying questions and share a personal view on the problem. Often such exploratory conversations help "difficult" board members to see the situation in a different light and to alter their behaviour.

The second strategy is to proactively transform the problematic behaviour, which may take the form of mentoring sessions, one-to-one conversations to set expectations and rules of engagement before the board meeting, feedback after the board meeting, follow-up phone calls or e-mails with specific requests. Chairs use 360-degree board evaluation as an additional instrument to create awareness of deviant behaviour and to change it.

In the spirit of open disagreement and direct negative feedback, chairs in Denmark do not hesitate to confront deviant directors' behaviour in the boardroom if offline interventions have not brought about the desired change. The respondents spoke about: repeating board rules before the meeting—and during the meeting, if the non-conforming behaviour recurs; "cold calling" silent directors and cutting short talkative ones; reminding egotistic members of the collective nature of the board's work; and not giving the floor to non-conforming directors for some time—or even the whole meeting. Some mentioned humour as a way to get a message across. Others involved the whole board in discussing deviant behaviour to strengthen the message.

If nothing works, Danish board leaders resort to the radical strategy of removal. Sometimes the chair suggests that a deviant director resigns; sometimes the matter is escalated to the shareholders, who elect a new board. But such cases are very rare. One chair says: "*I lay out the conditions under which I expect a person to function on this board, and I end by asking them: 'Do you want to stay on the board under these conditions?' If they don't want to comply I always get them to resign.*"

Unlike their counterparts in the Netherlands, Russia or Turkey, chairs in Denmark have a strong preference for resolving problems with difficult board members themselves or at the board level rather than involving external help from shareholders, consultants or professional coaches. Independent directors and CEOs also expect the chair to address the deviant behaviour of a board member personally, preferably outside the boardroom.

Working with Employee Representatives on the Board

Although employees have the right to the board representation in relatively small companies (35 employees or more), they do not always get organized to elect their representatives, so even some larger companies do not have employees on their boards of directors.

When employee representatives are part of the board, the tradition of collaboration helps to make their participation productive. In Denmark, which has been governed by coalition governments for more than a century, most laws are negotiated by political parties with fundamentally different beliefs and agendas. Similarly, negotiations between unions and employers' organizations are usually quite constructive. Danish people have not only the mindset but the skills for collaboration. Board leaders build on this when they integrate employee representatives. Often they start by making sure the board does not become a place for employer-employee negotiations and then gradually involve employee representatives in decision-making. As one of them said to us:

> *I used to accept them [employee representatives] but not really include them in our work. One day we were in a critical situation and an employee representative spoke up and prevented us from taking a disastrous decision. I realized that they have valuable knowledge about things on the ground—knowledge which we should be much more exposed to on the board. After that I started to invest time in them. I want to know them and understand how they can contribute, and what motivates them.*

Some respondents reported that they provided personal mentoring for employee representatives to make them more comfortable in the boardroom.

One experienced chair summarized his approach to working with employee representatives in five bullet points:

- *They bring deep insights of the organization to the board.*
- *They complement non-executive directors.*
- *They need to feel they are fully-fledged board members.*
- *They need to receive a solid induction training and to be supported throughout their journey.*
- *They have to work in board committees.*

Relationships with the CEO and Management

All the chairs interviewed work closely with the CEOs of their companies, an interaction that is often complex and followed no strict rules. The two predominant types of the interaction are collaboration and mentoring (see Chap. 1).

The first chapter of this book defines collaboration as "a close, intense and well-structured interaction between professionals with equal status and shared goals". As our interviews in Denmark demonstrate, both chairs and CEOs believe in intense collaboration based on a shared understanding of what is good for the company, mutual respect, transparency and predictability, and active information exchange. This approach resonates with Higgs' idea of a chair as a "trusted partner of the CEO".[21] The common practices of collaboration are joint development of board agendas and annual board plans, reviews of board materials before they go to the directors, customer visits and business trips. Some respondents mentioned that the chair and CEO may make some decisions between themselves and only inform other directors about them later. One chair explains: "*First you need to agree with the board that you work with the CEO in this way. I log all these decisions and inform them monthly or in the material for the next board meeting.*"

Some chair-respondents emphasized the importance of understanding the CEO as a human being, rather than just a professional, and of investing time in doing so: "*You need to know more details about the world of the CEO's everyday life, but you don't have to be an (industry) expert.*"

CEO-respondents shared that effective chairs respect their autonomy and professionalism, listen well and help when asked to. Danish shareholders want board leaders to work closely with CEOs, but do not interfere

---

[21] Higgs, D. (2003). Review of the Role and Effectiveness of Non-Executive Directors. Available from: http://www.ecgi.org/codes/documents/higgs.pdf [Accessed 26 March 2018].

with these relationships. They also appreciate having direct contact—without the mediation of the chair—with the CEO.

According to Chap. 1, mentoring "occurs when a senior professional (the chair) interacts with a junior partner (the CEO). The main goal is for the former to provide the latter with the knowledge, experience and resources to perform the CEO's functions." As one respondent put it: "*It is your job to guide the CEO to be good at receiving and processing the response from the board, no matter if it is positive or negative.*" In Denmark, chair-CEO mentoring is highly informal. Respondents spoke about face-to-face meetings without a formal agenda, both planned and impromptu phone calls, exchange of messages, meals together and introductions to the chair's social and professional networks. The content of the mentoring varies greatly and reflects the personalities, backgrounds and experiences of the people involved. The most popular themes are general management acumen, strategy and people management. One chair mentioned that he always enters a relationship with a CEO on the assumption that he/she is the best CEO for the company and asks himself: "*How can I help this CEO to succeed?*" This means that what works with one CEO does not necessarily work with another. This board leader believes that a chair has to protect a CEO from excessive criticism by directors during tough times.

In Denmark board chairs recognize the challenge of information asymmetry between the board and management and try to deal with it in a pragmatic way. They serve as a link between non-executive and executive directors, namely the CEO. One respondent shared his practice of "*the chair's minutes*", whereby he starts every meeting by summarizing the important issues he might have raised with the CEO since the last meeting. Other respondents prepare write-ups of their discussions with the chief executive or ask the CEO to write short updates for the whole board. Chairs encourage other directors to reach out to the company and its executives.

In fact, this is a distinctive feature of board-chair-CEO-management dynamics in Denmark. Unlike chairs in some other countries, board leaders follow Higgs' advice and do not try to monopolize the role of interacting with the CEO.[22] Both CEO- and shareholder-respondents recognized this as a positive element. As one owner put it:

---

[22] Ibid.

We want a flat organizational structure where the decisions can be made by the relevant people when it is necessary. The structure should not limit the quality of the work between our people. Therefore we need to have the same dynamics between board, owner and management. However, this requires mutual trust to work.

Chair Succession

There was consensus among all respondents that chair succession was the business of the shareholders. Danish chairs do not nominate or prepare their successors, leaving it entirely to the owners. As one put it: "*If the owner is not fully satisfied with the work of the chair, he will look for a new one.*" At the same time, resignation—in cases of serious disagreement with the shareholders, the board or even the CEO—is a tool Danish chairs are prepared to use. If they feel they have exhausted all possible ways of achieving alignment, they step down.

The approach to chair succession varies across ownership structures. In equity funds with active ownership, formal evaluation takes place on a regular basis and both sides can make a decision to end the relationship. In private companies, evaluation happens more informally, usually every two to three years. Owner-respondents reported that the chair is a very important figure for them. They pay attention to his or her performance and think about the future, although nobody reported having formalized succession planning.

Summary

While many practices identified by our research are similar to those in other European countries, some aspects of the chair's work have national roots and are specific to Denmark. We found that the values defined for Danish people by the nineteenth-century philosopher Nikolaj Grundtvig—a spirit of freedom, disciplined curiosity and equality—had an impact on the ways chairs think about and execute their job.

The research confirmed our initial hypothesis about chairs being proactive in understanding shareholders' concerns and bringing them to the board, as well as feeding information back to the owners. However, our interviews revealed an additional and very important element in Danish chair-shareholder dynamics: asserting the board and the chair's independence. In Denmark, an important condition for being an effective chair is to feel in control of the board, its dynamics and workings—and board leaders stand up for this right.

We hypothesized that, in the Danish context, board leaders operate as facilitators, striving for harmony and consensus and effectiveness at the same time. They are informal, candid and accessible. The research added more colour to that picture. Creating transparency, putting all the facts on the table and shedding light on all matters are important to Danish board leaders. Negative feedback is provided honestly and frankly. They encourage everyone to speak their minds with vigour and determination, are not afraid of conflicting views and deal with disagreements in a pro-active way.

Danish chairs run meetings in an interactive and lively manner. Procedural fairness is important for them, but formalities are of little value. They allow directors to formulate their opinions in multiple ways but do not shy away from taking an active part in the discussion They make sure that every director feels his/her opinion has been heard and counts. Above all, they are pragmatic and driven by a desire for effectiveness: the board has to make decisions.

Chairs in Denmark care about the collective capability of the board and strive to improve it through regular evaluations, providing coaching and mentoring to directors and even replacing board members. Surprisingly this proactivity does not extend to their own succession, which they leave to shareholders.

Danish board leaders partner with their CEOs for the benefit of the company and mentor them, mostly informally. These are relations between professionals of equal status, although chairs never forget that they represent the board and encourage other directors to engage with executives.

In the next decade, we foresee the following trends in Denmark.

- There will be more female board leaders, but their number will not exceed a quarter of all incumbents.
- The number of chairs under the age of 50 will increase.
- There will be more non-Danish chairs of Danish companies than today, but the majority of board leaders will remain Danes.
- Diversity will increase noticeably. We will see more chairs without CEO experience, though this will remain the main career path for future board leaders.

- The complexity of the chair's work will increase and will require more time and knowledge. Few people will chair more than two boards.
- Information technology will become an integral part of the chair's work. Many meetings will move online and paper will disappear from the boardroom.

References

Andersen, P. K. (2003). Corporate Governance in Denmark. Available from: http://www.scandinavianlaw.se/pdf/45-1.pdf [Accessed 3 December 2018].

Brodbeck, F.C., Frese, M., and el. (1998). Leader Perceptions in Europe: A 21 Nations Study Based on the GLOBE Project. Paper presented at the 14th EGOS colloquium. Maastricht, The Netherlands.

Christensen, S., and Westenholz, A. (1999). Boards of Directors as Strategists in an Enacted World – the Danish Case. *Journal of Management and Governance*, 3(3), pp. 261–286.

Committee on Corporate Governance. (2013). Recommendations on Corporate Governance. Available from: https://corporategovernance.dk/sites/default/files/recommendations-ebs-12401-rapport-selskabsledelse-uk-5k-nov-2014.pdf [Accessed 3 December 2018].

Goethals, G. R., Sorenson, G. J. and Burns, J. M. (2004). *Encyclopedia of Leadership*. Thousand Oaks: SAGE Publications.

Hansen, J. L and Lønfeldt, C. (2014). Corporate Governance in Denmark. In: P. Lekvall, ed., *The Nordic Corporate Governance Model*. Stockholm: SNS Förlag.

Higgs, D. (2003). Review of the Role and Effectiveness of Non-Executive Directors. Available from: http://www.ecgi.org/codes/documents/higgs.pdf [Accessed 26 March 2018].

Jakobsen, M. (2018). Janteloven/Jantelagen (Scandinavia). In: A. Ledeneva, ed., *The Global Encyclopedia of Informality*. London: UCL Press, pp. 254–259.

Lausten, M. (2002). CEO Turnover, Firm Performance and Corporate Governance: Empirical Evidence on Danish Firms. *International Journal of Industrial Organization*, 20(3), pp. 391–414.

Meyer, E. (2014). *The Culture Map: Breaking Through the Invisible Boundaries of Global Business*. New York: PublicAffairs.

Official Journal of the European Union. (2014). Commission Recommendation of 9 April 2014 on the Quality of Corporate Governance Reporting. Available from: https://eur-lex.europa.eu/legal-content/EN/TXT/?uri=CELEX%3A32014H0208 [Accessed 3 December 2018].

Randøy, T., Thomsen, S., and Oxelheim, L. (2006). A Nordic Perspective on Corporate Board Diversity. Available from: http://www.nordicinnovation. org/Global/_Publications/Reports/2006/The%20performance%20 effects%20of%20board%20diversity%20in%20Nordic%20Firms.pdf [Accessed 3 December 2018].

Schramm-Nielsen, J., Lawrence, P., and Sivesind, K. H. (2004). *Management in Scandinavia: Culture, Context and Change*. Cheltenham: Edward Elgar.

Simons, T., Pelled, L. H., and Smith, K. A. (1999). Making Use of Difference: Diversity, Debate, and Decision Comprehensiveness in Top Management Teams. *Academy of Management Journal*, 42(6), pp. 662–673.

Spencer Stuart. (2017). Nordic Board Index 2017. Available from: https://www. spencerstuart.com/research-and-insight/nordic-board-index-2017 [Accessed 30 November 2018].

Stewart, R. (1991). Chairman and Chief Executive: an Exploration of their Relationship. *Journal of Management Study*, 28 (5), pp. 511–527.

The World Bank. (2018). World Development Indicators. GDP Ranking. Available from: https://datacatalog.worldbank.org/dataset/gdp-ranking [Accessed 28 September 2018].

Thomsen, S., Rose, C., and Kronborg, D. (2016). Employee Representation and Board Size in the Nordic Countries. *European Journal of Law and Economics*, 42(3), pp. 471–490.

CHAPTER 6

Italy: Alignment for Effectiveness

Anna Zanardi

The Chair's Work in Context

Italy is a parliamentary republic, a founding member of the European Union and defined as a developed market economy. In 2016, its GDP was US$1.9 trillion,[1] US$39,426 per capita.[2] Italy is the only G7 country to register a negative percentage change (−0.2%) in per capita GDP since 1997. The service sector accounts for over 70% of GDP, industry around 24% and agriculture just above 2%.[3]

Italy has 3.7 million enterprises, which employ about 14.3 million people.[4] Privately held companies account for the majority of active businesses,

---

[1] The World Bank (2018). World Development Indicators. GDP Ranking. Available from: https://datacatalog.worldbank.org/dataset/gdp-ranking [Accessed 10 May 2018].

[2] The World Bank (2018). World Development Indicators. GDP per capita, PPP, in international dollars. Available from: http://databank.worldbank.org/data/reports.aspx?source=2&series=NY.GDP.PCAP.PP.CD [Accessed 16 May 2018].

[3] The World Bank (2018). Services, Value Added. Industry, Value Added. Agriculture, Value Added. Available from: https://data.worldbank.org/indicator/NV.IND.TOTL.ZS [Accessed 10 May 2018].

[4] European Commission (2017). SBA Fact Sheet. Italy. Available from: https://ec.europa.eu/docsroom/documents/26562 [Accessed 16 May 2018].

A. Zanardi (✉)
Independent Board Advisor, Zurich, Switzerland
e-mail: anna@annazanardi.com

© The Author(s) 2019
S. Shekshnia, V. Zagieva (eds.), *Leading a Board*,
https://doi.org/10.1007/978-981-13-3197-8_6

99% of them are SMEs.[5] Around 320 companies are listed on *Borsa Italiana* (Italian Stock Exchange). The concentration of ownership is very high: 46% of listed companies are controlled by a shareholder with more than 50% equity, and over 60% of listed companies have significant family shareholders.[6] The government is a controlling shareholder in 9% of public companies, which represent around 40% of Italian stock market capitalization.

Over the last 30 years, attention to corporate governance has significantly increased among governments, shareholders and other stakeholders. The creation, in 1985, of *Commissione Nazionale per le Societa' e la Borsa* (CONSOB), an independent authority responsible for regulating Italian financial markets, was an important step in this direction. It has a division dedicated to corporate governance, which monitors compliance by public companies against regulatory requirements and best practice. The Code of Corporate Governance has had six revisions since its inception in 1999. The last, in July 2018, further advanced the "comply or explain" principle, explicitly discouraged golden parachutes for executives, emphasized the importance of periodic board reviews and promoted gender parity for directors.[7]

The Code does not impose a mandatory structure for boards. In practice most Italian listed companies operate under a traditional governance system whereby the general shareholders' assembly elects a board of directors and a board of statutory auditors. The board of directors is responsible for approving strategic, operational and financial plans and monitoring their respective implementation; defining the risk profile of the company; ensuring an adequate organizational, administrative and accounting structure; approving extraordinary financial operations; and adequate disclosure and control as required by law. It also makes key executive appointments. The Code prescribes that the board should make decisions with the objective of creating shareholder value over the medium-to-long term.

---

[5] Ibid.

[6] Mandl, I. (2008). Overview of Family Business Relevant Issues: Final Report. Available from: https://ec.europa.eu/docsroom/documents/10389/attachments/1/translations/en/.../native [Accessed 3 December 2018].

[7] Corporate Governance Committee (2018). Corporate Governance Code. Available from: https://www.borsaitaliana.it/comitato-corporate-governance/codice/codiceeng2018.en.pdf [Accessed 2 November 2018].

The Code recommends that boards establish separate committees for remuneration, nomination and control and risk. In practice, nomination and remuneration responsibilities often come under the remit of one committee. In special circumstances, other committees are established to deal with specific tasks (such as self-tender offers, critical branding decisions and synergies after a merger or acquisition). On average, Italian boards have 3.4 committees.[8]

The board of statutory auditors (*collegio sindacale*) is an independent controlling and monitoring body made up of three standing and two alternate auditors. It is elected for three financial years and monitors compliance with the law, company by-laws and the principle of sound governance. It also gives an opinion on the appointment of internal auditors, compliance officers and risk managers. The members of the statutory auditors board attend all board of directors and committee meetings without voting rights. All statutory auditors are required to be chartered accountants or practising business faculty.

Italian boards have 11.5 members on average (the EU average is 12.3).[9] The number of independent directors on boards has increased steadily over the last two decades to an average of 5.9.[10] Women represent 31% of board members and 9% of chairs.[11] A new regulation, Law 120/2011,[12] requires one-fifth of board members to be women, rising to one-third when the board comes up for re-election. Since the enactment of Law 120/2011, directors have tended to be younger, more educated and less tied to the controlling shareholder. Only 4% of boards have a mandatory retirement age, indicating a culture that still values networks and connections more than new technology and innovation. The average number of board meetings in a year is 11.6.[13] However, this number is skewed by the

[8] Spencer Stuart (2017). Italy Board Index 2017. Available from: https://www.spencerstuart.com/-/media/pdf%20files/research%20and%20insight%20pdfs/italy%20board%20index%202017.pdf [Accessed 16 May 2018].

[9] Ibid.

[10] Ibid.

[11] Ibid.

[12] European Parliament. Policy Department C: Citizens' Rights and Constitutional Affairs (2014). The Policy on Gender Equality in Italy. Available from: http://www.europarl.europa.eu/RegData/etudes/note/join/2014/493052/IPOL-FEMM_NT(2014)493052_EN.pdf [Accessed 16 May 2018].

[13] Spencer Stuart (2017). Italy Board Index 2017. Available from: https://www.spencerstuart.com/-/media/pdf%20files/research%20and%20insight%20pdfs/italy%20board%20index%202017.pdf [Accessed 16 May 2018].

number of board meetings held by financial institutions. The boards of banks, for example, can meet as often as twice a month, while those of other companies tend to meet every other month, except in extraordinary circumstances.

The Code of Corporate Governance recommends the separation of the CEO and chair positions—as is the case at most publicly owned companies. In fact, the same person occupies both the chair and CEO roles at just 19% of publicly traded Italian companies.[14] Italian chairs are among the highest paid in Europe—in 2017 the average compensation for a chair of a public company was €879,000.[15] They also chair a significant number of boards—3.8 on average.[16]

Among the duties and responsibilities of the chair (*Presidente*) outlined in the Code are the following.

- To create effective board dynamics by the timely provision of quality materials, setting productive agendas for board meetings, facilitating board discussions and holding induction sessions to ensure directors update their skills and familiarity with the company. The induction of new directors is also advocated by the Corporate Governance Code of the Italian Stock Exchange, to provide them with information on the company, its financials, management systems, risks and so on.
- To ensure effective liaison between the board and management. Chairs are entrusted with organizing the board's work, liaising with executive and non-executive directors and between the board and the management. They ensure that directors do not interfere with or influence management beyond the purview of the board.
- To ensure effective communication between members of the board of directors and the board of statutory auditors, and to guarantee the latter with access to key information.
- To conduct board evaluations. These are generally carried out once a year, either as a self-evaluation exercise by the board or with the help of external consultants.[17]

---

[14] Ibid.
[15] Ibid.
[16] Ibid.
[17] Corporate Governance Committee (2018). Corporate Governance Code. Available from: https://www.borsaitaliana.it/comitato-corporate-governance/codice/codiceeng2018.en.pdf [Accessed 2 November 2018].

EXISTING RESEARCH

One of the better-researched themes in Italian corporate governance is CEO-chair duality. Studies have revealed a strong negative correlation between CEO-chair duality and firm performance.[18] Another observation is that the combination of the chair and CEO roles leads to an increase in the number and the influence of external directors.[19] This is consistent with the results of empirical research showing that the number of external directors increases as the CEO's influence increases, because they are required to counterbalance the power of the chair-CEO.[20] In addition, the chair and CEO roles tend to be performed by the same person in companies where there is less separation of ownership from control.[21]

In relation to the structure of Italian boards, it has been established that companies where a family is the largest shareholder and the chair comes from the controlling family tend to appoint more family representatives to board positions.[22] However, there is no research specifically dealing with the working practices of Italian board leaders.

ITALY CULTURE MAP

According to INSEAD Professor and cross-cultural expert Erin Meyer, Italy has a relationship-based, confrontational, top-down, flexible-time, principles-first and high-context culture (see Appendix A for full explanation). This description allows us to make a number of hypotheses about Italian chairs' behaviour and habits. We can expect informal connections between directors to be strong, with chairs working intensely outside the boardroom and some decisions being made informally (relationship-based culture). We also expect Italian chairs not to be afraid of debate and that they will perceive disagreement as an integral part of the decision-making process (confrontational). They will have no problem pushing their own

[18] Ciampi, F. and Gordini, N. (2013). The Potential of Corporate Governance Variables for Small Enterprise Default Prediction Modeling. Statistical Evidence from Italian Manufacturing Firms. *Preliminary Findings. Proceedings of the Cambridge Business and Economics Conference*, pp. 1–19.

[19] Belcredi, M. and Rigamonti, S. (2008). Ownership and Board Structure in Italy (1978–2003). *Proceedings of the EFMA Annual Meeting*, Athens, pp. 1–36.

[20] Linck, J. S., Netter, J. M. and Yang, T. (2008). The Determinants of Board Structure. *Journal of Financial Economics*, 87 (2), pp. 308–328.

[21] Ibid.

[22] Ibid.

point of view, especially on issues that are important to them (top-down, confrontational). In addition, we anticipate that agendas and timing will often change at the last minute (flexible time). Furthermore, Italian chairs will lean towards inductive reasoning, starting by defining the general concept and approach to an issue before presenting their own assumptions and only then moving on to examining the facts and finding specific solutions (principles first). Finally, they may leave a lot to be read between the lines, rather than explaining everything in detail (high context) (Fig. 6.1).

DATA

For this research project we interviewed 15 chairs, one-third of them women. Eight interviewees chaired listed companies; seven presided over family businesses or mid-sized private companies. None of them combined the role with that of CEO. Three had a mandate with regard to institutional communications. None of those chairing a listed company were the founder or a major shareholder. Two of those chairing family-owned companies were shareholders. All were "professional" chairs,

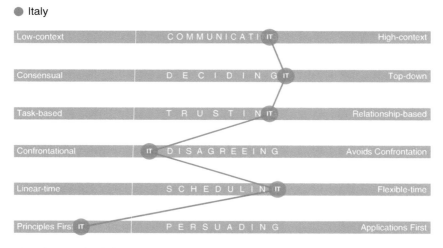

Fig. 6.1 Italy Culture Map (Source: Based on the work of INSEAD Professor Erin Meyer, and her *The Culture Map* book [Meyer, E. (2014). *The Culture Map: Breaking Through the Invisible Boundaries of Global Business.* New York: PublicAffairs])

insofar as they had no other job. On average, they had held their positions for four years (shortest two years, longest ten years). Nine presided over two boards, two over four boards and four over a single board.

Four of the 15 chairs defined the role of the board as "ceremonial". The other 11 saw its function as "principally supervisory and highly strategic". All of their boards had nominating, remuneration and risk committees.

The average number of board meetings per year was 10 (minimum 6, maximum 13). There was a positive correlation between market capitalization and the number of board meetings, probably related to the fact that higher capitalization is often associated with larger size and complexity, making frequent meetings necessary. The rate of participation in board meetings was 92%.

Meetings on average lasted two and a half hours (shortest one hour, longest up to six hours). Banking boards met more often and for longer, a trend that we believe is a direct effect of regulatory provisions aimed at increasing directors' accountability.

To complement interviews with the chairs we spoke to three directors, two CEOs and three shareholders' representatives—one from a family, one from a private equity firm and one from an investment institution.

Challenges and Practices

The interviews revealed valuable insights into how the leaders of Italian boards operate. We will present our findings based on the major challenges identified in the INSEAD Global Chair Survey 2015.[23]

Relationships with Shareholders

Chair-respondents considered establishing and maintaining good relationships with shareholders one of the most important aspects of their job. Non-chair-respondents seconded this view. Individual conversations, usually before board meetings, were the most common technique—and were especially important when deliberating on crucial decisions. For logistical reasons, these one to ones mainly took place by phone. While pre-board meetings were initiated equally by chairs and shareholders (or their representatives in the case of minority shareholders), the follow-up was mainly driven by the chair. In fact all but one of the chair-respondents made

[23] Shekshnia, S. and Zagieva, V. (2016). Chair Survey 2015. Available from: https://www.insead.edu/sites/default/files/assets/dept/centres/icgc/docs/chair-survey-2015.pdf [Accessed 3 December 2018].

follow-up calls within a week to update shareholders on board decisions and listen to their reactions. "*It's very important to solicit follow-up without leaving too much time to distort memories,*" said one.

Respondents felt that meeting in person with shareholders was important for maintaining good relationships, and held meetings at least every quarter on average. As one said:

> *Face-to-face meetings are very much part of the Italian culture. We need to sit at the same table and look at each other to reinforce the trust and sense of sharing goals. Often, I organize a business lunch or dinner with a shareholder. I understand that it's more than sharing updates—we need to share live moments to feel comfortable about discussing critical business issues.*

Respondents also underlined the need to provide both majority and minority shareholders with the same information.

From the shareholder's perspective, there are a variety of definitions of an "effective chair". For family shareholders, an effective chair guarantees harmony within the family while growing and diversifying the business for future generations. For private equity shareholders, an effective chair "*ensures that all important matters get onto the board's agenda*" and "*gets each director to contribute his/her best to the value of the company*". For institutional shareholders, the effective chair is a trusted guarantor of corporate governance. Many respondents underlined the legitimizing role of a board chair in the Italian context. As one CEO-respondent put it: "*The chair is a guarantor of the company's reputation.*" This partly explains the fact that many Italian chairs are older, well known in the business community and generally well paid.

Relationship with the CEO and Management

Contrary to our culture-based hypothesis, relationships between Italian chairs and CEOs are not hierarchical, even though board leaders are, in most cases, older and more experienced than CEOs. None of the respondents from any category used words like "boss" or "commanding" to describe chair-CEO interactions. In nine cases, chair-respondents defined themselves as "coaches" to the CEO and two mentioned being "mentors". The CEOs, for their part, talked about "partners" and "advisors". One put it this way: "*An effective chair is someone with experience, leadership and competence, who can be my sounding board and advisor.*"

Director-respondents emphasized the supporting aspect of the role, including one who described an effective experienced chair as "*very involved in the company's transformation as a support to CEO*".

Chairs and CEOs of Italian companies interact in a variety of ways: meeting in person, communicating via email and speaking on the phone. These encounters are often informal, unstructured and initiated by both parties—who value their relationships and try to avoid surprises and mis-understandings. One respondent described the practice of setting mutual expectations, whereby an incoming chair sits down with the CEO and asks a straightforward question, "*Where do you want me to contribute?*"—so as not to be perceived as a threat. However, we did not come across certain practices that are common in other European countries, such as formal feedback sessions between the chair and CEO, the setting of objectives for the former by the latter or periodical letters from the CEO to the chair.

CEO-respondents described an effective chair as someone who under-stands and supports the chief executive's agenda by aligning the board around it. One said that such chairs "*listen, ask questions, get the message and translate it to the whole board in an effective manner*". They also sup-port the CEO and the management by leading board meetings smoothly and efficiently, which allows for quick decisions and productive relation-ships with executives. One experienced CEO mentioned that good chairs help CEOs with external stakeholders, such as banks, customers and regu-lators, by putting their reputation and network behind the company's interests. One director recalled a case when a board chair joined negotia-tions with the bank and "*brought credibility*" into the process.

Shareholder-respondents also emphasized the collaborative aspect of chair-CEO relationships, but pointed to involvement with other senior executives, understanding of the business and challenging management as important practices of effective board leaders. One described an informal "management committee" set up by a chair—comprising the chair, CEO, some board members and selected senior executives—as a venue to chal-lenge management and have candid discussions.

Leading the Board

Board meetings at Italian companies are often formal—and even formali-ties, as many important decisions are taken outside the boardroom. Chairs along with the CEO play a critical role in securing this offline agreement through individual and small-group discussions with directors. As one

CEO put it: "*We work together to convince directors to agree to a certain decision; our unity is critical for achieving it.*" Yet sometimes discussions become quite heated, and chairs need to control directors' emotions and channel them into a productive direction.

In our conversations with Italian chairs and directors, the concept of "alignment" emerged as a central theme for a board leader. As one respondent put it:

> *Alignment is the most important dynamic a chair can put in motion when arriving in a board. Alignment means that, after having freely expressed our own ideas and dissent, we make an effort to be convergent on the final version of what we'll present outside the board—without exception, so that people feel how strong we are, all together in the same boat.*

We believe that the importance of alignment reflects some specific features of Italian boards and corporate governance. Not only are Italian boards of directors large (averaging 11.5 for public companies), they also have a high percentage of affiliated directors representing specific shareholders and interact with an independent board of statutory auditors, who participate in all board meetings.

Thirteen out of 15 chair-respondents felt their role was central to maintaining good relationships between board members, and that it was important to give equal attention to the different interests represented. These chairs worked hard on aligning their boards before, during and after board meetings.

In facilitating boardroom discussion, chairs of Italian companies strive for equality and balance by calling on reticent directors to speak up and containing talkative types. One director described an effective chair who always combined a strategic focus with attention to the human dynamics in the boardroom, never failed to see the wood for the trees and, at times of difficulty, could bring the discussion back on track. He called this practice "*content-based mediation*".

Most respondents open board meetings by presenting the agenda and then move on to the first item without further delay. However, a few ask the CEO or corporate secretary to introduce the agenda. Usually meetings end with a quick recap from the chair and an invitation to continue the discussion informally over drinks or a light lunch.

Half of the respondents dedicated 70% of board-meeting time to presentations and the remaining 30% to discussion; the other half tried to reach a 50:50 balance. As one said: "*The most difficult task is to explain effective rules for the executive presentations, so that the time is spent mainly on discussion, not on the narcissistic needs of the manager.*" Some chairs established formal rules for management presentations, such as a maximum of three slides and ten minutes.

For all respondents the preparation of board meetings required a substantial amount of time. It was considered best practice to send board material to directors six days prior to the meeting. However, only two respondents reported consistently following the rule—three days prior to the board meeting was more common. Many chair-respondents delegated the task of organizing the board materials to the board secretary.

In their personal preparation for the board meeting, chairs of Italian companies focus mostly on familiarizing themselves with the materials and proposed resolutions, although some respondents reported that they think about how to frame discussion questions, how to allocate time and how to manage potential conflicts and disagreements. All board leaders interviewed had done some work on improving their chairing skills and understanding the human side of their boards. One of them said: "*I've spent some time in the recent past getting to know myself better: my deep-rooted beliefs and also my reactions. It is time well spent to be more self-aware and available for the collective interest of the board.*"

Meals are important instruments of alignment for chairs of Italian companies. Pre-meeting dinners are quite common and usually well attended—by around 75% of board members on average, according to our respondents. In addition to dinners for the whole board, which usually take place before board meetings or the annual shareholders' meetings, chairs organize meals for smaller groups of directors—and some find them more effective. One respondent alternates dinners with committee chairs and dinners with independent directors, gathering the whole board to eat together only once a year.

The Code of Corporate Governance requires that the chair organize an annual evaluation of the board and its committees. This is a new practice for most Italian boards—and chairs are learning alongside their boards. Three respondents carried out a board assessment every year, while the other 12 did so only once every two years. Twelve used external consultants, while three conducted an internal evaluation. Evaluations covered items such as board size and composition; the professional competencies and experience of directors; and gender composition.

Ten of the 15 chairs interviewed had implemented a formal induction process for new members. The remaining five planned to implement one soon.

Managing Difficult Board Members

Chairs of Italian companies prefer to prevent misalignment or conflict among board members rather than manage it. As one director-respondent put it: "*Effective chairs have the experience and personal charisma to avoid conflicts on the board.*" Italian board leaders must be good at this, since only four of our respondents reported experiences of managing "difficult" board members!

In these rare cases, the first step was to make the person aware of the deviant behaviour by having a one-to-one discussion after the incident. Then it was possible to have another conversation before the next board meeting to warn the director not to destroy group dynamics.

In the boardroom, chairs played a finely balanced game of allowing productive dissent and containing open confrontation. As one respondent put it: "*You have to give enough space for expressing individual positions and also intervene with the right timing in order to avoid disruption. It's not very easy to be unpleasant but sometimes it's needed. You have to cut in gently but firmly.*" One director-respondent mentioned that in the Italian context a chair can just say "Let's give another person time to speak," if a director takes too long to express an opinion or loses track of the subject. Another practice is to involve other directors, to ask their advice and to make them allies in containing a deviant colleague in the boardroom. None of the respondents mentioned involving shareholders or firing as strategies for managing a "difficult" director.

Relationships with External Stakeholders

In Italy board chairs have a higher external visibility than in other European countries such as Denmark, the Netherlands or Russia. In many cases they take on a significant part of the legitimization function that the board plays.[24] This is another reason for the comparative seniority of people occupying the chair position in Italy and virtually full-time status that many of them have. One director-respondent shared an illustrative story:

[24] Johnson, J.L. Daily, C.M. and Ellstrand, A.E. (1996). Board of Directors: A Review and Research Agenda. *Journal of Management*, 22 (3), pp. 409–438.

In one company where I was on the board, the shareholders wanted to sell their stake and attracted a very seasoned chair to improve the company's image and help in negotiations with potential buyers. The chairman was known as a very honest and reliable person, so the other side took it very positively. The company was successfully sold.

This view is seconded by a CEO-respondent: "*A good chair is one who sends a convincing message to the external world: 'this is an all right company, you should do business with us'.*"

All chair-respondents considered institutional and external communication to be important tasks and constantly worked to maintain a positive image of the company in the eyes of the wider business community, not only shareholders. Meetings with institutional stakeholders, such as regulators, banks and suppliers, were carefully planned in advance but often held in informal settings over lunch or dinner. One director-respondent mentioned that the chairs he worked with met suppliers, banks and clients on behalf of the company and "*opened new doors for the CEO*". Interestingly, some chair-respondents met with business associates during the summer holidays and even took vacations with them. Professional and personal lives and networks often intertwine in Italy.

A few respondents mentioned that, in times of crisis, the chair's duties as representative of the company to the external world increased, as did the pressure to choose the right moment, means and words to communicate—while respecting the constraints of the law and the Code. This requires experience and training, but effective chairs, in the words of one director, "*must take to it like a duck to water*".

Chair Succession

The Code recommends that boards of directors "evaluate the adoption of executive succession plans" but says nothing specific about chair succession. We also know that transparent and well-planned preparation of future leaders has never been a strength of Italian business culture; succession decisions have traditionally been made when a sense of urgency prevails. Unsurprisingly, succession is not a top priority for chairs of Italian companies.

Nevertheless, our research revealed some positive dynamics. Five chair-respondents reported that they are working on—or have already prepared—their succession plans with the help of an external consulting company. Four, on the other hand, all from the banking and insurance sectors, had not concerned themselves with such matters. One director told us how the board nomination committee prepared a competencies-based profile of the future chair to guide the chair-succession process.

SUMMARY

In Italy the roles and practices of chairs are defined not only by law and a constantly evolving Code of self-discipline and cultural traditions, but also by such factors as company ownership, size, financial health and lifecycle. As one experienced director put it: "*In a startup board all boundaries are blurred. The chair drives an agenda, but he is the equal to other directors. In a public-company board, the chair should have an authority and stand apart.*" The composition of the board and the personality of the chair also impact what chairs do and how they do it.

As in other European countries, board chairs in Italy play three core roles: leading the board; interacting with shareholders; and maintaining relationships with the CEO and senior executives. In addition to these roles, they often represent the company in relationships with other external stakeholders and serve as "guarantors" of its reputation. Chairs in Italy represent a somewhat exclusive and predominantly male group of senior, well-connected and highly paid professionals. Most of them have been CEOs in the past, although a significant number have backgrounds in academia and politics. Some have family links to the key shareholders of the companies whose boards they chair.[25]

Alignment is the word that best describes both the mindset and the key practices of board chairs in Italy. They integrate directors with different backgrounds and agendas into a cohesive working system that produces board decisions; they maintain productive relationships with the board of statutory auditors; they inform and engage shareholders; and they collaborate with and support the CEO. They prevent rather than stifle conflict, synthesizing and compromising rather than pushing for the "best option". A lot of this work is accomplished outside the boardroom over coffee, lunches and dinners, or during joint trips, informal personal meetings and phone calls.

---

[25] Spencer Stuart (2017). Italy Board Index 2017. Available from: https://www.spencer-stuart.com/-/media/pdf%20files/research%20and%20insight%20pdfs/italy%20board%20index%202017.pdf [Accessed 16 May 2018].

Chairs balance a focus on performance with compliance, working with directors on strategy and value creation and aligning with the board of statutory auditors on audits and controls. They actively contribute to a positive image of the company in the outside world and do not shy away from the media.

In the next ten years, we predict that the following trends will have an impact on the work and personalities of board chairs in Italy.

- There will be more diversity in terms of gender and age on boards of Italian companies and, as a result, among their chairs. Progress will be faster at director level and slower at chair level. Men will remain in the majority among Italian chairs and the average age will not change significantly.
- There will be a noticeable increase in the number of foreign nationals chairing boards of Italian companies, as well as in the number of chairs with substantial experience outside Italy. Yet the majority of chairs will remain Italian.
- Digital technology will make its way not only into Italian companies, but also into their boardrooms. Chairs will become more technology savvy and will move their boards onto digital platforms.
- Companies, professional/industry organizations and governments will provide more formal induction and training programmes both for board members and for their chairs. The latter will take a more active personal role in developing directors and their own successors.
- Chairs will become more involved in the nomination process of new directors. They will work closely with nomination committees both on defining profiles of future board members and on screening them.
- The balance between decisions developed and made at formal board sessions and informal meetings between chairs and some board members will shift in favour of the former. However, coffees and dinners will continue to play an important part in the work of the board.

References

Belcredi, M. and Rigamonti, S. (2008). *Ownership and Board Structure in Italy (1978–2003)*. Proceedings of the EFMA Annual Meeting, Athens, pp. 1–36.

Ciampi, F. and Gordini, N. (2013). *The Potential of Corporate Governance Variables for Small Enterprise Default Prediction Modeling. Statistical Evidence from Italian Manufacturing Firms*. Preliminary Findings. Proceedings of the Cambridge Business and Economics Conference, pp. 1–19.

Corporate Governance Committee (2018). Corporate Governance Code. Available from: https://www.borsaitaliana.it/comitato-corporate-governance/codice/codiceeng2018.en.pdf [Accessed 2 November 2018].

European Commission (2017). SBA Fact Sheet. Italy. Available from: https://ec.europa.eu/docsroom/documents/26562 [Accessed 16 May 2018].

European Parliament. Policy Department C: Citizens' Rights and Constitutional Affairs (2014). The Policy on Gender Equality in Italy. Available from: http://www.europarl.europa.eu/RegData/etudes/note/join/2014/493052/IPOL-FEMM_NT(2014)493052_EN.pdf [Accessed 16 May 2018].

Francesco Napoli, The Board's Strategic and Control Tasks; Family Firms and their Search for outside Directors to Support Growth: Empirical Evidence from Italian Publicly Listed Companies. *Journal of General Management*, 37, 4 (1), (2012).

Ginesti, G., Sannino, G. and Drago, C. (2017). Board connections and management commentary readability: the role of information sharing in Italy. *Corporate Governance: The International Journal of Business in Society*, 17, 1 (30).

Johnson, J.L., Daily, C.M. and Ellstrand, A.E. (1996). Board of Directors: A Review and Research Agenda. *Journal of Management*, 22 (3), pp. 409–438.

Linck, J. S., Netter, J. M. and Yang, T. (2008). The Determinants of Board Structure. *Journal of Financial Economics*, 87(2), pp. 308–328.

Mandl, I. (2008). Overview of Family Business Relevant Issues: Final Report. Available from: https://ec.europa.eu/docsroom/documents/10389/attachments/1/translations/en/.../native [Accessed 3 December 2018].

Spencer Stuart (2017). Italy Board Index 2017. Available from: https://www.spencerstuart.com/-/media/pdf%20files/research%20and%20insight%20pdfs/italy%20board%20index%202017.pdf [Accessed 16 May 2018].

The World Bank (2018a). World Development Indicators. GDP Ranking. Available from: https://datacatalog.worldbank.org/dataset/gdp-ranking [Accessed 10 May 2018].

The World Bank (2018b). World Development Indicators. GDP per capita, PPP, in international dollars. Available from: http://databank.worldbank.org/data/reports.aspx?source=2&series=NY.GDP.PCAP.PP.CD [Accessed 16 May 2018].

The World Bank (2018c). Services, Value Added. Industry, Value Added. Agriculture, Value Added. Available from: https://data.worldbank.org/indicator/NV.IND.TOTL.ZS [Accessed 10 May 2018].

CHAPTER 7

Smooth Operator: The Chair as the Drive Belt of the German Governance System

Elena Denisova-Schmidt and Peter Firnhaber

THE CHAIR'S WORK IN CONTEXT

The Federal Republic of Germany (*Bundesrepublik Deutschland*) is a federal parliamentary republic. It consists of 16 states (*Länder*), each with some degree of autonomy, and has a population of nearly 83 million in total.[1] In 2017, its GDP was US$3.7 trillion,[2] (the fourth largest in the world, and the largest in Europe) and per capita GDP was US$50,638.[3] The automotive

---

[1] The German Federal Statistical Office (2018). Bevölkerung in Deutschland: 82,8 Millionen zum Jahresende 2017. Available from: https://www.destatis.de/DE/PresseService/Presse/ Pressemitteilungen/2018/09/PD18_347_12411.html [Accessed 6 November 2018].

[2] The World Bank (2018). World Development Indicators. GDP Ranking. Available from: https://datacatalog.worldbank.org/dataset/gdp-ranking [Accessed 10 May 2018].

[3] The World Bank (2018). World Development Indicators. GDP per capita, in international dollars. Available from: https://data.worldbank.org/indicator/NY.GDP.PCAP. PP.CD?year_high_desc=true [Accessed 13 August 2018].

E. Denisova-Schmidt
University of St. Gallen, St. Gallen, Switzerland
e-mail: elena.denisova-schmidt@unisg.ch

P. Firnhaber (✉)
Independent Executive Coach and Coaching Supervisor, London, UK
e-mail: Peter.FIRNHABER@insead.edu

© The Author(s) 2019
S. Shekshnia, V. Zagieva (eds.), *Leading a Board*,
https://doi.org/10.1007/978-981-13-3197-8_7

industry, energy, industrial production, pharmaceutical and medical technology, media and telecommunications, transportation, logistics, retail and healthcare are the economy's main driving forces.[4] In early 2018, the labour force numbered about 44 million people working in 3.5 million enterprises, 82% of which were partnerships and public utilities, while only 18% were corporate entities.[5] Since the reunification of Germany in 1990, the unemployment rate has remained stable at around 5%. Germany is ranked fifth in the world on the Human Development Index.[6]

Germany has a system of corporate governance that is distinctive both in spirit and in form—often referred to as "stakeholder" capitalism. Under this model the company is governed for the long-term interests of all stakeholders, not only shareowners. Profits and value creation are not the ultimate measures of success in corporate Germany. This underlying philosophy translates into such characteristics as a two-tier board system with a non-executive supervisory board (*Aufsichtsrat*) and collective executive body or management board (*Vorstand*) and co-determination or employees' representation on a workers' supervisory board (*Mitbestimmung*).

There are two types of companies in Germany: public limited companies (*Aktiengesellschaften, AG*), which are comparable with public limited companies (PLCs) in the United Kingdom and private limited companies (*Gesellschaften mit beschränkter Haftung, GmbH*), which might be considered the equivalent of the limited liability company (Ltd) in the United Kingdom. There are some differences in terms of corporate governance between the two. Every AG, for example, is obliged to elect a supervisory board (*Aufsichtsrat*), while a GmbH must do so only if the number of employees in Germany exceeds 500.

The supervisory board is responsible for nominating key executives, establishing their compensation, approving business strategy and overseeing management. An AG must also have a management board (*Vorstand*), where all decisions are made collectively, while a GmbH may be managed by a single managing director (*Geschäftsführer*) acting alone. The management board is responsible for strategy development and implementation. Both types of companies are obliged to have an employee representative

⁴PricewaterhouseCoopers (2018). Doing Business in Germany. Available from: https://www.pwc-wissen.de/pwc/de/shop/publikationen/Doing+business+and+investing+in+Germany+2018/?card=22162 [Accessed 6 November 2018].

⁵Ibid.

⁶UNDP (2018). Human Development Indices and Indicators. 2018 Statistical Update. Available from: http://hdr.undp.org/en/2018-update [Accessed 28 September 2018].

(*Betriebsrat*) on their supervisory boards if the workforce numbers more than 2000.

In addition to the relevant legal framework—the Stock Corporate Act (*Aktiengesetz, AktG*), Laws on Co-Determination, EU directives (*Societas Europaea SE*) and the Equality Act—the work of both management and supervisory boards of publicly listed companies have to comply with the German Corporate Governance Code (*Deutscher Corporate Governance Kodex*). The Code "presents essential statutory regulations for the management and supervision of German listed companies and contains, in the form of recommendations and suggestions, internationally and nationally acknowledged standards for good and responsible corporate governance".[7] The document is written and periodically revised by the Commission (*Regierungskommission*), "as a rule, [...] annually in light of national and international developments and is adapted if necessary".[8]

The Code describes the obligations of both management and supervisory boards "to ensure the continued existence of the company and its sustainable value creation in line with the principles of the social market economy", as well as the chair's roles and responsibilities, which include[9]:

- coordinating the supervisory board's activities;
- making oneself available to investors and others over supervisory-board-related issues;
- staying in regular contact with the management board, in particular the chair of the management board, in order to discuss with them issues of strategy, planning, business development, risk management and compliance of the company;
- informing the supervisory board about events at the company and calling extraordinary meetings if necessary;
- outlining to the shareholders' general meeting the salient points of the executive remuneration system and informing subsequent general meetings about any amendments and chairing the meetings of the supervisory board so as to "safeguard the matters of the Supervisory Board externally".

[7] Regierungskommission (2017). German Corporate Governance Code. Available from: https://www.dcgk.de/en/code.html [Accessed 30 October 2018].
[8] Ibid.
[9] Ibid.

The latest revisions of the Code (February 2017) include new requirements to provide up-to-date information on the background, qualifications, previous experience and financial activities of supervisory-board members, as well as issues pertaining to executive remuneration and some ethical questions covering the independence of auditors, compliance management systems and whistle-blowing. The new revision of the Code states that "the principles not only require compliance with the law, but also ethically sound and responsible behaviour" (i.e., the "reputable businessperson" concept, *Leitbild des Ehrbaren Kaufmanns*).[10]

German boards are quite large with 16.3 members on average for *Deutscher Actienindex* (DAX, the German stock index) 30 companies. The proportion of independent directors has now reached 60% for the same sample. Women represent 29% of board members and 3.3% of chairs. The average age of German chairs is 68 (the highest in Europe).[11]

EXISTING RESEARCH

Corporate governance in Germany has been the subject of numerous studies. However, the role of the chair has been examined only to a limited extent. The supervisory-board chair is expected to maintain constant communication between supervisory and management boards in order to keep the exchange of information flowing within the company.[12] Schilling claims that the specifics of a supervisory-board chair's work in Germany are largely defined by the co-determination principle, which allows employees to elect representatives to the supervisory board. Co-determination often works as an excuse to keep supervisory-board members out of important issues that cannot be discussed in the presence of employee representatives. Thus, the chair has to play the role of a behind-the-scenes *éminence grise*, discussing and fixing important issues so that there are no surprises during board meetings. As a result, the

---

[10] Ibid.

[11] Spencer Stuart (2017). UK Board Index 2017. Available from: https://www.spencer-stuart.com/research-and-insight/uk-board-index-2017 [Accessed 10 May 2018].

[12] Tüngler, G. (2000). The Anglo-American Board of Directors and the German Supervisory Board – Marionettes in a Puppet Theatre of Corporate Governance or Efficient Controlling Devices. *Bond Law Review*, 12, pp. 230–271.

chair's workload can be three to five times higher than that of the other board members.[13]

Another characteristic of corporate governance in Germany is the widespread practice of "executive continuity", whereby a retiring CEO assumes the role of the supervisory-board chair. Bresser and Thiele have shown that there is a correlation between executive continuity and the dismissal of CEOs for poor performance. However, executive continuity does not influence the ability of their successors to improve business performance during the two-year post-dismissal period.[14]

GERMANY CULTURE MAP

According to Erin Meyer's research, German culture is low-context, task-based, confrontational and principles-first with a consensual decision-making style (see Appendix A for full explanation). The most distinctive characteristic of German culture is its linear-time orientation. We therefore would expect chairs in Germany to set detailed board agendas ahead of time and rarely make ad hoc changes. We also hypothesize that, while they may not shy away from candid conversations in and outside the board-room, they will try to build consensus and avoid making unilateral decisions. Similarly, we envisage that chairs in Germany invest time and effort in planning and preparing board meetings, including board materials, and pay special attention to the wording of board resolutions, as well as following up on their implementation. Finally, we expect German chairs to encourage a clear and precise manner of communication during meetings, without hesitating to express their own thoughts openly (Fig. 7.1).

DATA

For the Global Chair Research Project, we conducted semi-structured interviews with 11 experienced and mostly professional chairs: 2 women and 9 men, aged from 59 to 75. All were highly educated—and five had a

---

[13] Schilling, F. (2001). Mitbestimmung und Corporate Governance. Available from: https://www.board-consultants.eu/docs/schilling1-faz-mit-cg.pdf [Accessed 3 December 2018].

[14] Bresser, R. K. and Thiele, R. V. (2008). Ehemalige Vorstandsvorsitzende als Aufsichtsratschefs: Evidenz zu ihrer Effektivität im Falle des erzwungenen Führungswechsels. *Journal of Business Economics*, 78 (2), pp. 175–203.

● Germany

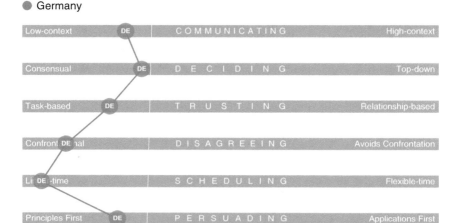

Fig. 7.1   Germany Culture Map (Source: Based on the work of INSEAD Professor Erin Meyer, and her *The Culture Map* book [Meyer, E. (2014). *The Culture Map: Breaking Through the Invisible Boundaries of Global Business.* New York: PublicAffairs])

PhD. Nine were native Germans, one came from Austria and one from the Netherlands. All had significant international experience. They chaired both listed DAX and unlisted companies, including some family-controlled firms. They had held two to four chairs, in each case for an average of three to five years, and most were also independent directors on other boards. The boards they chaired comprised 6 to 12 members—half shareholders' representatives, half employee representatives (*Mitbestimmung*)—with an employee representative usually holding the vice chair position. All of the boards concerned had audit, nomination and remuneration (and sometimes additional) committees based on the Corporate Governance Code.

To provide a 360-degree view of the chair's work, we interviewed six board members, including one employee representative, five CEOs and two shareholders. The majority of them were over 50 years old and of German origin. Each of them had experience of serving on the boards of public, private and charitable organizations in various sectors.

The 2015 INSEAD Global Chair Survey identified the following key challenges for the chairs of German companies (in descending order of importance):

- Relationships with shareholders
- Managing non-conforming board members (special cases)
- Relationships with CEO and senior executives

During the interviews, all of our respondents agreed that relationships with shareholders and collaboration among board members were top priorities. They also emphasized the importance of interaction with employee representatives and external stakeholders. Before we describe how chairs of German companies deal with those challenges, we would like to present how they and other respondents see their work.

WORK OF THE CHAIR THROUGH THE EYES OF RESPONDENTS

All respondents—both chairs and their colleagues—agree that the job of a chair of a supervisory board in Germany is very important and very challenging. As one director put it, "*In Germany chairs do not have much formal power* [although, in contrast to other European countries they have a decisive vote (*Doppelstimme*) in cases of stalemate]. *They have to align diverse actors—directors elected by shareholders, directors elected by employees, management board, shareholders, very often family members, governments at different levels, banks, etc. It's hell of a job.*" The complexity of this job stems from: the two-tier board system; the requirement for co-determination (which leads to large and often split boards); Germany's social market philosophy; and the attention traditionally paid to all of the company's stakeholders. The underlying role of the chair is to keep this very complex governance system running smoothly and producing both economic results and stakeholder satisfaction. It is a tricky balancing act, which requires, according to our respondents, patience, tact, good questioning and listening skills on the one hand, and firmness, discipline and determination on the other.

When asked "Who does the supervisory-board chair work for?" none of the respondents provided a one-word answer. They referred to multiple "masters": the company, shareholders, employees and all stakeholders. Surprisingly, none of them mentioned the board itself. We believe that this reflects the predominant view among our respondents that the main role of the chair is to connect and align different stakeholders.

This chapter will demonstrate that chairs of German companies use various strategies to get their jobs done. They invest *time*. They thoroughly prepare for board meetings, both by planning the discussion flow and by meeting with key players. They use committees to delve into important or complex issues and to prepare specific proposals. They interact with directors individually and in small groups, and chair separate informal meetings with groups of directors elected by shareholders or employees. They meet with shareholders in person and correspond with them in writing. They reach out to other stakeholders and participate in public forums and events. Unlike their counterparts in some other European countries, they often represent not only the board but also the company to the outside world.

The directors interviewed for this research emphasized that effective chairs understand and manage the dynamics between the two boards of German companies and their external stakeholders. They also involve all directors in discussions and decision-making, see the big picture and focus on strategic issues. They demonstrate critical and complex thinking, listen well and have an eye for how people are engaged.

Relationships with Shareholders

Germany has one of the most developed stock markets in Europe and, at the same time, relatively high levels of ownership concentration.[15] Many German public companies have significant shareholders, such as families, private equity investors, investments funds and local and regional governments, with different investment horizons and risk profiles, and often directly represented on the board. The shareholders' map of Germany is one of the most heterogeneous in Europe, which adds extra complexity to the chairs' work.

All of our chair-respondents agreed that building and developing relationships with shareholders of all types was their top priority. The main challenge in this respect is to find a balance between complying with regulations and achieving productive shareholder engagement with the board and the company. The respondents emphasized the principle of equal treatment of all shareholders, especially in the case of publicly listed companies. At the same time, many of them spoke about the need to find a unique way to work with every shareholder. As one respondent put it: *"I try to have one-on-one meetings with shareholders, where I deal with each of*

---

[15] Brendel, M., Schwetzler, B. and Strenger, C. (2017). Ownership Structure, Firm Value and Government Intervention: The Case of the German Tax Reduction Act. Available from: https://ssrn.com/abstract=2440706 [Accessed 3 December 2018].

them differently, according to her or his background, experience, knowledge of the business, etc."

Chairs of German companies interact with significant shareholders on a regular basis (many respondents mentioned "monthly encounters") and when important board decisions need to be made. One respondent said that he always reaches out to the representatives of large shareholders before deciding on an acquisition or a big strategic move. Another respondent consults on M&As, large investments and key nominations. All respondents emphasized that such conversations do not undermine the independence of their boards—one chair explained that he "*doesn't take orders for the board from shareholders, but solicits their views.*" Often shareholders ask for a meeting and most chairs try to accommodate that request. Most meetings with shareholders are informal, off the record and without minutes. They rarely take place on the company's premises. Chairs often see owners and their representatives over coffee, lunch or dinner.

At some family-controlled companies, chairs of supervisory boards take on additional functions, such as advising on family succession, next-generation development and investment strategy. As one respondent put it: "*It helps to solidify relationships, which helps the company in the long run, so it's a part of my job.*"

Some respondents reported on their recent experience with *activist* shareholders.[16] The consensus was that activists represent a real threat for the company and have to be dealt with carefully. In Germany, the chair of the supervisory board is responsible for coordinating communication with all shareholders, including activists—who generally correspond in writing and expect to be answered. The key issue, according to our respondents, is what information to release to them. One chair summed up the problem: "*Whatever you say can be twisted, turned around and misinterpreted.*" Perhaps for this reason, it is a common practice among chairs of German companies to engage a professional communications agency to assist them in dealing with activist shareholders.

For non-chair-respondents, the effective management of shareholder relationships is a must for a good chair of a supervisory board. According to them it is usually achieved through personal contacts and the chair's ability to engage and listen to people from diverse backgrounds—and then feed information back to the board. Effective board leaders allocate

---

[16] Logsdon, J. M. and Van Buren III, H. J. (2008). Justice and Large Corporations: What Do Activist Shareholders Want? *Business & Society*, 47(4), pp. 523–548.

significant time to relationships with shareholders, show respect and attention, but protect the board's independence. They recognize the threats posed by activist shareholders early, communicate them to the board and lead the company in organizing an effective defence.

Relationships with External Stakeholders

Several chair-respondents shared that developing good relations with such stakeholders as government bodies, customers, suppliers, industry associations and others was an important part of their work. The government—both on the regional (*Landesebene*) and on the federal (*Bundesebene*) levels—is a key economic agent in Germany, as an active regulator, mediator in employer-employee relationships and shareholder in many companies. Interaction with representatives of the government and other external stakeholders takes various forms. Some chairs visit contacts in their offices; some organize open events on their company premises and invite stakeholders; and others use external gatherings like industry conventions to meet with them. One respondent said that he regularly attended exhibitions and conventions in order to keep on top of what was going on in the industry. He did not, however, discuss any company-specific issues with clients, suppliers or government officials. Rather, his objective was to check "the pulse of the times".

Leading the Board

Supervisory boards in Germany are large and exclusively non-executive. They consist of two categories of directors—shareholder and employee representatives—and deal with high-level and compliance-driven issues. They meet rarely, usually four to five times a year. This combination of factors is not found anywhere else in Europe and leads to some unique strategies and practices (see Table 7.1 for a list of chairs) on the part of Germany's chairs.

German board meetings are quite formal and chairs consider it one of their key tasks to ensure order and discipline and avoid any surprises. As one international director noted: "*The board meetings I attend in Germany are by far more formal and disciplined than the ones I am part of in the Netherlands and the UK.*" For all respondents it was very important that meetings start and finish on time, that all items on the agenda get discussed and that all decisions are made. One chair expressed it as

Table 7.1 Chairs' strategies and practices in Germany

Stage	Strategies	Practices
Pre-meeting	Get the right people on the board Set expectations Create a framework for each individual meeting Provide data Reach out to directors Avoid surprises Align different directors' groups	Drawing up a director's profile Discussing requirements for future directors with stakeholders Interviewing candidates Organizing and participating in induction programmes for new directors Calling some directors before the board meeting to re-engage them Meeting with the CEO and/or management board to discuss preparation of the upcoming board meeting Ensuring board committees prepare draft board decisions Creating temporary board subcommittees to address a specific issue Defining the format of board materials Checking board materials before they are sent to directors Creating a digital board book Meeting with directors elected by shareholders and by employees separately Organizing a dinner for the whole board
In-meeting	Keep to the agenda and clear criteria for decision-making Provide data and information Ensure fairness and equal treatment of all directors Facilitate discussion Remove barriers to effective discussion Exercise self-restraint	Allocating significant time to management and committee presentations Stating criteria for decision-making Asking every director to state their position Asking what the "best owner" would do in any given situation Speaking last Not indicating a personal position Casting a decisive vote in case of deadlock Conducting an "express evaluation" at the end of the meeting
Post-meeting	Continue board discussions informally Learn from evaluations Stay connected with both groups of directors	Hosting a lunch for all board members after the board meeting to discuss and evaluate it Conducting formal 360-degree board evaluation Holding feedback sessions with each director Meeting directors elected by shareholders and by employees separately Having informal meetings and meals with directors

follows: "*For every item put on the table we have to make a decision. It's a failure to bring it back next time.*"

To make their large boards effective, chairs work actively inside and outside the boardroom, demonstrating 3E-leadership—engage, enable and encourage—with a strong German accent.[17] As one director-respondent put it: "*An effective chair involves all players, makes sure they have access to all information, provides them with equal opportunities to speak in the boardroom and steers them to a decision.*"

Pre-meeting

Supervisory-board chairs in Germany do not have direct influence over the nomination process for directors, but they try to ensure the quality of their boards by articulating their expectations of future board members and discussing these requirements with the stakeholders—shareholders, employees and nomination committees. As one chair explained: "*The selection process is consensus driven.*" Chair involvement can be formal—through written communication—or less formal—through personal meetings. Some chairs reported having full assessment interviews with candidates before their nomination.

Since discipline is very important in the German context, chairs make sure that new directors have sufficient time to attend all board and committee meetings, and articulate severe consequences for non-attendance at an early stage. Some respondents reported formal rules that require directors to resign if they miss two board meetings in one year. In Germany video-conferencing is still the exception: the majority of board meetings take place in a corporate boardroom.

Chairs in Germany start planning board meetings well in advance. They are the sole masters of the agenda, although it is heavily influenced by the law and the Code and the corporate secretary has an input. A typical board agenda has four to five important items plus some technical questions. Four to six weeks before the board meeting, the chair meets with the CEO, sometimes together with the CFO and other members of the management board, to go through the agenda and discuss what documents need to be produced. The board book usually contains detailed presentations and proposed resolutions with a short rationale for each of them. The materials are extremely detailed. As one director-respondent

---

[17] See Chap. 1 for the description of 3E-leadership model.

remarked: "*Five hundred-plus pages are the norm rather than the exception.*" Some respondents defined an exact format for contributors, while others left it to the management, but all approved the board materials before sending them out, usually one week before the meeting. None of the respondents checked every single line of the board book but ensured that all agenda items were covered adequately. Most boards in our sample used digital platforms, but some chairs liked to have additional hard copies in the boardroom.

Supervisory-board chairs use committees extensively, a practice that is largely driven by such country specifics as large boards, co-determination and the limited number of meetings a year. Committees play a major part in the analytical work and are expected to prepare draft decisions for the board. One chair described his way of organizing committee work as follows: "*I articulate clearly what I need from them: description of the problem, specific recommendation for the board decision, supporting argument, data, criteria applied and methods used.*" This chair and many of his colleagues personally participate in some committees, actively manage their membership through nomination and rotation and set up temporary board subcommittees to look at specific problems. As one respondent said: "*I love to rotate committee members—it gives directors a 360-degree picture of the company.*"

None of the chair-respondents mentioned reaching out to each board member before the meeting as a standard practice. Perhaps the large size of many German boards makes this rather impractical. However, supervisory-board chairs often meet with the two groups of directors—shareholder and employee representatives—separately. As one respondent explained, such meetings allow them to discuss items on the next board meeting agenda "*less formally, more frankly and without always looking at your watch*". Some respondents said they used such sessions to achieve alignment and agreement between the two groups on decisions to be formally approved at the board meeting. Chairs also interact with vice chairs, who are always employee representatives, to gauge the position of other employee representatives, to discuss potential disagreements and to find mutually acceptable solutions. Such meetings usually take place in cafes, pubs or over the phone.

Board chairs in Germany pay a great deal of attention to planning board meetings. They allocate time for each item, splitting it between presentation, Q&A, discussion and decision-making. Board leaders carefully frame discussion questions, outline criteria for decision-making, think about the order in which directors will express their views, analyse what could potentially disrupt board discussion and prepare mitigation strategies. As one of them put it, "*When you have only four hours, five important questions and twenty board members, you have to plan every detail and be prepared for every eventuality.*" Another chair shared his practice of drafting the meeting plan on a piece of paper, outlining time allocation, exact wording of discussion questions and detailed decision criteria.

Some chairs organize dinners for their directors on the eve of the board meeting to talk informally, to probe for potential disagreements, to get directors on the same wavelength and to put them at ease. One respondent said: "*It is an opportunity to talk about our families, to have a glass of good wine, to become more social, to have some fun and to bond as a team.*"

In-meeting

We did not discover a typical German way to start a board meeting. Some chairs open by sharing news from the company. Other chairs greet everyone and go straight to the agenda.

One unexpected finding of our research is the attitude of German chairs to management presentations during board meetings. While their counterparts in other European countries try to minimize or even eliminate them, board leaders in Germany allocate significant time to them. As one of them explained: "*You should assume that nobody read the board materials and provide them with all data necessary for decision making.*" Although other respondents were less radical in their assessment of directors' preparedness (and one of them shared his practice of cold calling board members to identify the unprepared), they all attributed high importance to presentations and worked with the management to structure them to their taste.

Committee reports are also an important element of board meetings in Germany. Again chairs are involved in structuring and polishing them. As one respondent explained, he is interested to hear "*not only a suggestion but a description of the problem, method and data—the way it was analyzed, how the decision was reached and the mechanics behind the recommendation.*"

During the meeting the chair functions as a facilitator and coordinator who encourages discussion, ensures more or less equal allocation of airtime and avoids imposing or even articulating a personal point of view.

Both the chairs and the directors we interviewed described this as a very challenging task, because of the specifics of German supervisory boards. As one of them put it: "*Some people might be well prepared, some people are not; some people are talkative, some not; some people know the company well; others do not.*" Time constraints make facilitation even more difficult, so effective chairs combine an engaging approach with discipline and reining in talkative or disruptive members (see below).

In Germany, the chair of a supervisory board has a deciding vote in cases of stalemate. However, our respondents considered exercising this right a very ineffective practice, as it undermines the board's unity in the long run. They preferred to extend or even postpone the discussion to reach a decision acceptable to all board members. Chairs are also very careful not to impose their opinions on other board members. One said that he prefers "*not to state my views at all, but when I do it I always emphasize that this is just an opinion of one board member.*"

At the close of the board meeting some chairs give three to four minutes to every board member to state their key impressions of the meeting or something that might be on their minds as they are going home. In the words of one respondent: "*It is very helpful—issues are mentioned that were not discussed because they were forgotten or very sensitive topics.*"

In contrast to other European countries, there is almost no humour in German board meetings. Although one respondent mentioned that "humour does not contradict efficiency", another, the chair of a listed company, explicitly forbade it. When asked about this, he responded that it reflects the way he prefers to work: "*The board meets to conduct business.*" Only one chair from our sample (younger and more international) said that he explicitly introduces humour into his sessions to create a relaxed and constructive working atmosphere.

Post-meeting

Organizing a lunch for the whole board immediately after the board meeting is quite common in Germany. Many chairs use this opportunity to continue discussions informally, for example, to reflect on the meeting itself. One respondent extends the reflection to questions about the directors' engagement with the board, the time commitment required, the effectiveness of communication between board meetings and the quality of materials.

Board evaluation is a standard routine for German companies. Following the Code's recommendation, most chairs organize self-evaluation once a year and use external help every three years. The self-evaluation is often organized in two stages: first all directors fill in a questionnaire and second aggregated data is presented to the board and discussed. Some chairs also conduct individual meetings with directors to provide personalized feedback and discuss improvements.

Managing Difficult Board Members

Our respondents classified as "difficult" several categories of board members: people who constantly try to impose their own very different opinions on the rest of the board; people who speak too much or too little; certain directors representing the founding family; and directors representing minority/activist shareholders. One respondent also remarked that *"the most difficult are directors who do not have enough time."* We discovered some interesting strategies and practices for working with deviant board members.

The first strategy is to formalize behavioural norms for directors. Some boards have a code of conduct (*Verhaltenskodex*) that describes the rules of engagement and in cases of deviation chairs refer to this document. Some chairs reported that they had established a "meeting code", obliging each member of the supervisory board to voice her or his opinion and refrain from dominating the discussion.

The second strategy is intervention outside the boardroom. This takes the form of a one-to-one meeting or even a phone call to provide feedback and ask for a change in boardroom behaviour. Usually conversations are polite but straightforward as suggested by the "culture map" earlier in this chapter.

The third strategy is direct confrontation in the boardroom. We collected some specific phrases that board chairs use to improve the performance of deviant directors.

To silence domineering board members:

- *"Could you please allow others talk as well? You are dominating the discussion."*
- *"Could you please make some space for others?"*
- *"You have made 20 comments, while others have made none."*

To encourage more silent board members:

- "*Could you speak up a little bit more?*"
- "*I would like to hear more from you, especially when it comes to your field of expertise.*"
- "*I'd love to hear your voice; I'd love to hear your opinion.*"

Interactions with Employee Representatives on the Supervisory Board

The law on co-determination (*Mitbestimmunsgesetz*), giving employees at large German companies the right to elect up to half the members of a supervisory board, was adopted in 1976. Since then, according to our respondents, chairs have come a long way—from outright hostility towards directors representing employees, through the acceptance stage, to considering them as valuable members of the board. As one chair-respondent put it: "*You need to understand where they are coming from, what they can and cannot bring to the table, and treat them fairly.*"

Fairness and non-partiality are the main expectations of directors representing employees on the boards of German companies. As one of them remarked to us: "*The best chair treats all board members with respect. He ensures that all are given the same attention and remains neutral.*" According to this very experienced director, the main function of the chair of a supervisory board is "*to align directors representing shareholders and employees behind the common strategy*" and the main attributes of a good chair are "*non-political, open, good communicator, strong personality and good industry knowledge*". He mentioned "*domination, arrogance and non-inclusiveness*" as the three deadly sins of chairing a board.

Chair-respondents said that they try to engage employee-directors, make them part of a collective process and help them to contribute—as they do with all board members. The tactics, however, may be different. One respondent said that he helps employee-directors to see the bigger picture, understand how the business world operates and recognize the expectations of other stakeholders. Another chair meets with them to talk about their roles and responsibilities as members of a supervisory board in informal and simple language.

While interacting with employee representatives on the board, chairs may make some adjustments to their style in order to appear on a more equal footing: for example, wearing less-formal clothes, driving a different car or selecting a pub to have beer and sausages. As in some other countries discussed in this book, we found that a shared meal—with traditional German bread rolls (*Brötchen*) or seasonal foods like asparagus—helps facilitate collaboration.

Relationships with the CEO and Management

German companies are formally managed by a group of senior executives (*Vorstand*), where the CEO according to one chair-respondent is the "*primus inter pares*". This feature means that the supervisory-board chair interacts with all members of the management board, although our research found that their main contacts are the CEO and CFO. Other senior executives get involved with board committees and work with the chair occasionally rather than systematically.

Chair-respondents reported that their interaction with the CEO is intense, complex, multi-faceted and multi-format. It is not uncommon for the chair of a German company to have an office on the company premises and it is often the venue for regular chair-CEO meetings. As one respondent explained: "*I have an office where I meet with the CEO every two weeks for a couple of hours. The agenda is not formal. First we discuss his points, then I ask him my questions.*" Chairs and CEOs also meet for coffee or a meal, speak on the phone, correspond by e-mail and use messenger applications.

Although the German model of corporate governance draws a clear line between the non-executive supervisory board and the executive management board, chairs and CEOs collaborate on a number of issues from preparing board meetings to working with external stakeholders and the mass media. One director-respondent even talked of "*co-management*", while a chair-respondent called himself "*a business sparring-partner for the CEO*".

At the same time, the chairs in our study considered challenging the CEO and other senior executives of one of their key roles: "*As soon as you see them* [the CEO and CFO] *walking on water, take the water away.*" "Challenging" takes place in the boardroom and one-to-one meetings. According to our respondents it has to be specific, supported with facts, non-emotional and non-aggressive but firm.

Chairs give performance feedback to CEOs and sometimes to other members of the management board. We learnt about two principal formats: formal annual evaluation, which takes somewhere between one and three hours, and involves quantitative as well as qualitative metrics, and less-formal feedback sessions, which follow important events or are organized on the CEO's request. Both types of feedback sessions usually take place behind closed doors, although in some cases chairs involve members of the compensation committee.

Many chair-respondents told us that they mentor the CEO and, in some cases, other senior executives. Mostly this is a matter of informal, unstructured mentoring, which takes place during regular or specially organized meetings initiated by either party. Sometimes it is situational—after a board meeting, presentation to investors, company conference and so on. One chair-respondent said that at one company he participated in management meetings in order to observe the CEO and provide developmental advice.

One of our unexpected findings was that in Germany some board chairs are involved with leadership development at their companies. Chair-respondents reported inviting high-potential managers to make presentations to the board and its committees, attending company events for "hi-pos" and speaking to groups of middle managers. One of them defined one of his personal tasks as *"looking for internal high-potentials who could fill the pipeline for the management board."*

CEO-respondents reported that effective chairs interact with them on a regular basis (*"we meet face-to-face every three to four weeks, but we constantly communicate via secure messenger"*), treat them as equal and are available and ready to help with advice or an introduction to an important person. All the CEOs we interviewed emphasized the importance of mutual trust and predictability as the foundations of effective chair-CEO collaboration. As one of them put it: *"What I know he knows (was ich weiss, weiss er)."*

Chair Succession

In Germany board chairs do not consider their succession a priority or even a task for themselves. The selection and nomination of candidates is carried out by nomination committees. As one chair-respondent commented: *"I am not involved with my succession—it would be inappropriate for me to influence its* [the committee's] *work."* Significant shareholders, on the other hand, are very much involved in selecting the next chair—and are often the de facto decision-makers. One family-business shareholder explained that his family was in charge of finding successors for their firm's chairs. They involve an executive search company to co-define a profile and source candidates, keeping the incumbent chair out of the process entirely. In general, personal and professional networks are important avenues for finding future chairs—both significant shareholders and nomination committees actively use them.

However, the current situation with respect to chair succession may change in the near future. The most junior chair we interviewed expressed a very different attitude—he is thinking about his successor and intends to be a part of the succession process.

Summary

According to our research, a "typical" supervisory-board chair in Germany is male, German, aged 60 or above, well educated, has significant international experience and was previously a CEO. His work is complex and requires significant time commitment. Most chair-respondents reported spending one to two weeks a month on their role.

In Germany chairs are first and foremost enablers of a very complex system of corporate governance. Their skill and will make this sophisticated machinery run. Their function as "smooth operators" includes the roles that are traditional in other European countries, such as leading the board, maintaining relationships with shareholders and interacting with the CEO and management. However, it also requires chairs in Germany to take on some additional duties, such as representing the company to the outside world.

Understanding and aligning the interests of diverse stakeholders is critical for the effectiveness of chairs in Germany. To achieve this they need to demonstrate patience, empathy and great questioning and listening skills. They must be able to synthesize and articulate. To do all this under the significant time constraints of a part-time job they have to be highly disciplined and capable of instilling discipline on their boards.

According to our respondents, there are three significant trends that will affect the work of chairs in Germany over the next decade: digitalization; increasing diversity; and mounting regulatory pressure.

Digitalization will make all boards paperless and will reduce information asymmetry between supervisory and management boards by making data available to non-executive directors in real time. Video-conferencing will become a viable alternative to traditional board meetings and most committee meetings will be virtual. However, most chairs will preserve the traditional format of personal attendance in the boardroom.

The number of female directors will increase, probably reaching 40% ten years from now and expanding the pool of potential female chairs significantly. As a result, there will also be more female chairs, especially in the second half of the next decade. However, the percentage of women chairing supervisory boards will not match the percentage of women directors any time soon. Age diversity will also increase: technology will catapult younger (under 50) people into chair positions, while increasing longevity will make people in their 80s perfectly fit for the job of chair. The chief executive position will remain the principal career path, but there will be more chairs with backgrounds in academia, consulting and government.

Increasing regulatory pressure will make the chair's job more demanding, more risky and perhaps less attractive. People will chair fewer boards simultaneously and their tenures will shorten.

References

Bresser, R. K. and Thiele, R. V. (2008). Ehemalige Vorstandsvorsitzende als Aufsichtsratschefs: Evidenz zu ihrer Effektivität im Falle des erzwungenen Führungswechsels. *Journal of Business Economics*, 78(2), pp. 175–203.

Brendel, M., Schwetzler, B. and Strenger, C. (2017). Ownership Structure, Firm Value and Government Intervention: The Case of the German Tax Reduction Act. Available from: https://ssrn.com/abstract=2440706 [Accessed 3 December 2018].

Delamaide, D. (2018). German Economy Faces Shortages as Growth Tests Limits. *Handelsblatt Global*. Available from: https://global.handelsblatt.com/companies/german-economy-faces-shortages-as-economy-reaches-capacity-limits-895822 [Accessed 3 December 2018].

Deutschlandfunk (2018). Erstmals seit der Wiedervereinigung Unter 5 Prozent Arbeitslose. Available from: https://www.deutschlandfunk.de/erstmals-seit-der-wiedervereinigung-unter-5-prozent.1939.de.html?drn:news_id=940556 [Accessed 30 October 2018].

Du Plessis, J., Grossfeld, B., Luttermann, C., Saenger, I., Sandrock, O. and Casper, M. (2017). *German Corporate Governance in International and European Context*. Berlin: Springer-Verlag.

Fiss, P.C. (2006). Social Influence Effects and Managerial Compensation Evidence from Germany. *Strategic Management Journal*, 27, pp. 1013–1031.

Franks, J.R. and Mayer, C.P. (2001). The Ownership and Control of German Corporations. *Review of Financial Studies*, 14, pp. 943–977.

Kreijger, G. (2018). Why German Corporate Governance is So Different. *Handelsblatt Global*. Available from: https://global.handelsblatt.com/companies/why-german-corporate-governance-is-so-different-892389 [Accessed 30 October 2018].

Logsdon, J. M. and Van Buren, H. J., III (2008). Justice and Large Corporations: What Do Activist Shareholders Want? *Business & Society*, 47(4), pp. 523–548.

Meyer, E. (2014). *The Culture Map: Breaking Through the Invisible Boundaries of Global Business*. New York: PublicAffairs.

Maier, A. (2018). Der Schmitt im Leben. manager magazin, 9/2018. 37–41.

PricewaterhouseCoopers (2018). Doing Business in Germany. Available from: https://www.pwc-wissen.de/pwc/de/shop/publikationen/Doing+business+and+investing+in+Germany+2018/?card=22162 [Accessed 6 November 2018].

Regierungskommission (2017). German Corporate Governance Code. Available from: https://www.dcgk.de/en/code.html [Accessed 30 October 2018].

Schilling, F. (2009). Altvorstände sind die besten Aufsichtsräte. *Frankfurter Allgemeine Zeitung*. Available from: http://www.faz.net/aktuell/wirtschaft/wirtschaftswissen/unternehmen-altvorstaende-sind-die-besten-aufsichtsraete-1626592.html [Accessed 3 December 2018].

Schilling, F. (2001). Mitbestimmung und Corporate Governance. *Frankfurter Allgemeine Zeitung*. Available from: https://www.board-consultants.eu/docs/schilling1-faz-mit-cg.pdf [Accessed 3 December 2018].

Spencer Stuart (2017). UK Board Index 2017. Available from: https://www.spencerstuart.com/research-and-insight/uk-board-index-2017 [Accessed 10 May 2018].

The German Federal Statistical Office (2018). Bevölkerung in Deutschland: 82,8 Millionen zum Jahresende 2017. Available from: https://www.destatis.de/DE/PresseService/Presse/Pressemitteilungen/2018/09/PD18_347_12411.html [Accessed 6 November 2018].

The World Bank (2018a). World Development Indicators. GDP per capita, in international dollars. Available from: https://data.worldbank.org/indicator/NY.GDP.PCAP.PP.CD?year_high_desc=true [Accessed 13 August 2018].

The World Bank (2018b). World Development Indicators. GDP Ranking. Available from: https://datacatalog.worldbank.org/dataset/gdp-ranking [Accessed 10 May 2018].

Tüngler, G. (2000). The Anglo-American Board of Directors and the German Supervisory Board – Marionettes in a Puppet Theatre of Corporate Governance or Efficient Controlling Devices. *Bond Law Review*, 12, pp. 230–271.

UNDP (2018). Human Development Indices and Indicators. 2018 Statistical Update. Available from: http://hdr.undp.org/en/2018-update [Accessed 28 September 2018].

CHAPTER 8

Turkey: Between Traditional and Modern Leadership

Hande Yaşargil and Elena Denisova-Schmidt

THE CHAIR'S WORK IN CONTEXT

Turkey is a transcontinental country linking Europe, the Middle East, North Africa and Central Asia. It is a constitutionally presidential republic. It has a population of over 80 million.[1] Since 2000 the country has urbanized significantly and opened up to foreign trade and finance. Many laws and regulations have been harmonized with European Union (EU) standards, and access to public services has been greatly expanded. The driving forces of the Turkish economy—the 6th largest in Europe and 17th in the world[2]—are light and heavy industry (textiles, vehicles, chemicals,

---

[1] The World Bank (2018). World Development Indicators. Population, total. Available from: http://databank.worldbank.org/data/reports.aspx?source=2&series=SP.POP.TOTL [Accessed 22 September 2018].

[2] The World Bank (2018). World Development Indicators. GDP Ranking. Available from: https://datacatalog.worldbank.org/dataset/gdp-ranking [Accessed 22 September 2018].

H. Yaşargil
Women on Board Association of Turkey, Istanbul, Turkey
e-mail: hyasargil@mentor-tr.com

E. Denisova-Schmidt (✉)
University of St. Gallen, St. Gallen, Switzerland
e-mail: elena.denisova-schmidt@unisg.ch

© The Author(s) 2019   161
S. Shekshnia, V. Zagieva (eds.), *Leading a Board*,
https://doi.org/10.1007/978-981-13-3197-8_8

machinery, electrical industry) and the service sector, with a significant contribution from agriculture. Family businesses of many different types, from "mom-and-pop shops" to multi-industry conglomerates, dominate the Turkish economy, accounting for almost 90% of all companies.[3]

In 2017, Turkish GDP was US$851 billion[4] or US$27,916 per capita,[5] and inflation reached 8%. The high unemployment rate—10.6%[6] as of May 2018—and the significant economic gap between rural areas (located mainly in the east and in the southeast) and rapidly growing industrial centres are the main challenges for the labour market. Moreover, the Turkish labour market suffers from a relatively low employment rate for women (about 30%)[7] and a significant percentage of off-the-books employment. Turkey is ranked 64th on the Human Development Index.[8]

Domestic and international political challenges, as well as security concerns, have led to volatility in Turkey's financial markets and threaten economic growth in the country (cf. Index of Economic Freedom, 2018[9] and the German Federal Foreign Office, 2018).[10] In the summer of 2018, the domestic currency—the lira—lost 40% of its value against the dollar.

Corporate governance in Turkey has undergone profound changes in the last decade. The Turkish Commercial Code (TCC) and Capital Markets Law (CML) set out the main principles of corporate governance for public and private joint-stock companies (JSCs). Both largely reflect

[3] Tasman-Jones, J. (2013). Infographic: Turkish Family Businesses. *CampdenFB*, 59. Available from: http://www.campdenfb.com/article/infographic-turkish-family-businesses [Accessed 22 October 2018].

[4] The World Bank (2018). World Development Indicators. GDP Ranking. Available from: https://datacatalog.worldbank.org/dataset/gdp-ranking [Accessed 22 September 2018].

[5] The World Bank (2018). World Development Indicators. GDP per capita, in international dollars. Available from: https://data.worldbank.org/indicator/NY.GDP.PCAP.PP.CD?year_high_desc=true [Accessed 22 September 2018].

[6] Eurostat (2018). Unemployment by Sex and Age – Monthly Average. Available from: http://appsso.eurostat.ec.europa.eu/nui/show.do?dataset=une_rt_m&lang=en [Accessed 8 October 2018].

[7] Auswärtiges Amt (German Federal Foreign Office) (2018). Turkey Country Profile. Available from: https://www.auswaertiges-amt.de/de/aussenpolitik/laender/tuerkei-node/wirtschaft/201964 [Accessed 8 October 2018].

[8] UNDP (2018). Human Development Indices and Indicators. 2018 Statistical Update. Available from: http://hdr.undp.org/en/2018-update [Accessed 28 September 2018].

[9] Heritage Foundation (2018). Turkey Country Profile. Available from https://www.heritage.org/index/country/turkey [Accessed 14 August 2018].

[10] Auswärtiges Amt (German Federal Foreign Office) (2018). Turkey Country Profile. Available from: https://www.auswaertiges-amt.de/de/aussenpolitik/laender/tuerkei-node/wirtschaft/201964 [Accessed 14 August 2018].

the spirit and the Principles of Corporate Governance developed by the OECD. The Capital Markets Board (CMB) is an independent regulatory and supervisory body overseeing Turkey's capital markets. The Corporate Governance Code in Turkey is represented by the Principles on Corporate Governance[11] first issued in 2003 by the Capital Markets Board (CMB) and revised several times, most recently in 2014. Some of the provisions of the Principles are mandatory; others are to be implemented under the "comply or explain" approach.

Turkey has a one-tier board system, under which both executive and non-executive members make up the board of directors, the highest governing body in the company. The board has full authority to manage the company. In practice, it delegates managing powers to the CEO or, in some cases, to more than one managing director with equal powers.

The responsibilities of the chair and the CEO are clearly delineated. Indeed, the Principles on Corporate Governance recommends that these positions be filled by two individuals and stipulates that, if they are combined, the board should disclose the reason.[12] There are currently only three BIST companies (the 30 largest corporations listed on the Istanbul Stock Exchange) where the chair and the CEO is the same person.[13] By law, the CEO is required to sit on the board of Turkish banks, although the role cannot be combined with that of chair.

Non-transferable powers of the board include the appointment of key executives, approval of the management structure, supervision of executives (including appraisal and remuneration), compliance with laws and regulations and organization of shareholder meetings. The board is also responsible for effective communication with shareholders. The Principles of Corporate Governance prescribes a board with no less than five members, at least half of whom should be non-executive directors and one-third independent directors.[14] In early 2018, there were 513 companies listed

---

[11] The Capital Markets Board (2014). Communiqué on Corporate Governance. *Official Gazette*. Available from: http://www.cmb.gov.tr/SiteApps/Teblig/File/479 [Accessed 22 October 2018].

[12] Ibid.

[13] Türkiye Kurumsal Yönetim Derneği (Turkish Corporate Governance Association) (TKYD) (2016). BIST Yönetim Kurullari Araştirmasi 2016. Available from: http://www.kobirate.com.tr/content/BIST-YONETIM-KURULLARI-ARASTIRMASI.pdf [Accessed 22 October 2018].

[14] The Capital Markets Board (2014). Communiqué on Corporate Governance. *Official Gazette*. Available from: http://www.cmb.gov.tr/SiteApps/Teblig/File/479 [Accessed 22 October 2018].

on the Istanbul Stock Exchange (BIST) with on average 6.5 board members[15] and 26% independent directors. Only 12% of all directors were women, while 5.8% of boards had a female board chair. Around 10% of all board members are non-Turkish, but only 7% of companies have non-Turkish board chairs. Most non-Turkish board members sit on the boards of the largest companies—those with a market value of more than 3 billion (US$500 million).

According to the Principles on Corporate Governance, the chair is responsible for setting the board agenda, providing materials, ensuring directors' attendance and conducting board meetings in such a manner that every director contributes to the collective work.[16]

Turkey has one of the highest levels of ownership concentration in Europe, and shareholders often play a prominent role in managing and governing their businesses. Large shareholders are often emotionally attached to their companies and "owners' pride" plays an important role in their decision-making. Half of all listed companies in Turkey are majority owned by individuals or families, and boards at 80% of Turkish public companies have at least one board member who is a member of the controlling or founding family.[17] Many chairs are also significant shareholders—or their representatives.

EXISTING RESEARCH

In spite of a growing interest in researching corporate governance in Turkey over the last decade, the literature on the subject is limited. One study devoted to board chairs in Turkey,[18] based on interviews with chairs of eight Turkish public companies and ten board members, describes the

[15] Türkiye Kurumsal Yönetim Derneği (Turkish Corporate Governance Association) (TKYD) (2016). BIST Yönetim Kurullari Araştirmasi 2016. Available from: http://www.kobirate.com.tr/content/BIST-YONETIM-KURULLARI-ARASTIRMASI.pdf [Accessed 22 October 2018].

[16] The Capital Markets Board (2014). Communiqué on Corporate Governance. *Official Gazette.* Available from: http://www.cmb.gov.tr/SiteApps/Teblig/File/479 [Accessed 22 October 2018].

[17] Kula, V. (2005). The Impact of the Roles, Structure and Process of Boards on Firm Performance: Evidence from Turkey. *Corporate Governance: an International Review*, 13 (2), pp. 265–276.

[18] Kakabdse A., Kakabadse, N. and Yavuz, O. (2009). Turkish Chairmen: Contrasting the Art of Dialogue against the Discipline for Governance. In: A. Kakabadse, and N. Kakabadse, eds., *Global Boards*. Basingstoke: Palgrave Macmillan.

context in which the chair operates and the scope of the role. The research-ers concluded that, because of the complexity of personal relationships and the active role of shareholders in Turkey, "delicacy of touch" and the abil-ity to nurture balanced power structures within the board were particularly important qualities. The study also highlighted that, due to internal and external relationship exposure, the spread of the chair's responsibilities is extensive and the chair's influence on the organization is extensive.

A number of studies examine the impact of the structure of boards on the performance of Turkish companies. Some of these are of interest for our analysis, since among other issues they focus on the relationship between CEO-Chair duality and company performance. Most of the research reveals that CEO-Chair duality is negatively associated with performance.[19]

Other studies cover the relationship between certain aspects of the chair's role and the company's performance. For example, one study, based on a sample of 266 Turkish firms with majority family ownership, showed that in the highest-performing companies, chairs are rarely replaced—except in cases of death and old age. In addition, chairs in higher-performing companies tend to be less involved with routine affairs. Finally, the better the company's performance, the more the chair deter-mines the board agenda.[20]

TURKEY CULTURE MAP

Using Turkey's position on Professor Erin Meyer's "Culture Map", we can develop some hypotheses about the working practices of board chairs of Turkish companies (see Appendix A). In Turkey communication is medium-to-high context, so board discussions may be nuanced and far from straightforward. If this hypothesis is correct, effective chairs will spend a lot of time clarifying assumptions and establishing relevant facts for their boards. In most principles-first cultures, such as Turkey, the chair

---

[19] Kula, V. (2005). The Impact of the Roles, Structure and Process of Boards on Firm Performance: Evidence from Turkey. *Corporate Governance: an International Review*, 13 (2), pp. 265–276; Kaymak, T. and Bektas, E. (2008). East Meets West? Board Characteristics in an Emerging Market: Evidence from Turkish Banks. *Corporate Governance: An International Review*, 16 (6), pp. 550–561.

[20] Kula, V. and Tatoglu, E. (2006). Board Process Attributes and Company Performance of Family-Owned Businesses in Turkey. *Corporate Governance: The International Journal of Business in Society*, 6 (5), pp. 624–634.

is likely to focus on clarifying the logic behind certain decisions and the board's overall mission. Decision-making is top-down rather than consensual in hierarchical cultures like Turkey, so we would expect chairs to be somewhat authoritarian. Turkish culture is relationship-based, which implies that chairs will pay attention to building and maintaining relationships with all stakeholders, both formally and informally. Turkey is medium ranked in terms of confrontation, which should translate into chairs preventing arguments and heated debates in the boardroom—and avoiding tough face-to-face conversations outside it. Turkey operates in flexible-time mode, which is likely to make chairs adaptable in their attitude towards timings of board meetings and deadlines (Fig. 8.1).[21]

DATA

We conducted semi-structured interviews with six board chairs—five men and one woman—aged between 55 and 65 years. With one exception, they were all based in Istanbul. Two are second-generation owners; four are professional chairs with a CEO background. Together the respondents

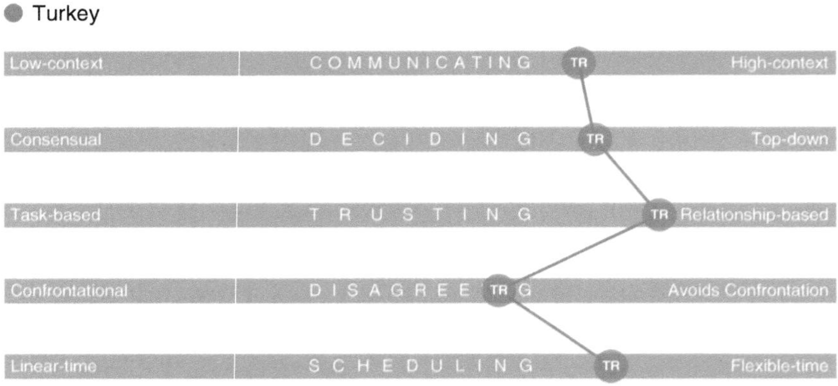

● Turkey

Fig. 8.1 Turkey Culture Map (Source: Based on the work of INSEAD Professor Erin Meyer, and her *The Culture Map* book [Meyer, E. (2014). *The Culture Map: Breaking Through the Invisible Boundaries of Global Business.* New York: PublicAffairs])

[21] The Persuading scale does not plot all world cultures as the concept of Applications-first and Principles-first only applies to western environments. For this the Turkey Culture Map does not have the Persuading scale.

have chaired the boards of 43 companies with significant private share-holders, 3 of which were publicly traded. They have all served as the chair of at least one charity in the past. All have a full-time engagement with the organizations whose boards they currently chair. Their experience of chairing boards varies between 6 and 16 years.

The interviewees' boards meet either monthly or every two months, in most instances for half a day. Some of their companies have only share-holders as board members, while others have executive, non-executive and independent directors. Most chairs in the sample actively use committees, especially those mandated by the Turkish Capital Markets Board, such as risk and audit. Optional committees, such as ethics and human resources, operate in only a few of the companies.

To provide a 360-degree view of the chair's work, we interviewed six other respondents—three women and three men—including three inde-pendent directors, one private shareholder, one representative of a share-holding family and one CEO. Five of them were over 50 years old and one was under 35. All were of Turkish origin and had CEO experience or rep-resented a family. They also had significant experience of serving as board members for the public, private and charity sectors in different industries.

CHAIRS IN TURKEY: KEY CHALLENGES AND PRACTICES

Relationships with Shareholders

In Turkey, where there is a high concentration of ownership and share-holders are very involved with the businesses they own, board chairs con-sider relationships with shareholders to be their top priority. The fact that in most cases shareholders are members of their boards makes managing these relationships even more challenging. In our research we observed a number of modes of chair-shareholder interaction and some specific prac-tices supporting them. The modes are defined by the ownership structure, family ties, personalities and social status of the parties involved.

Some chairs operate under the "I work for the company" model. As one experienced independent director noted: *"He [the chair] works for and looks after the interests of the company, and nothing else, while looking after relevant stakeholders."* Under this model an independent chair is aware of the interests and expectations of all shareholders, conveys them to the board and makes sure the latter takes them into consideration while making decisions. The interests of the company do not always match those of the shareholders, and the board under the chair's leadership has to

advance the former. The chair and the board need a high level of independence from shareholders and those who sit on the board are required to
leave their shareholders' hats at the door of the boardroom. We came
across this model at public companies with dispersed ownership and at
private ones with three or more shareholders. In all cases, the chairs were
independent, very experienced professionals with high social status. One
particularly interesting occurrence of the model was at a public company
where the chair was the majority shareholder. This required considerable
autonomy, maturity and resilience from the chair as well as highly developed communication and moderating skills.

By contrast, the "I work for the shareholders" model implies that a
board chair puts the interests of shareholders above those of the company
and other stakeholders. As one chair-respondent said: "*He can have a
small share in a business, but be a wise and experienced man. I want him to
feel that I value him as much as I do large shareholders.*" We observed this
attitude in the board of a private company chaired by a minority shareholder. In his work the chair strived to understand and align the interests
of all shareholders, and viewed the board's decision-making through the
prism of maintaining and strengthening this alignment.

Another model that we discovered could be called "I work for an individual." One chair of a subsidiary, who had been nominated by the CEO
(and majority shareholder) of the holding company, operates in such a way as
to satisfy the latter above all else. Similarly, the chair of a public company may
work for a controlling shareholder who sits next to her in the boardroom as
a director. One variation on this model is "I work for a family," where a chair
(family member or non-family member alike) owes a duty to the founding
family and orchestrates board business to the tune of its interests.

Neither the "I work for the shareholders" nor the "I work for a person"
model implies that the chair and the board ignore the interests of the company or forget about other shareholders. On the contrary, they respect the
law and the Code. It is simply that they have a specific sense of duty and priorities. Furthermore, in reality, none of the models we have described exists
in its pure form. The boundaries between them are somewhat blurred, but
they allow us to capture the variety of approaches to chairing a board in Turkey.

In terms of practices, chairs use both formal and informal tools to interact with shareholders. Five of the chairs interviewed rely on regular reporting to keep shareholders informed and engaged. Most of them send all
board materials to the shareholders before the board meeting, so that the
latter feel in control and trust the former. One chair does not share board
materials but organizes a meeting for shareholders—with the CEO's

participation—to discuss the upcoming board meeting. Another goes to see a shareholder to prepare for all the decisions to be made by the board. Some chairs take shareholders and their representatives out for dinner to discuss the upcoming board meeting informally. One respondent conducts an annual strategy meeting with shareholders to review and document strategy and board agendas for the next year. He then relies on the agreed points to navigate the board during the next 12 months.

Board Dynamics

In Turkey, with its hierarchical but non-confrontational culture, authority has to be visible yet warm. According to our respondents, effective chairs are welcoming, communicative, have high levels of energy and, at the same time, are capable of using power to make difficult decisions. We discovered three approaches to running board meetings among Turkish chairs, referred to as "structured", "semi-structured" and "delegated" (or "professional") facilitation.

Structured facilitation: Proponents of this approach believe in planning, timing and controlling. They set the agenda and allocate time for each item in advance, establish the rules of engagement and enforce them. One chair always opens the meeting with procedural questions, tightly controls the time, the order and the flow of the discussion, disciplines anyone who deviates, solicits the opinions of silent directors and closes the meeting. He does not allow interruptions by phone or in person. Another chair insists on sticking to the pre-defined agenda and timetable.

Semi-structured facilitation: One chair subscribes to a more flexible approach. She allows new items to be added to the agenda, but keeps them for the end. She organizes breaks when she feels directors need some fresh air. Another tries to lead with emotional intelligence: "*You should be in the meeting, but also look at it from the outside to see what's going on—and intervene accordingly.*"

Delegated facilitation: One of our interviewees is the chair of several companies where he is also a controlling shareholder. He delegates the job of chairing board meetings at some of these companies to lead independent directors (LIDs), who are usually experienced professional directors and sometimes professional facilitators. Under this model, the LID runs the meeting while the chair participates in it as a director. Another tries to create an inclusive, collaborative environment for active participation of board members, and in cases of non-constructive behaviour, he intervenes with authority.

Based on our research, structured facilitation is the most popular approach among chairs of Turkish companies. Although chairs are responsible for setting the board agenda, sometimes they do so in consultation with shareholders or the CEO. The agenda will reflect the company's size, stage of development, industry and the complexity of its environment, but boards in Turkey examine not only strategic but operational issues. As one experienced director explained, a typical agenda would be "*60–80 percent strategic and the rest operational*".

We learnt that there is more or less a traditional way to start a board meeting in Turkey. The chair opens with a greeting and a short summary of what was decided at the previous meeting and then goes over the agenda, which in most cases remains as planned. Each item on the agenda has a time allocation and the chair brings the board's attention to it.

In conducting board discussions, effective chairs strive for a balance between effectiveness and efficiency. On the one hand, they encourage directors to speak up and let the discussion unfold while keeping personal egos in check. As one independent director, a pioneer in Turkish corporate governance, put it: "*A chair tries to create a platform for a constructive and focused discussion and not let personal animosity take over the discussion.*" On the other hand, well aware of flexible attitudes to time in Turkey, experienced chairs keep an eye on their watches to ensure every director gets an opportunity to speak up. As one of the chair-respondents put it: "*Timing is of the essence; each member should be given a sufficient time for his or her contribution.*"

Everyone we interviewed agreed that the ability to involve all directors and organize a productive discussion within a limited amount of time is one of the most important competencies of a board chair. As one respondent said: "*The most important feature of an effective chairperson is [his/her] 'effectiveness', not only in terms of preparation of the agenda and the meeting, but also in facilitating discussion during the board meetings, and stipulating short- and medium-term risks and opportunities for the company.*"

Effective chairs create a productive environment for their boards by treating directors equally, encouraging everyone to speak up their minds, containing egotistic directors (discussed below) and setting an example of discipline and punctuality. "*A good chair ensures a climate that allows the board to ask the right questions and harmonizes the environment to have maximum contribution from a diverse board,*" in the words of one of the independent directors we interviewed. Another respondent shared the **CRAFTE**D approach to building trust: **C**onsistency, **R**esponsibility, **A**ccountability, **F**airness, **T**ransparency and **E**ffectiveness (see box).

Building Trust: CRAFTED Approach
The key to a successful board is to have trust among its members and between the board, the management and the shareholders. The main role of the chair is to ensure that a culture and climate of trust is established and maintained. This can only be accomplished by following the CRAFTED principles of good governance:

Consistency: A key element in gaining the trust of others is demonstrating consistency in behaviour. This is true not only where the board is gaining the trust of the stakeholders, but also where members of the board are gaining trust among themselves so as to create the proper climate to handle difficult decisions.

Responsibility: As the board is the final decision-making authority for corporate decisions, the ability to take the initiative, say "no" and bring tough issues onto the agenda is a valuable attribute for board members.

Accountability: The board and its committees have to demonstrate humility, conduct an annual self-evaluation process in order to identify areas for improvement in their own composition and operations and bring about the changes required.

Fairness: The choice of a board member should not be based on their relationship with the chairperson, the CEO or other members, but on the value they could add to the board. Also, in balancing the interests of various stakeholders, fairness is a key principle in gaining the trust of others.

Transparency: Board members need to have the self-confidence and skill to be able to explain the basis for their decisions to each other, and to the management, in order to develop and maintain the right climate for raising challenging issues and help the management internalize the reasoning of board decisions for better implementation.

Effectiveness: Both the ability to demonstrate intellectual independence, in order to bring different perspectives to bear on board decisions, and the regular benchmarking of both corporate and board performance are essential for effectiveness.

Source: Arguden, Y. (2009). *Boardroom Secrets. Corporate Governance for Quality of Life*. Basingstoke: Palgrave Macmillan

The enabling approach applied by many effective chairs translates into the decision-making pattern on Turkish boards. Based on the characterization of Turkish culture as hierarchical, we expected board leaders to be "more equal" than other directors in articulating and influencing board decisions. We found this to be the case when the chair is also an important shareholder. However, we also discovered that many boards make decisions collectively with the equal participation of all directors, including the chair. As one respondent put it: "*A board member, individually, has no authority to make decisions on behalf of the company. However, collectively, the board is the ultimate decision-making body. So the best practice of the chair is to enable this through effective facilitation and agenda management.*" Not surprisingly, all the directors we interviewed spoke against voting and in favour of consensus as the best way to make board decisions.

Collaboration Outside the Boardroom

To create a smoothly operating board effective chairs undertake various activities outside the boardroom. One respondent emphasized taking "*great care to ensure that the team is formed properly from the outset*". This view is seconded by another chair: "*Team members should spend time together and exchange ideas and views so the board works as a unified team, not as individual stars.*" Specific activities include meetings to discuss ideas and projects without keeping minutes; informal gatherings around meals or coffee; and one-to-one conversations with the chair.

One board leader who emphasized the power of joint intellectual effort organizes brainstorming sessions for board members with the participation of external speakers. He brings directors to product launches and customer meetings and even sets specific performance-improvement projects. Another appoints board members (including independent ones) as sponsors of executive initiatives.

One chair considers board committees to be an important venue for directors, and encourages and supervises committee work. He believes that competition between the committees to produce high-quality work increases collaboration among committee members. He invites them to company-sponsored events like art exhibitions and award gatherings to enhance their feeling of belonging and togetherness. Some chairs also organize lunches after board meetings. As one of them said: "*It is never enough just to come, have the meeting and go. They need to enjoy each other as well.*"

Managing Difficult Board Members

Maintaining discipline among board members is one of the main challenges board chairs face in Turkey. One type of disrupter is the "multitasking director" who tries to do several things in parallel during board meetings, such as talking on the phone or messaging. Effective chairs, according to directors and CEOs, lead the process with discipline, serving as role models to prevent the event from spiralling out of control. "*A fish stinks from the head*," as one respondent so colourfully expressed it.

Another problem is "challengers", who interrupt other directors and make critical comments during the discussion. While we expected Turkish chairs to avoid direct confrontation, the majority of them do not shy away from it, replying directly to challengers and cutting interruptions short. They may even abandon a meeting altogether. One chair shared a dramatic story: "*When everything was clear, but one member wanted to continue talking about the topic in spite of my warnings, I stood up, told them that I was cancelling the meeting and walked away.*"

In addition to open confrontation, chairs may use subtler practices. One handles difficult directors by talking to them one to one before a board meeting, or discussing critical issues at pre-meeting dinners or other social occasions. As one respondent accurately observed: "*Difficult members get even more difficult if excluded; it is easier to manage those members by involving and engaging them.*" Another professional chair stressed the importance of a non-judgemental attitude:

> *The most important thing is to understand. If she/he has a tough reaction, that means we brought her/him to that stage. When we listen and show that we understand the point, it resolves automatically, and we see points where she/he is right too. It is important to listen to someone who is labelled a troublemaker with a non-judgmental attitude. When you listen to them genuinely, you deserve the right to say something.*

This approach calls for emotional intelligence from the chair. Another director confirmed: "*If the chair is impulsive in his reactions to the challenges coming from the directors, they will most likely be discouraged from sharing their views, which would be a waste of the value they can add.*"

"Quiet" and "non-contributing" directors present another challenge. Understanding why they abstain from discussions is of crucial importance for a chair. One respondent had realized that a director was afraid to speak up because he lacked industry expertise. The former sent the latter some additional materials and previous board books, as well as arranging meetings with executives to learn about the business. After a couple of meetings the director began to participate much more.

A very effective way to manage difficult board members is to avoid them altogether. One professional chair described making sure that shareholders always seek clearance from him before appointing a new director, so that the chances of having a destructive board member are low from the beginning. In general, we found that chairs in Turkey are quite active in influencing board composition through defining profiles of directors and "selling them to shareholders" (often informally); suggesting candidates and interviewing them; and conducting induction sessions and programmes.

Unfortunately, chairs may themselves become a problem for the board. Abrasive behaviour from a board leader reduces directors' willingness to participate and diminishes the board's effectiveness. One director-respondent articulated the chair traits that may become destructive for the board: *"partiality, a loss of control, an authoritative tone, complacency"* and/or *"opinionated reactions to news or new ideas and enforcing his own views"*.

Board Evaluation

Regular board evaluations are relatively new in Turkey and we came across a variety of approaches. Some chairs organize *"an in-camera executive session at the end of each board meeting to receive frank feedback from board members"*; others involve an external consultant. Some respondents shared that they had developed a questionnaire for each director to assess each other on standard dimensions—followed by whole-board discussions of the results. As one respondent pointed out, the key challenge with board evaluations is *"to make every director contribute"*.

Relationships with the CEO and Management

"The chair manages the board, the CEO manages the company" might be easier said than done in Turkey. Our research found two principal types of Turkish board leaders—chair-principals and professional chairs. The former have power over the organization because of their ownership stake, family ties, CEO position, social status or all of the above. They call the shots, no matter what the org charts or bylaws say. Directors and executives often work for chair-principals rather than for the board or for a nominal CEO. Under this scenario, the relationship between the chair and the CEO is hierarchical. The former is the boss and the latter a subordinate, although sometimes the CEO plays an advisory role vis-à-vis an all-powerful chair.

Professional chairs have no power base, except for their position. They work for the board and in some cases for the specific shareholders who appointed them. In the latter case, the shareholders tend to remain very involved and influential in board matters, while the chair sometimes plays a more technical role. Under this scenario, the relationship between the chair and the CEO is one of two professionals with equal or similar status and usually falls into the "collaboration" and "mentoring" categories described in Chap. 1. One respondent described the chair's role in such relationships as "*a sounding board and counsellor to the CEO—the chair should help the CEO through bad times with advice and support.*" Another added that, although an effective chair challenges the CEO and management in a constructive way: "*The chair should let neither personal aggressiveness nor complacency take over interactions with the CEO/management.*" A third respondent summed it up as follows: "*A good chair is a person who is challenging at good times and supportive at bad times—and never vice versa!*"

The research identified a number of specific—and sometimes unorthodox—practices that Turkish chairs use to interact with CEOs.

Clearly dividing areas of responsibilities: One respondent called himself an "*executive chair*". Under his model the CEO is 100% responsible for execution and the chair for governance and strategy. All executives report to the CEO, but audit and risk report to the executive chair.

Regular communications with the CEO: The optimal frequency for some respondents is daily: "*A chair who does not cooperate with the management daily cannot portray the company's dynamics to the shareholders in a correct or timely manner.*" However, others mentioned only monthly meetings. The chair also brings information to the management team from the shareholders or from other companies in the group.

Managing CEO performance: One chair told us how he supervises the CEO. The board has established KPIs and the chair reviews progress in formal meetings with the CEO. In addition, there are less-formal mentoring sessions. Other respondents are also involved in direct supervision of CEOs and provide performance feedback, in some cases after each board meeting—particularly when the chair is the controlling owner or former CEO of the company.

Mentoring: Advice and patronage are often the basis of the relationship with the CEO. One respondent explained: "*Since I groomed and promoted the CEO, he consults me as he would an older brother, and I mentor him.*" This kind of mentoring from a position of seniority has its drawbacks, as some CEOs try to devolve responsibility upwards. One chair said that he always pushes back on such attempts.

Mentoring sessions for the CEO–1 level: One chair provides mentoring not only to the CEO but to his direct reports. This enables the board leader to gauge the company's leadership talent.

Recognition: The chairs we interviewed always make CEOs aware that their contributions are noticed and appreciated. They do not always wait for a formal performance appraisal session but give praise informally when the opportunity emerges, including during board meetings.

Rehearsing meetings with the CEO: One chair-respondent rehearses upcoming board meetings with the CEO. He considers this not only a good way to ensure an effective meeting, but also a means to motivate and train the CEO. He observed that "*Turks are less prepared than international CEOs and need more support.*"

Initiative sponsorship: One chair uses the practice of assigning a board member as curator of each major initiative that management has to implement. The curators work closely with the CEO and other executives, providing mentoring, advice and feedback.

Chair Succession

Independent chairs in Turkey are not actively involved in their succession, leaving the decision to the shareholders. However, chairs who are large shareholders or CEOs of the company often think about and plan for their succession very carefully. One respondent shared that his successor is almost ready to take over, now that they have worked together for several years. One chair-owner of a large holding takes his succession particularly seriously—he selects external governance and business experts as independent directors for some of his companies and looks at them as potential candidates. One chair-CEO has two potential candidates to succeed him in both positions and another five years to make his choice.

Summary: Profile of the Chair in Turkey

There are two types of board chairs in Turkey: chair-principals, who are significant shareholders or members of founding families, and professional chairs, who have no connection with ownership. Both groups share some important characteristics and use similar practices, yet there are significant differences in how they see and do their jobs. The former use their position as a platform for leading the whole organization, including board, management and employees, while the latter manage the board only.

In recent years, there have been significant changes in the way chairs of Turkish companies approach leading the board. Our research has identified two major trends, which to some extent run counter to the national culture and long-standing tradition of ceremonial boards and nominal chairs. Both professional chairs and chair-principals are becoming expert facilitators, enabling every director to speak her mind and allowing constructive collective discussions to take place in the boardroom. They proactively manage board agendas, strive for balance between strategic and operational issues, balance presentations, discussions and information exchange, and set the tone for the meeting. Board leaders are also acting more like mentors who support and give guidance, rather than senior leaders who decide and have the last say. These trends are in line with what is happening in other European countries, but they contradict some cultural elements and established practices. As a result some incumbents have been forced out of their comfort zones. Another role that is increasingly similar to that of their counterparts across Europe is acting as a "bridge" between the board and the shareholders or management. In these relationships, chairs in Turkey are increasingly acting as representatives of the board rather than individual agents—as are chairs in other European countries.

Although the formal corporate governance framework in Turkey is very similar to that in other European countries, our research revealed some notable characteristics of chairs in Turkey. A number of factors are behind these specifics: prevalence of private and family businesses with active physical shareholders; a hierarchical, relationship-based and male-dominated business culture; and dynamic co-existence of formal "global" governance rules and standards alongside traditional models and instruments of informal governance. We have identified a number of elements of the "Turkish chairing style". For example, in Turkey chairs often have a family-style view of the organization, whereby the chair accords attention and respect based on individual status—as defined not only by formal affiliations or position but also by a whole web of social ties. This view translates into chairs paying attention both to performance (making effective decisions) and to relationships (keeping the board a "happy family"). Board leaders value social events, such as dinners, outings and conferences, and often rely on social contacts and informal ties to get things done. Chairs in Turkey do not shy away from emotions, even at formal board meetings, and conduct their business in an authoritative but diplomatic style.

The tension between global and local trends will influence how the work of chairs in Turkey evolves over the next decade. In the meantime, our interviews suggest some specific trends.

- The informal elements of the chair's work will increase in volume and importance. More meetings will be held off site, without minutes and even without all directors present.
- Value protection for shareholders (rather than value creation) will become a top priority for chairs and their boards in Turkey. Chairs will use all their resources, including personal networks, to ensure business and ownership continuity.
- Government and government-linked individuals and institutions will require more and more attention and time from boards and their leaders. Reliability, predictability and personal loyalty to key shareholders will be important chair-selection criteria.
- Boards of Turkish companies will become more diverse. There will be more female directors and chairs, because initiatives such as "Women for Boards" will increase awareness and produce capable candidates. Yet, despite significant efforts to increase the number of women board members—from cross-company mentoring to board-ready-women programmes—women will remain a small minority, unless quotas are applied.
- The CEO position and links to owners will remain the two principal avenues for becoming a board chair in Turkey.
- Information technology will conquer Turkish companies and make significant incursions into their boardrooms, but many chairs will stick to the traditional way of doing things and boards will not become fully digitalized in the next five years. We will probably have to wait a decade for digital savvy to become indispensable for board leaders in Turkey.

REFERENCES

Ararat, M., Alkan, S., Aytekin, B. and Büyükabacı, O.S. (2017). *Women on Board Turkey: 2017.* Working Paper, Sabanci University.

Aras, G. (2015). The Effect of Corporate Governance Practices on Financial Structure in Emerging Markets: Evidence from BRICK Countries and Lessons for Turkey. *Emerging Markets Finance and Trade,* 51, pp. 5–24.

Arguden, Y. (2009). *Boardroom Secrets. Corporate Governance for Quality of Life.* Basingstoke: Palgrave Macmillan.

Avcin, M. and Balcoiglu, H. (2017). Corporate Governance: A Comparative Study of Firms in Northern Cyprus and Turkey. *Revista De Cercetare Si Interventie Sociala,* 57, pp. 182–201.

Auswärtiges Amt (German Federal Foreign Office) (2018). Turkey Country Profile. Available from: https://www.auswaertiges-amt.de/de/aussenpolitik/laender/tuerkei-node/wirtschaft/201964 [Accessed 8 October 2018].

Ciftci, I., Tatoglu, E., Wood, G., Demirbag, M., and Zaim, S. (2019). Corporate Governance and Firm Performance in Emerging Markets: Evidence from Turkey. *International Business Review,* 28, pp. 90–103.

Eurostat (2018). Unemployment by Sex and Age – Monthly Average. Available from: http://appsso.eurostat.ec.europa.eu/nui/show.do?dataset=une_rt_m&lang=en [Accessed 8 October 2018].

German Federal Foreign Office, 2018. Turkey. https://www.auswaertiges-amt.de/de/aussenpolitik/laender/tuerkei-node/wirtschaft/201964.

Heritage Foundation (2018). Turkey Country Profile. Available from https://www.heritage.org/index/country/turkey [Accessed 14 August 2018].

Kakabdse A., Kakabadse, N. and Yavuz, O. (2009). Turkish Chairmen: Contrasting the Art of Dialogue against the Discipline for Governance. In: A. Kakabadse, and N. Kakabadse, eds., *Global Boards.* Basingstoke: Palgrave Macmillan.

Kaymak, T. and Bektas, E. (2008). East Meets West? Board Characteristics in An Emerging Market: Evidence from Turkish Banks. *Corporate Governance: An International Review,* 16(6), pp. 550–561.

Kula, V. and Tatoglu, E. (2006). Board Process Attributes and Company Performance of Family-Owned Businesses in Turkey. *Corporate Governance: The International Journal of Business in Society,* 6(5), pp. 624–634.

Kula, V. (2005). The Impact of the Roles, Structure and Process of Boards on Firm Performance: Evidence from Turkey. *Corporate Governance: An International Review,* 13(2), pp. 265–276.

Meyer, E. (2014). *The Culture Map: Breaking Through the Invisible Boundaries of Global Business.* New York: PublicAffairs.

Sonmez, M. (2014). *The Role of Better Transparency Law in Corporate Governance and Financial Markets, and Its Practicability in Legal Systems: A Comparative Study Between the EU and Turkey.* Durham theses, Durham University. Available from http://etheses.dur.ac.uk/1080 [Accessed 8 October 2018].

Tasman-Jones, J. (2013). Infographic: Turkish Family Businesses. *CampdenFB*, 59. Available from: http://www.campdenfb.com/article/infographic-turkish-family-businesses [Accessed 22 October 2018].

The Capital Markets Board (2014). Communiqué on Corporate Governance. *Official Gazette*. Available from: http://www.cmb.gov.tr/SiteApps/Teblig/File/479 [Accessed 22 October 2018].

The World Bank (2018a). World Development Indicators. GDP per capita, in international dollars. Available from: https://data.worldbank.org/indicator/NY.GDP.PCAP.PP.CD?year_high_desc=true [Accessed 22 September 2018].

The World Bank (2018b). World Development Indicators. GDP Ranking. Available from: https://datacatalog.worldbank.org/dataset/gdp-ranking [Accessed 22 September 2018].

The World Bank (2018c). World Development Indicators. Population, total. Available from: http://databank.worldbank.org/data/reports.aspx?source=2&series=SP.POP.TOTL [Accessed 22 September 2018].

Türkiye Kurumsal Yönetim Derneği (Turkish Corporate Governance Association) (TKYD) (2016). BIST Yönetim Kurullari Araştirmasi 2016. Available from: http://www.kobirate.com.tr/content/BIST-YONETIM-KURULLARI-ARASTIRMASI.pdf [Accessed 22 October 2018].

UNDP (2018). Human Development Indices and Indicators. 2018 Statistical Update. Available from: http://hdr.undp.org/en/2018-update [Accessed 28 September 2018].

CHAPTER 9

Russia: Powerful Moderation

Ekaterina Ryasentseva and Veronika Zagieva

THE CHAIR'S WORK IN CONTEXT

Russia is the largest country in the world, extending across Eastern Europe and Northern Asia. With 146.9 million inhabitants (77 per cent of whom live in Europe),[1] it is also the ninth most populous country[2] in the world. Russia is a federation with 85 "subjects" (constituent units) and a presidential-parliamentary republic. The president is an elected head of state, while the prime minister is appointed by parliament as the head of government.

Russia's gross domestic product (GDP) in 2017 was US$1.5 trillion,[3] the 6th highest in the world[4] (using purchasing power parity), but in terms

---

[1] Russian Federation Federal State Statistics Service (2018). Population. Available from: http://www.gks.ru/wps/wcm/connect/rosstat_main/rosstat/ru/statistics/population/demography/# [Accessed 10 May 2018].

[2] The World Bank (2016). Population Ranking. Available from: https://datacatalog.worldbank.org/dataset/population-ranking [Accessed 10 May 2018].

[3] The World Bank (2018). World Development Indicators. GDP Ranking. Available from: https://datacatalog.worldbank.org/dataset/gdp-ranking [Accessed 28 September 2018].

[4] The World Bank (2018). World Development Indicators. GDP Ranking, PPP based. Available from: https://datacatalog.worldbank.org/dataset/gdp-ranking-ppp-based [Accessed 28 September 2018].

E. Ryasentseva • V. Zagieva (✉)
Ward Howell Talent Equity Institute, Moscow, Russia
e-mail: e.ryasentseva@wardhowell.com; v.zagieva@wardhowell.com

© The Author(s) 2019
S. Shekshnia, V. Zagieva (eds.), *Leading a Board*,
https://doi.org/10.1007/978-981-13-3197-8_9

of per capita GDP ($25,533) it ranks 54th in the world.[5] Russia is one of the world's leading producers of oil and natural gas and a major exporter of steel and aluminium. This reliance on commodity exports makes it vulnerable to swings in global prices. On the Human Development Index, it ranks 49th in the world.[6]

About 4.7 million Russian companies[7] employ more than 66 million people.[8] The government plays a significant role in the economy. State and state-owned companies account for almost 70 per cent of GDP, up from 40 per cent in 2008.[9]

The primary sources of corporate governance regulations are the law on joint stock companies and the law on the securities market. In 2001, a Code of Corporate Governance was adopted and implemented on a so-called comply or explain basis. On the initiative of the Central Bank, it was revised in 2013 and a new Code enacted in 2014.[10] This specifies the functions of a board of directors, the organization of its work and that of its committees, the criteria for independent directors, and recommendations on developing a remuneration system for executives.

Russian companies operate under a one-tier governance system, with a single board composed of non-executive and executive directors. By law, the functions of CEO and chair must be separate. Based on a survey of 43 of the largest public companies, Russian boards are not small (10.4 members on average) and have limited gender diversity (only 8 per cent of directors are women and none of them holds chair positions).[11] According to the Corporate Governance Code, boards should have "a sufficient

[5] The World Bank (2018). World Development Indicators. GDP per capita, in international dollars. Available from: http://databank.worldbank.org/data/reports.aspx?source=2&series=NY.GDP.PCAP.PP.CD [Accessed 28 September 2018].

[6] UNDP (2018). Human Development Indices and Indicators. 2018 Statistical Update. Available from: http://hdr.undp.org/en/2018-update. [Accessed 28 September 2018].

[7] EMISS (2018) Number of Organisations According to Official Registration. Available from: https://www.fedstat.ru/indicator/42930 [Accessed 10 May 2018].

[8] Russian Federation Federal State Statistics Service (2017). Labor and Employment in Russia. Moscow: Rosstat.

[9] Federal Antimonopoly Service of Russian Federation (2017) Russia' Competition Report 2016. Available from: https://fas.gov.ru/documents/596439 [Accessed 10 May 2018].

[10] Bank of Russia (2014). Russia Corporate Governance Code. *Bank of Russia' Vestnik*, 40 (1518), pp. 3–63.

[11] Spencer Stuart (2017). Russia Board Index 2017. Available from https://www.spencerstuart.com/research-and-insight/russia-board-index-2017-russian [Accessed 28 September 2018].

number" of independent directors—Russian boards have 3.8 independent directors per board on average.[12] Russian directors are also the youngest in Europe—with an average age of 54.3 years.[13]

The Code recommends appointing a chair with an impeccable business and personal reputation and extensive executive experience but limits guidelines on the chair's role and responsibilities to the following:

- *Communication with shareholders.* The chair of the board of directors should make himself/herself available to interact with company shareholders.
- *Management of the board.* The chair should ensure that board meetings are held in a constructive atmosphere and that all items on the meeting agenda are discussed freely. The chair should ensure effective organization of the board's work and its interaction with the other bodies of the company.
- *Providing information for directors.* The chair should take "any and all measures required to provide board members in a timely fashion with information required to make decisions about issues on the agenda".
- *Conducting board performance evaluations.* The chair and nominating committee shall organize periodical evaluation of the board's performance and, if necessary, develop proposals on how to improve board and work committees, taking into account the results of such evaluations.

EXISTING RESEARCH

The role of the chair in Russian companies is not well researched, but there are some studies that help to shed some light on this subject.

In a survey of 50 members of the Russian Managers Association, chairs and directors were asked to rate the different aspects of chairs' qualities and performance.[14] Unsurprisingly, chairs rated themselves more highly than their fellow directors did on almost every aspect, especially styles and qualities. Compared to directors, chairs particularly overestimated their own

---

[12] Ibid.
[13] Ibid.
[14] Kakabadse, A., Kakabadse, N. and Myers, A. (2009). Chairman of the Board Research: a Survey of Russian Organisations. Cranfield School of Management.

"availability to talk", "encouragement of feedback on own performance", and "seeking of consensus". The authors conducted the same survey in the UK and Australia and found that Russian chairs scored higher in "enabling an understanding of organizational strategy" and "directors' contribution to the board agenda" than their counterparts in the other countries.

Another survey of 116 Russian managers from the three centrally located industrial regions of Russia, conducted in 2002, revealed the phenomenon of "informal CEO duality".[15] This occurs when the CEO tends to accumulate power over the board, even though the CEO and chair roles are formally separated. The research also revealed a negative relationship between informal CEO duality and firm performance.

The number of "outsider chairs" in Russia has been growing steadily since the 1990s, when insider control prevailed.[16] Data collected from 741 enterprises in 2008 showed that 46 per cent of all chairs were promoted from within the company and the remaining 54 per cent were from outside. The research also confirmed a strong positive correlation between the appointment of an outsider chair and the extent of outsider directorship in Russian firms.[17] The increase in outsider chairs can be explained by the growing professionalization of Russian corporate boards and the availability of professional chairs.

One final study worthy of note established a positive correlation between the tenure of a board chair and the quality of corporate governance at a company.[18]

Russia Culture Map

According to cross-cultural management experts, Russia has a high-context, relationship-based, principles-first, and confrontational culture with a strong top-down approach to decision-making and a flexible-time scheduling style (see Appendix A for full explanation). On this basis, it can be assumed that Russian chairs are less straightforward and more sophisti-

[15] Judge, W. Q., Naoumova, I. and Koutzevol, N. (2003). Corporate Governance and Firm Performance in Russia: an Empirical Study. *Journal of World Business*, 38 (4), pp. 385–396.

[16] Radygin, A. D. (1998). Russian Privatization: National Tragedy or Institutional Platform for Post-Soviet Reforms. *Mir Rossii*, 7 (3), pp. 3–32.

[17] Iwasaki, I. (2008). The Determinants of Board Composition in a Transforming Economy: Evidence from Russia. *Journal of Corporate Finance*, 14 (5), pp. 532–549.

[18] Kapalyushnikow, R. and Demina, N. (2005). Concentrated Ownership and Management Turnover: The Case of Russia. *Russian Economic Barometer*, 14 (1), pp. 10–21.

cated in delivering indirect messages than their Western European colleagues. At the same time, we would hypothesize that Russian board leaders do not shy away from open confrontation in the boardroom and are ready to face down deviant directors. As they operate in a strongly relationship-based environment, Russian chairs presumably have to pay a lot of attention to managing their networks and are likely to have some connection to the company's shareholders or management prior to their appointment. We also theorize that the hierarchical culture and top-down decision-making style results in comparatively little collaboration and egalitarianism inside the boardroom—with consensus not the primary goal of any discussion and voting considered a legitimate mechanism. Finally, it seems safe to assume that Russian chairs are highly disciplined in ensuring performance but can be flexible in terms of timing and agendas (Fig. 9.1).

DATA

We interviewed nine chairs (one woman and eight men), aged between 44 and 63. All but one (who is British) are Russian citizens. They have extensive corporate governance experience: together they have chaired 28

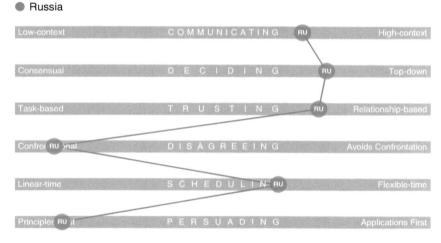

Fig. 9.1 Russia Culture Map (Source: Based on the work of INSEAD professor, Erin Meyer, and her *The Culture Map* book [Meyer, E. (2014). *The Culture Map: Breaking Through the Invisible Boundaries of Global Business.* New York: PublicAffairs])

boards and have served on a total of 57 other boards as directors. Currently they chair 13 boards. Five lead one board each (three are owners of the companies; two others—formerly top-ranking government officials—respectively chair a state-owned company and a private company). Two of them chair two boards each (one is an independent chair of two private companies; the second is an affiliated chair in two joint ventures that belong to the parent company, where he is deputy CEO). One chairs four large public companies, while another is no longer active but previously led four boards. Five of these nine respondents had been CEOs beforehand.

To provide a comprehensive perspective, we also interviewed:

- three professional directors who have sat on over 30 boards between them;
- three shareholders (a representative of an investment fund, who has sat on more than 12 corporate boards, and two business owners who sit on the boards of their own companies as well as those of companies they have invested in); and
- two CEOs—both executive members of two boards of directors.

RUSSIAN CHAIRS: GLOBAL CHALLENGES AND PRACTICES

The INSEAD Global Chair Survey 2015[19] identified a number of key challenges for chairs in Russia—such as relationships with large or controlling shareholders, managing difficult board members (special cases), and relationships with other key stakeholders. Our research questions were organized accordingly; we asked respondents to what extent they considered them relevant and how they dealt with them. We also enquired about other challenges, strategies, and practices used to manage them.

Relationships with Shareholders

For all respondents, the shareholder was the number one stakeholder. But that specific shareholder has to be big and powerful. Many interviewees admitted that they work for the interests of shareholders (not the company or all stakeholders). One even explained that he worked for a specific shareholder: "*I always remember who nominated me as chair!*"

---

[19] Shekshnia, S. and Zagieva, V. (2016). Chair Survey 2015. Available from: https://www.insead.edu/sites/default/files/assets/dept/centres/icgc/docs/chair-survey-2015.pdf [Accessed 3 December 2018].

Since relationships with shareholders were high on the agenda of the chairs we interviewed, they all spent a significant amount of time interacting with these people or their representatives. Specific practices for dealing with shareholders were primarily defined by whether they were government representatives, private owners or another legal entity—although the individual chair's personality and attitudes clearly played a role.

In working with the government as a shareholder, chairs consistently relied on formal mechanisms such as registered mail, official minutes, written requests stating the shareholder's position and so-called directives—formal instructions from the government to its directors about how to vote on a certain item on the board's agenda. When the government is a majority shareholder, the chair is often a conduit of its will rather than its partner. One respondent commented: *"It is a highly political function: 70 per cent of initiatives come from the government and only 30 per cent are generated by the board."* Another said: *"I try to act in accordance with government interests, but in the rare cases when the government can't see that its decisions contradict its interests, I speak up, clearly expressing my disagreement, and vote according to my conscience."*

In Russia's relationship-based culture, informal ties were acknowledged as playing an important role in connections between the chair and the shareholders. Chairs with extensive social networks actively used them to build relationships with, and influence, the government shareholder. One explained:

> *The government is an institution, but there is always a real person behind the institution. There are people who are responsible for the government stake in our company and I have good working relationships with them. Most of the time we find common ground. In rare cases when we don't agree, I speak to people in my network who are above them or can influence them.*

In the joint venture (JV) context, a chair who was also a senior executive at one of the partners considered himself a representative of the shareholders—and acted to advance those interests. He did not interact with other JV partners directly but had created a system under which junior staff members from each organization prepared board decisions in advance and had them approved by the relevant parties before the board meeting. He had delegated the shareholder-management function to a specially created JV management and coordination department.

At private and public companies, chair-shareholder interaction is intense but usually less formal. At one private company covered by our study, the chair met the CEO, who was also the majority shareholder, once a month to informally discuss various issues related to the board and the company. At each meeting, among other things, they reviewed progress in preparing the CEO's successor. Conversations were candid but the chair insisted on retaining independence of action.

Another chair invites two large shareholders of a private company for an informal dinner before every board meeting and organizes a more formal shareholders' get-together every six months to ensure alignment between their expectations and those of the board: "*To be effective you need to be in virtually permanent contact with the key shareholders. They built this business and they care about it as if it was their baby, but they are also very dynamic individuals and develop new ideas quickly.*" He also created a WhatsApp group for shareholders and they exchanged messages on a daily basis.

One shareholder, who had independent chairs on the boards of his companies, confirmed the importance of informal meetings: "*An effective chair connects shareholders and helps them to find a common language. Among good practices I have seen are informal shareholders' meetings with an agenda (but without minutes), dinners at the chair's house (especially if he cooks well) and Telegram chats.*"

The chair of the board (who is also a large shareholder) of a private company (in which a global corporation owns a 50 per cent stake) told us that he made an annual trip to meet the CEO of the major shareholder in person to discuss dividend distribution and the investment programme. They also spoke over the phone every six to eight weeks.

All respondents agreed that working with large shareholders was a top priority that required time, patience, and flexibility. As one put it: "*You just need to be available. They may have what they think is a brilliant idea and want to share it with you at the most inconvenient moment, but if you are not there they will share it with somebody else, and the whole governance system will be at risk.*" Another agreed: "*I think I spend 60 to 70 per cent of my time working with shareholders. If you get it right, the rest is easy.*"

For board directors and CEOs, the chair should be a mediator between executives, shareholders, and other important stakeholders. To do this effectively he or she should develop not only communication skills but also political instincts. As one of the CEOs we interviewed confessed: "*In theory, a chair should be able to tell to a shareholder, 'I do not agree.' But I never heard it in real life.*" Another CEO commented that effective chairs should ensure that shareholders do not overfill the agenda with their favourite topics, such as executive compensation.

Respondents generally did not spend a great deal of time interacting with minority shareholders. Most did not consider this part of their work a significant challenge. They did what the law requires but no more. One chair of a public company said that this was the responsibility of the investor relations manager, who reported to the board on a quarterly basis, together with the CEO. However, three respondents emphasized the importance of regular communication with minority shareholders. As one put it: "*Minority shareholders are like a thermometer—they have no direct influence on the company but a sincere interest in its success. It is always interesting to talk with them and to listen to them. I try to make sure their rights are protected and their voices are heard.*"

Board Dynamics

Pre-meeting

According to the INSEAD Global Chair Survey 2015,[20] the second major challenge for Russian chairs was managing difficult board members (special cases). We discussed this within the larger topic of managing board dynamics.

Respondents took a pragmatic view of the board, its purpose, and interpersonal dynamics: it exists to make major decisions in the interests of shareholders. One respondent said: "*The board should work for the company not for the stakeholders.*" The chairs we interviewed did not waste time discussing the board's mission or operating principles with directors—they got straight down to business. But as one of the respondents put it:

> *In Russia, the board can play dozens of different roles—and the chair's responsibility is to determine for himself what is the role of this board: to be an advisor to shareholders, collective mentor to the CEO or strategic decision maker? When you understand its identity, do not try to change it—just accept it.*

None of the chairs we interviewed had tried to turn the board into a "team," as one of them explained: "*The board is not a team! According to the law, each member has a personal responsibility.*" Unlike their peers in some other countries, chairs of Russian companies did not organize strategic off-sites or team-building events.

---

[20] Ibid.

At the same time, Russian chairs believe that their work outside the boardroom is crucial to the board's effectiveness. They start with themselves, their own preparation and their own positioning. This is less about preparing for a specific meeting than making the board a platform for long-term effectiveness. All the respondents invested significant time in getting to know the company and its key players and in becoming known and visible in the organization. As one shareholder put it: "*The chair links all board members with the company. He makes sure directors understand this expectation, and have time and opportunities to visit the company and speak with executives and rank-and-file employees.*"

One chair spent up to three days a week in the company, during which he worked with the CEO and other senior executives, attended management meetings, reviewed reports, and worked with the company secretary. He had a personal office next to the CEO's and shared the CEO's assistant: "*When I was just a 'visiting chair,' things did not work as well as they do now. My relationships with management were a lot more formal, materials less convenient and board meetings long and poorly structured.*"

Others likewise emphasized the importance of their physical presence at headquarters to being effective. One recalled:

> *A few years ago I became the chair of the board at a large company. It was in the process of moving offices and planned to have a huge one for me. I refused at first, only to reconsider six months later. When you have a permanent office, you send a strong signal to all key stakeholders: "I am here. I am real. I care—and you'd better collaborate with me."*

Another added: "*Physical presence gives you legitimacy in the eyes of shareholders, directors and management.*" One CEO-respondent shared his view that conducting board meetings at different company locations allows directors to know the organization better, meet executives outside of the headquarters and get valuable insights.

Reflecting on the effectiveness of chairs, the directors and CEOs interviewed agreed that presence and involvement is crucial. In their opinion, a chair should not have a full-time job (such as being a CEO elsewhere), as he or she would always be distracted by executive responsibilities.

In addition to presence, substance matters. One experienced chair said: "*In Russia you need to understand the business very well. Some directors are often founders or their representatives, who eat, sleep and breathe this business. In order to gain legitimacy in their eyes, a chair has to develop industry and company knowledge.*" The chair of two JV boards used his staff to generate this knowledge: "*It gives me the opportunity to get any information and data I need.*" Another used site visits, management meetings, and interviews with executives. A number held meetings with the CEO to discuss the upcoming board meeting a couple of days beforehand.

Respondents considered board committees a vital tool for making good decisions. One said:

> *We do three-quarters of the work during committee meetings. Some directors confirm that putting the majority of the discussion into committee work makes the board much more effective. Committees are small, their members possess relevant expertise and discussions are always candid. Board meetings are more formal, so I try to have good discussions at the committee level and ask the board to approve the proposed resolutions.*

Another added: "*Our committees are staffed not only with board members but external experts. We also invite consultants a few times a year to be part of the process. Committees do all the analytical work; the board does not need to spend much time on decision making.*"

Some chairs in our sample actively managed committee membership. One said that he did not try to influence who was elected to the board but cared instead about the selection of committee chairs: "*I look for competent and honest ones.*" Although they relied on committees to prepare decisions, the final decision-making power was rarely delegated to the committees.

We found different degrees of chair involvement in managing board materials. One respondent had established strict rules for all the boards he chairs—materials were sent to all directors ten days before a meeting (others had seven- and five-day rules). Some verified the materials before they went out ("*I always look at the materials first and sometimes I ask management to rework them*") and others delegated the task to executives. Many reported that they no longer sent materials by e-mail or post but downloaded them onto the board website.

From the director's perspective, it is the chair's responsibility to make sure that board members are not overloaded with data. Information overload is even more dangerous than scarcity of information, as it makes directors reluctant to ask additional questions, in case the information was in materials that they failed to read!

To ensure good attendance at board meetings, chairs used different strategies. Some scheduled an informal dinner the evening before, especially when the meeting was not due to be held on company premises, and in some instances dined one to one with directors. Others saw no point in sharing a meal.

Two respondents reported that they included "come prepared" in the list of formal board rules. One experienced professional chair said: "*In Russia you have very strict rules, but everybody bends them. You have to be flexible and use multiple tactics to make sure your board members come prepared.*" Others called their directors a few days before the board meeting, not to discuss specific topics or secure support, but to remind them informally of their duties and encourage preparation and participation.

Leading the Meeting

Our interviews revealed specific ways in which chairs in Russia lead a board meeting. They tend to be quite formal and forceful: they sit at the head of the table; set a detailed agenda and have the board stick to it; keep detailed minutes; allocate strict time slots for presentations, questions, and comments; actively manage the discussion process; and insist on detailed board resolutions. Directors do not mind submitting to such strict discipline in the boardroom. Some director-respondents shared that they appreciated chairs who were openly critical of latecomers ("*How can you manage a big company if you can't manage your schedule?*") and insisted on a "no cell phone" policy.

However, we found that Russian chairs often demonstrate flexibility, if they believe it is beneficial to the outcome of the discussion or social cohesion of the board. One commented: "*The [board] process is flexible. First people tread a path and then it gets covered with asphalt.*" This blend of authority and flexibility produces a particular style, which we refer to as "domineering facilitation" (see the following).

Additional Specific Practices

Establishing and reinforcing the rules of engagement: Some chairs set formal rules for board work. One set a strict "30-20-40-10" schedule: 30 per cent of board time spent on presentations, 20 per cent on Q&A, 40 per cent on discussion, and 10 per cent on making and articulating the decision. Others provided a timeframe for every agenda item:

> *When we have to approve the annual auditors' report, I would give 10 minutes to the chair of the audit committee to speak, allow 15 minutes for questions and*

5 minutes for discussion—the committee has done most of the work. When we need to approve an annual business plan there is no presentation—we go straight to the Q&A and spend the lion's share of the time on discussion.

Many respondents had a set length of time for management presentations and numbers of slides: one limited slides to five; another allowed 12–15 slides for management presentations and set specific formats for budgets and investment projects.

Actively managing board discussion: Within a formal framework, respondents actively managed board dynamics, sometimes breaking their own rules: "*Yes, we have this '30-20-40-10' rule, but when I feel that directors are well prepared I may ask the CEO to skip the presentation and go straight to the conclusions.*" They did not hesitate to interrupt board members who had spoken for too long or off subject or call on a specific director to speak when deemed necessary. Some regularly went "round the table" asking each director to state their position on a specific question. Postponing a decision or moving an item to the next board meeting was a routine tactic. As one of the shareholders shared: "*A good chair controls the flow of the board meeting without being too assertive. He knows when to stop and when to let go.*"

Management participation: This has in board meetings prompted controversy among interviewees. Those with CEO experience tended to have senior executives present throughout board meetings, except for discussions of confidential matters. Others were more selective, inviting the CEO and the most senior managers for a limited number of agenda items.

Voting: As we predicted in the section earlier on the Russian "culture map," reaching a consensus is not a must for chairs of Russian companies. One respondent said: "*It's nice to have everybody aligned, but we have to be efficient. When I feel the majority supports a specific decision, I put it to a vote as some directors may have a different view. We vote and move on.*" Another added: "*Voting is a legitimate instrument. When I use it, board members do not have bad feelings, even those who voted against the decision taken.*" One of the directors confirmed the critical role of hierarchy in the boardroom: "*One independent chair also asked the most powerful guy in the room to vote first, so other directors could form their views.*" The voting also helps shareholders understand what is going on in the boardroom, when they see the voting protocols. Two respondents were categorically against voting, as they believe it destroys board unity. Both had attended executive development programmes at top international business schools.

If the discussion is going to be hard or the topic is complicated, some chairs work in "reverse order"—that is, at the beginning of the exchange they formulate an example of the kind of decision to be made. This helps to frame the debate and demonstrate the kind of outcome needed. Some chairs also set time limits for discussions of no more than one or two hours—if the board cannot come to a conclusion, the chair puts the decision to a vote or postpones the discussion.

Post-meeting
When it comes to post-board meeting practices, arranging a dinner after a board meeting is the most common. Some chairs we interviewed had organized New Year parties for board members and senior executives: "*At such events, real board issues are rarely discussed, but people get to know each other better.*" One left time for informal discussion after the board meeting finished. Others met with directors informally and privately, to discuss specific business issues and strengthen social ties. One chair spent a day a month at company headquarters, keeping the office door open for both board members and executives. Several had created WhatsApp and Telegram group chats for their boards.

Board evaluations: They are not a favourite tool for all our respondents. Three were champions of evaluation, five used it because they felt it had to be done and one was openly critical. The "believers" conducted a short oral assessment at the end of each board meeting and a 360-degree online evaluation once a year, followed by individual meetings with directors and discussion with the entire board. One said:

> *The annual evaluation is a major tool for improvement. In one of my boards, we let go of two directors and brought in three new ones following last year's assessment. In the other board, we overhauled the work of our committees. I don't know how I would have done it without the annual evaluation.*

One chair-founder was dubious about board evaluation: "*How could they evaluate themselves? They will only say good things about themselves! I am watching them and I tell them what does not work.*" At the same time, our non-chair respondents—CEOs and directors alike—considered annual evaluation a very important tool. Comments included "*360-degree assessment helps to get rid of deviant directors*" and "*annual evaluation legitimizes board composition decisions and disciplines directors, who know that their behaviour will be assessed in the end of the year*".

Managing Conflict Within the Board

Arguments and emotions often flare up in the Russian boardroom, but our interviewees did not seem to worry about it. Coming from a culture of open conflict, they knew how to navigate heated debate. Respondents distinguished between "sincere" and "fake" disagreements. They praised the former—*"directors are sincerely looking for the best solution, albeit from different points of view"*—and encouraged healthy (even emotional) debates. However, they distinguished these from discussions where *"people argue for the sake of arguing or, worse, want to advance some political agenda"*. When "fake" disagreement emerged, they halted the discussion and dealt with it outside the boardroom, working individually with the interested parties and returning to the question at the next meeting.

Although comfortable with a highly emotional style, one respondent stepped in from time to time to manage conflict in a forceful manner: *"I don't like surprises, but when the discussion becomes too emotional and unproductive, I say, 'Cards on the table', give every director a minute to state his position, and then we vote."* Another affirmed: *"There are no conflicts, no disruptors, just different opinions. If you do your homework, prepare all the issues in committees, and all members know each other's position, you don't need to debate—just make the final decision by voting."* This chair, in some instances, formulated his position before the board meeting and sent it to the other directors in advance.

Managing difficult board members was not seen as a major challenge. "Talkative types", "silent types", "absent types", and "power types" were mentioned. The last of these was considered the most difficult and included directors who were large shareholders or their relatives and friends and important government officials. One professional chair said:

> *These people are used to telling others what to do and doing it on their own terms. They have a hard time listening to others. Large shareholders have another problem: most of them forget that the board is not a shareholders' meeting and put on their shareholders' cap in the boardroom. To deal with it you need to combine patience with firmness.*

Ways of working with power types included holding a private meeting before the board, reminding them of the rules before and during the meeting, interrupting the meeting to have a word, and even conducting an emergency shareholders' meeting. One chair shared his experience in dealing with a government official who considered himself an expert in everything and disagreed with everybody: "*Initially I would always let him speak at the board, then I involved him in committee work so he could speak there, and it helped to reduce his airtime in the boardroom.*" Another conceded: "*Sometimes you just let the power guy speak for as long as he wants, hoping that you will be able to bring the discussion back when he is done. Other directors understand.*" One CEO shared a practice used by the chair of his board: if the discussion became too heated with only one director arguing against everyone else, he postponed the voting and later allocated the decision to absentee voting, thus avoiding the next round of debate.

There was less tolerance of "talkative" and "silent" types. Interrupting the talkers and reminding directors in the boardroom of their duties as well as "cold calling" around the table were common practices. Some chairs pursued the matter outside the boardroom: one respondent had a one-to-one conversation with deviant directors and offered coaching help. Another applied *razgovor po dusham* (literally "heart to heart")—a tough conversation with the threat of dismissal, if the offending behaviour did not change. Four chairs interviewed indicated they had had to ask a director to resign.

There were two distinct approaches to managing "absent" (non-attending) directors among our interviewees. The first was to try all means available to get them to participate, such as allowing attendance via phone or Skype, soliciting their opinion in writing and transferring their vote to other board members. The chairs who subscribed to this strategy wanted to keep absent directors engaged; they always informed them about the meetings they had missed and reminded them of their obligations.

The second group subscribed to a more radical strategy: "*You are either in or out.*" One said: "*If a board member misses two or three meetings, he/she does not take the job seriously and should be removed.*" This particular chair asked shareholders to re-elect the director or, in the case of a state-owned company, send a written complaint to the government body. A softer option was: "*I make fun of him, emphasizing that he does not know much about the problem under discussion.*" Another said: "*I call him on the phone and beg him to come. Sometimes I say, 'I will send you a plane—please come to the meeting, it's very important.'*"

Relationships with the CEO and Management

The relationship with the CEO, and in some cases with other senior executives, is a top priority for all chairs interviewed but takes different forms

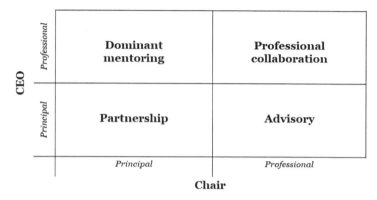

Fig. 9.2   Chair-CEO relationship matrix

largely defined by the parties' backgrounds. We identified two types of protagonists: principal (either a significant shareholder in the company or a fully empowered representative of it) and professional (someone who has no significant stake in the company and works for a salary). There were four resulting types of relationships between chairs and CEOs (see Fig. 9.2).

The principal chair-professional CEO dyad produces an intense relationship, which we refer to as **"dominant mentoring"**. The chair leads and the CEO accepts the role of follower. The former sets the agenda, chooses the forms of interaction, provides direct advice and feedback, and even gives informal orders to the latter. We came across three cases of dominant mentoring where company founders had handed over the reins to a professional executive and had become the chair. One was quite open: "*Of course, I know that I should not interfere in his [the CEO's] work, but I know this business inside-out and sometimes I just have a better feeling of what should be done, so I tell him. Most of the time he is grateful.*" Another agreed: "*I have a lot of experience and know many important people the CEO does not know. It's natural that I give him advice and introduce him to some people, not the other way around.*" With dominant mentoring, the chair acts not as a leader or a spokesperson for the board but as an expert with a specific background and a powerbase unrelated to his or her formal position. In this model, the chair sometimes has to shield the CEO from shareholders: "*Our principal shareholder is a board member. For him, if the year was successful, that was because of a growing market, but if the year was bad, it was the CEO's fault. I understand that it's not fair logic, and try to protect the CEO from unfair accusations.*"

When both the chair and CEO are principals, a different type of relationship emerges, which we call **"partnership"**. Both have a high degree of autonomy and room for independent action, but they have shared goals, align their agendas from time to time, and cooperate when required. A chair of a company with the government as its controlling shareholder described the relationship:

> We both represent government. The CEO is not appointed by the board, but by the Russian President. We both can open important doors, but we also can help each other to help the company. We agree on that, so he does his job and I do mine. But when required we join forces, for example on the business strategy, on regulatory constraints we have to overcome and in other cases. Sometimes he gets grilled by the board, but he accepts it. He knows that I am his great supporter.

When the chair is a professional and the CEO is a principal, the relationship turns into what we call an **"advisory"** model. Formally, the chair is in charge of the board, sets the agenda, and conducts the board meetings, but everyone in the system understands where the ultimate power resides. The board and its leader perform their functions but only up to a point, beyond which the power of the CEO-principal prevails. The chair advises and educates the CEO, brings important information to his/her attention, and assists him/her in preparing and making decisions. The CEO may also educate the chair about the business, share concerns and challenges, and ask for advice or a favour. The two cooperate but not on an equal footing. One chair respondent described his relationship with a founder-CEO in a way that typifies the advisory relationship:

> I come to see him every month. We speak one-to-one, very informally. I update him on the board's work, ask his opinion on important issues. He may ask my views on anything from US politics to the last remuneration committee meeting. Sometimes he asks for help in specific deals. I feel that he values my advice.

When the chair-CEO relationship involves two professionals, we call it **"professional collaboration"**. The chair of a JV, who is a senior executive at one of the partner organizations, described his work with the CEO, who is a former executive of the same company: "*I provide him with all the information I have and he does the same for me. I run all major decisions by him before they go to the board. You may call it informal mentoring, but he also mentors me in some areas such as regional politics or local markets.*"

Similarly, one ex-government official–turned professional chair said, *"[It's] partnership and cooperation, not mentoring! My office is next to the CEO's. It helps our close professional relations, as I can easily ask him: 'Sasha, please come to my office as there are questions regarding the investment programme.'"* Another chair described a specific instance, when the company he chaired was experiencing a major crisis: *"In this situation I supported the CEO, because I believed he could manage it. He just needed time. As chair I could have taken responsibility and tried to fix it, but I'm not sure it would have been a smart decision."*

In terms of specific communication between CEOs and chairs, respondents largely opt for informal one-to-one meetings with no minutes on the company premises, phone and Skype conversations, and texting. Some wine and dine with their counterparts, others do not: *"Dinner is useful to break the ice and establish relationships, but when you know a person it's better to meet in the office."*

Most of our respondents did not claim to mentor their CEOs. One was categorical: *"A chair should not be a mentor to the CEO, otherwise they become friends and the chair will start protecting management interests."* However, they all willingly introduced CEOs to the people in their social networks and provided other resources.

OTHER CHALLENGES

Most respondents regard relationships with external stakeholders, such as clients or suppliers, as less of a challenge than relationships with internal stakeholders, with one exception—the government. Chairs with a government background or high social status (e.g., large shareholders) tend to play a significant government relations and public relations role in addition to fulfilling their direct duties. They meet with government officials, speak at summits and conferences, supervise charity projects, and promote the company image in other ways. In contrast, professional chairs usually stay out of the public eye and undertake projects only when asked by the CEO.

Planning and preparing their own succession was not a priority for the chairs interviewed. Only one respondent was working on getting the CEO of a JV ready to succeed him as chair, but the decision in this case had been made by the chair's boss. Other interviewees mentioned "shareholders", a "dedicated board committee", and even a "corporate secretary" among the parties responsible for finding their successor. It is worth mentioning here that there is no culture of planning leadership succession in Russia, which makes the earlier observations less surprising.

Respondents actively used technology in their personal work and for the boards they chair, for example, video-conferencing for individual work with directors, committees, and even some board meetings. Most boards have their own online portals and some use digital voting. However, as one of respondents noted: "*Chairmanship is mostly about people and balance of interests—there is simply no place for disruptions caused by technology.*"

Russian chairs work hard and feel a huge responsibility on their shoulders. One said: "*I am representing the company all the time and everywhere. It is a huge responsibility, which creates some constraints. For example, I do not drink in public so as not to damage the image of the company I chair.*" Yet they still find room for humour: "*I am not afraid of joking, sometimes even to the point of absurdity. It helps to keep spirits up.*"

SUMMARY

Modern capitalism is only 25 years old in Russia and corporate boards as we know them in the West emerged only about two decades ago. The Russian model of corporate governance is still a work in progress and the chairs we interviewed are at the forefront of this. While it is too early to draw far-reaching conclusions, our key findings are as follows.

Public companies with dispersed ownership are virtually non-existent. Russia is dominated by first-generation private businesses or state-owned corporations. The owners or their representatives (in the case of government-owned companies) are powerful and have a strong impact on the work of board leaders in terms of their attention, time allocation, and even style. In this context it is understandable that chairs should work for shareholders, not all stakeholders or the long-term interests of the company.

Relationships are more important than institutions in Russia. While the authority and responsibilities of corporate boards are well defined and correspond to global standards, other factors have a stronger impact on board dynamics. Ownership structures and the power networks of key players such as shareholders, their representatives, board members, and top executives create specific constraints for chairs and largely define their roles and the practices they use.

Authority and facilitation: Russian chairs are pragmatic—they want their boards to be effective decision-making bodies. Yet they are ambivalent in the way they try to achieve this goal. On the one hand, they operate from a position of authority and often act in an authoritative and even authoritarian way. Yet they can instantly switch to a facilitating mode, ask other directors to speak their minds and reach a consensus—only to put the dictator's mask back on if things do not go their way. We believe that extensive use of voting is one manifestation of this ambivalence.

Traditional informal ways of getting things done, such as drinking sessions or sauna parties, are not in the arsenal of board chairs in Russia. They are quite modern in the way they work, opting for office meetings and Skype calls rather than drinking sessions. As one said: "*We all are busy people. I would rather spend my time on a one-to-one meeting with a director than arrange a big drinking party.*" Russian chairs also seem increasingly health-conscious and strive for a healthy lifestyle.

TRENDS FOR THE NEXT FIVE YEARS

Russia's history teaches us that it is hard to make accurate forecasts, but we believe the following trends will materialize.

- There will be more professional chairs who exclusively dedicate themselves to this type of work, but the percentage will be still lower than in more developed countries.
- The "professional collaboration" model of chair-CEO relationship will spread to many organizations, especially private and public businesses.
- Many government officials and ex-government officials will assume chair roles; for some it will be an informal retirement plan.
- Women chairs will remain a tiny minority.
- Chairs and their boards will become technology savvy. Information technology will have a transformative impact on the way Russian boards work.

REFERENCES

Bank of Russia (2014). Russia Corporate Governance Code. *Bank of Russia' Vestnik*, 40 (1518), pp. 3–63.

EMISS (2018). Number of Organisations According to Official Registration. Available from: https://www.fedstat.ru/indicator/42930 [Accessed 10 May 2018].

Federal Antimonopoly Service of Russian Federation (2017). Russia Competition Report 2016. Available from: https://fas.gov.ru/documents/596439 [Accessed 10 May 2018].

Judge, W. Q., Naoumova, I. and Koutzevol, N. (2003). Corporate Governance and Firm Performance in Russia: an Empirical Study. *Journal of World Business*, 38(4), pp. 385–396.

Iwasaki, I. (2008). The Determinants of Board Composition in a Transforming Economy: Evidence from Russia. *Journal of Corporate Finance*, 14(5), pp. 532–549.

Kakabadse, A., Kakabadse, N. and Myers, A. (2009). Chairman of the Board Research: a Survey of Russian Organisations. *Cranfield School of Management*.

Kapalyushnikow, R. and Demina, N. (2005). Concentrated Ownership and Management Turnover: The Case of Russia. *Russian Economic Barometer*, 14(1), pp. 10–21.

Meyer, E. (2014). *The Culture Map: Breaking Through the Invisible Boundaries of Global Business*. New York: PublicAffairs.

Radygin, A. D. (1998). Russian Privatization: National Tragedy or Institutional Platform for Post-Soviet Reforms. *Mir Rossii*, 7(3), pp. 3–32.

Russian Federation Federal State Statistics Service (2017). *Labor and Employment in Russia*. Moscow: Rosstat.

Russian Federation Federal State Statistics Service (2018). Population. Available from: http://www.gks.ru/wps/wcm/connect/rosstat_main/rosstat/ru/statistics/population/demography/# [Accessed 10 May 2018].

Shekshnia, S. and Zagieva, V. (2016). Chair Survey 2015. Available from: https://www.insead.edu/sites/default/files/assets/dept/centres/icgc/docs/chair-survey-2015.pdf [Accessed 3 December 2018].

Spencer Stuart (2017). Russia Board Index 2017. Available from: https://www.spencerstuart.com/research-and-insight/russia-board-index-2017 [Accessed 10 May 2018].

The World Bank (2016). Population Ranking. Available from: https://datacatalog.worldbank.org/dataset/population-ranking [Accessed 10 May 2018].

The World Bank (2018a). World Development Indicators. GDP per capita, in international dollars. Available from: http://databank.worldbank.org/data/reports.aspx?source=2&series=NY.GDP.PCAP.PP.CD [Accessed 10 May 2018].

The World Bank (2018b). World Development Indicators. GDP Ranking. Available from: https://datacatalog.worldbank.org/dataset/gdp-ranking [Accessed 10 May 2018].

The World Bank (2018c). World Development Indicators. GDP Ranking, PPP based. Available from: https://datacatalog.worldbank.org/dataset/gdp-ranking-ppp-based [Accessed 10 May 2018].

UNDP (2018). Human Development Indices and Indicators. 2018 Statistical Update. Available from: http://hdr.undp.org/en/2018-update [Accessed 28 September 2018].

CHAPTER 10

"Top Fives" of Chairing a Board in Europe

Stanislav Shekshnia and Veronika Zagieva

In this chapter we would like to synthesize the research findings presented in the country chapters to highlight commonalities and differences in how board chairs conduct their business in different European countries. We use a "top five" approach, identifying the five practices most widely used across Europe; the five most "destructive" practices or common traps for board leaders; and the five most important personal attributes that make chairs effective. We will make one exception to our rule of five and present the most original practice from each country—making eight in total.

THE FIVE MOST COMMON PRACTICES IN EUROPE

1. Arranging dinners with board members the evening before the board meeting: We found shared meals in the toolkit of board leaders in all of the countries we studied. One of the most experienced chairs from the Netherlands summarized the advantages of organizing a dinner for directors on the eve of the board meeting:

S. Shekshnia
INSEAD, Fontainebleau, France

V. Zagieva (✉)
Ward Howell Talent Equity Institute, Moscow, Russia
e-mail: v.zagieva@wardhowell.com

© The Author(s) 2019
S. Shekshnia, V. Zagieva (eds.), *Leading a Board*,
https://doi.org/10.1007/978-981-13-3197-8_10

You kill a few birds with this stone. First, directors usually travel for the meeting or had a committee meeting in the afternoon, so they are hungry and you feed them. Second, you do it in a nice restaurant and they see that you care. Third, you allow them to reconnect with the board and the company in a relaxed setting. Fourth, you create some positive group dynamics around a dinner table, which will hopefully migrate to the boardroom next morning. Fifth, you find out if there are any concerns and disagreements between directors with regard to the next morning's agenda and plan the discussion accordingly. Finally, you can have some content-rich discussions about current and future issues without the pressure of making a decision.

2. Reaching out to each director before the board meeting to discuss the agenda and seek input: This practice takes on a number of forms: one-on-one meetings, Skype calls, e-mail or messenger exchanges or a phone call—the last of these being the most popular. It is a way of re-engaging directors with the company and the board, showing their importance, soliciting specific input on the agenda and exploring other board-related issues. It takes little time but can be very effective. As one director-respondent put it: "*A 15-minute phone call gives me a chance to pick every director's brain before the board meeting. It also reminds them about the need to prepare for the meeting.*"

3. Speaking last during boardroom discussions: We explain later in this chapter how restraint is one of the key attributes of an effective board chair. One of the most popular ways to enable productive discussions and diversity of opinions in board meetings is for the leader to withhold his or her personal opinion until the last moment. We found the practice of taking the floor only after all other directors have spoken quite common among European chairs. It was best described in the words of one UK chair: "*I try to take up as little room as possible. My task is to help others to speak their minds.*" Another chair from Switzerland confirmed: "*I listen. I also decide when it is time to decide, but everyone can express himself without fear.*"

4. Meeting with shareholders to discuss an upcoming board meeting: In all of the countries, we studied that effective chairs are proactive and go beyond compliance in their relationships with shareholders. This proactivity takes on different forms—from diagnostic questionnaires to mentoring sessions—in different countries, yet respondents from all of them identified meeting active shareholders in advance of the board meeting as one of the chair's most productive practices. The meeting can cover a range of subjects, such as shareholders' strategies, their positions on specific items of the agenda or their general expectations of the board. Usually such meetings take place informally, without strict agendas and minutes, although some chairs reported writing informal summaries and sharing them with shareholders—and in some cases board members. Effective chairs consider such meetings as important venues for information exchange between the board and shareholders and between different shareholders but stand firm against any attempts to impose decisions on the board via its leader. As one chair-respondent put it: *"I am not promising them we will do what they want; I am promising that we will keep it in mind."*

5. Making yourself available to the CEO 24/7: The relationships between board chairs and CEOs are usually complex and intense and take different forms depending on both objective and subjective factors. However, we found that many board leaders in Europe make themselves available to the CEO on a "5/7 or 7/7" basis. As one chair from Russia explained: *"I tell all my CEOs to call me any time for any reason. I believe it sends the right message: 'You are important to me, I am here to listen and support.' They don't abuse my time, but I've had a few late-night calls that helped both the CEO and the company in a big way."* Another board leader seconds this view: *"Whenever the CEO calls me I thank her and repeat that I am available 24 hours 7 days a week. She knows that I care and she can rely on me."*

A supplementary practice to help close the troublesome information gap between executives and the board[1] is for the CEO to compile—and circulate to the chair and directors—a **regular update** about recent and future developments at the company. We came across different names for this document ("CEO report", "chair report", "board report", "management report", "monthly update"), different frequencies (monthly, bimonthly, quarterly) and lengths (from one to six pages), but the objective is always the same: to keep board members informed and engaged. Some chair-respondents leave it to the CEO to define the format and content of the report; others set their own standards. One veteran chair explained that he wants a two-page document every month with the first page devoted to what has already happened and the second to what is going to happen during the next month. He does not allow any financial

[1] Larcker, D. and Tayan, B. (2011). *Corporate Governance Matters*. Upper Saddle River (New Jersey): Pearson Education, p. 133.

information ("*we have it online*"), only qualitative descriptions. The chair reads the document first and then sends it to other directors with his comments.

The Five Most Important Traps to Avoid[2]

In our interviews with board chairs and their key stakeholders, we came across not only effective but also "destructive" practices. The latter reduce the effectiveness of the board or damage chair-CEO and chair-shareholder relationships. In most cases board leaders have developed these habits in other contexts where they might have worked well—and then unconsciously transferred them onto the chair's role. As one of the respondents put it: "*We are all creatures of habit, but we often refuse to recognize that habit.*" In his opinion, "experience" and "reflection" are the two best cures for the bad habits board chairs carry with them from previous undertakings. In the course of our research, we identified five behavioural traps that board leaders should be aware of.

1. Executive behaviour in the boardroom: Around 85 per cent of board chairs interviewed for this project had been CEOs earlier in their professional life (compared to 77 per cent in the whole population of chairs).[3] CEOs and other senior executives thrive by setting a vision, making bold moves, appointing people, giving them specific tasks, assuming responsibility and leading by example. Action- and result-oriented executives, they are at the centre of their companies. On becoming chairs, many former CEOs naturally adopt the same old behaviour patterns. Such leaders start treating directors as "members of my team". Some even organize team-building events, take the lion's share of airtime in the boardroom, offer decisions the board should make before other directors have expressed their views, talk more than listen and occupy centre stage. Instead of energizing and stimulating directors, such an approach often leads to disengagement and resentment at being treated as "subordinates".

---

[2] Some findings presented in this section were previously published as Shekshnia, S. (2018). How to Be a Good Board Chair. *Harvard Business Review*, March–April 2018, pp. 96–105.

[3] Shekshnia, S. and Zagieva, V. (2016). Chair Survey 2015. Available from: https://www.insead.edu/sites/default/files/assets/dept/centres/icgc/docs/chair-survey-2015.pdf [Accessed 3 December 2018].

Many respondents shared personal stories of how they discovered, sometimes painfully, that the work of a chair requires a very different type of leadership from that of a CEO. They reflected on how much more effective they could have been if only they had paid attention to this from day one. As a chair from Russia put it: *"My advice to novice board chairs is: 'What got you here will not make you successful. Unlearn your CEO activism and become a hands-off, reflective leader.'"*

2. Sweating the boardroom: We found a striking difference between experienced and inexperienced chairs in their attitudes towards the importance of actual board meetings. The latter think that it is all about the boardroom; the former consider the meetings just the tip of the iceberg. In reality, the work that takes place outside the boardroom creates a solid foundation for the meeting itself. The famous 80:20 rule applies to the board process: actions taken (or not taken) before and after the meeting determine 80 per cent of its effectiveness. This also means that effective chairs budget the lion's share of their time for working "offline".

One very experienced chair shared his approach to steering effective governance. It had four components: *planning, preparation, follow-up* and *communication with key players.* He plans the dates for board and committee meetings for the next 24 months on a rolling basis and tries to avoid changing the dates at all costs since it upsets directors and undermines respect for the board as an institution. His favourite formula is committee meetings in the afternoon, followed by a dinner for all non-executive directors (*"It saves me some time in the boardroom to get them going"*) and a board meeting the next morning. He does not believe in meetings that last more than five hours and avoids having any after lunch.

The preparation starts for him with the induction of a newly appointed director and includes committee work, preparation and distribution of board materials, and planning of the board meeting itself. According to this chair, committees are critical:

> *We do three-quarters of the work during committee meetings. Committees are small, their members possess relevant expertise and discussions are always candid. By definition board meetings are more formal, so I try to have profound discussions at the committee level, and have them do all the analytical work and prepare resolutions for the whole board.*

He keeps detailed minutes of his various meetings and quickly shares them with all board members. They are action oriented for the benefit of management as well as for the board. They cover different views and opinions as well as conclusions and resolutions. In addition to formal control mechanisms, the chair informally reaches out to the CEO and committee chairs once a month and, among other things, enquires about the outcomes of recent board decisions: "*It shows them that I remember and I care—and gives them an extra nudge.*"

Communication cuts across planning, preparation and follow-up. The chair reaches out to committee chairs, directors and the CEO via phone calls, e-mails and Skype on a regular basis and encourages them to contact him.

3. Building the team: Another practice that works well for executives but backfires for board chairs is team building. One of our respondents had become an independent board chair after being CEO of an international retail chain and explained how his firm belief in teamwork and team building failed him big time with his first board. Soon after becoming a chair he organized an off-site event to discuss shared goals, team rules and mutual expectations. All of the directors showed up, but two had to excuse themselves in the middle. The chair pressed on with his team-building agenda and scheduled a new off-site, but only six out of ten directors showed up. The board evaluation that took place a few months later yielded some surprising news: the directors did not appreciate their leader's efforts. After some reflection and discussions with other chairs, our respondent realized that there are fundamental differences between an executive team and a board of directors. While executives work for one company, and usually under one roof, see each other frequently and report to one boss, board members spend little time together (from four to six board meetings a year plus some committee meetings and phone calls), usually belong to more than one board and may have a very different full-time job. Most importantly they do not report to the chair, who has no administrative power to give them an order or to reward and punish them. Building a team from such people is an enormous task.

After realizing this, our respondent concentrated on creating conditions for the group to work collectively and make effective decisions when they were together. In fact, he started practising 3E leadership—engaging, enabling and encouraging directors' performances, as described in Chap. 1.

4. Trying to be the CEO's boss: Quite simply, the CEO is the boss, solely responsible for executive decisions and accountable for their outcomes. Other company executives report to him and in their turn have direct reports of their own. This logic of boss-subordinate relationships works well in most organizations and is deeply ingrained in the psyche of many executives who later become board chairs.

Board chairs typically have frequent interactions with the management, particularly the CEO. The chair and CEO may discuss board agendas and plans, review board materials, finalize a company press release, follow up on board decisions or meet regulators together. In some cases, chairs even visit customers or vendors, attend public relations events or hold meetings with government officials, all of which create additional opportunities to liaise with the CEO. It is not surprising, therefore, that some chairs come to see themselves as the CEO's boss.

Good chairs do not make this mistake. They always remember that they represent the board and keep other directors informed about all new developments and insights. They understand that the board serves as the "collective boss" of the CEO and that the task of the chair in this system is to make sure that the board creates a dynamic frame for management action, which includes setting goals, resources, rules and accountability for executives. A good chair orchestrates this process but never dominates it.

5. Looking for perfect metrics: "What gets measured gets done." This quote—at different times attributed to Edwards Deming, Peter Drucker and Tom Peters—has become a mantra of the executive world. Not surprisingly, many ex-CEOs when they become chairs start looking for metrics to evaluate the performance of the board of directors. Some even engage strategy consultants from McKinsey or BCG to help develop such indicators. However, we could not find any evidence that such efforts produce good results.

Instead we discovered that experienced chairs take a more holistic and long-term view of board performance. As one respondent who currently chairs the boards of two multinationals put it: "*The decisions our board makes today will shape the company for decades to come. It is naïve to think that we can find a metric or a set of metrics to apply at the end of the year to tell how effective the board has been.*" This chair, along with many other experienced board leaders, concentrates on measuring what can be measured and what he calls the "inputs": directors' competencies, board agendas, board materials, board processes and board minutes. If the quality of inputs is assured, the desired outputs will follow. Other respondents emphasized the importance of involving all directors in discussing board effectiveness, doing so regularly, not fixating on a limited number of specific indicators bur rather maintaining a big-picture outlook. This view was seconded by a non-chair-respondent—a seasoned private equity capitalist who has nominated a few hundred board chairs during the course of his career: "*When during an interview an aspiring chair answers my question about board effectiveness by suggesting quantitative metrics, it's a red flag for me.*"

FIVE ATTRIBUTES THAT MAKE A CHAIR EFFECTIVE

From our research we were able to distil a number of personal character-istics that incumbent chairs considered enablers of effectiveness: restraint; availability; patience; specific soft skills such as listening, questioning and framing; and the hard skills of systemic thinking and general business acu-men. Contrary to the myth, deep industry knowledge is not among the top five attributes—and can even be counterproductive for board leaders.

1. Restraint: One of the most experienced participants from the Netherlands put it this way: "*If you intend to use your chair position as a platform for self-aggrandizement, you are in for trouble.*" Terms like "restrained", "non-domineering" and "leaving room for others" were often used to describe the leading of productive board discussions. Effective chairs speak little, making their interventions sharp, encouraging and focused on process and people, rather than on content. One director-respondent talked about an effective chair he had known: "*She never said 'I', never spoke first and never took more than 10 per cent of the airtime dur-ing any board meeting.*" In fact, the figure of 10 per cent was mentioned by a number of respondents from several countries.

2. Patience: Like good CEOs, good chairs are passionate about their work. But in leading the work of a group of professionals, passion must be tempered by patience and the ability to pause and reflect. Good chairs do not rush to get things done quickly but focus on getting things done properly; they strive for effectiveness rather than efficiency. They become reflective leaders and enable their boards to operate in a reflective mode. One of the participants shared her practice of analysing and improving her board's effectiveness. At the end of each meeting, she asks board members to share their impressions. She discusses the board meeting with the CEO the next day and goes through her notes, reflects on them and decides what needs to change the day after that.

3. Availability: The chair's presence should be felt as little and as much as necessary. A good chair gives other directors room to speak and yet is there to direct the conversation. In the words of one respondent from

Denmark: "*It may be called a non-executive and part-time job, but I have no illusions: I have to be ready to mobilize and commit all my time to this board if the need arises. And I stay in a permanent contact with the company to make sure I don't miss this need.*" Availability is not so much about giving the board and the company an unlimited amount of time; it is the mental attitude of putting the interests of the institution first, of fully embracing the work and its consequences in spite of its part-time nature. One respondent explained: "*I always thank directors and the CEO when they call me, no matter what day or time it is, because they need to know that I care and I am available.*"

4. Specific soft skills: While to an outsider it may look highly technical or even purely ceremonial, the work of a chair is almost exclusively about human relations—often with specific types of people: senior, successful, action-oriented, performance-driven and sophisticated individuals from different backgrounds and countries. Managing these relations requires exceptional behavioural skills. Respondents most often mentioned the ability to listen, ask questions, frame issues and provide feedback. As one put it: "*It is important to listen to directors with a non-judgmental attitude. When you listen to them genuinely, you deserve the right to say something.*"

5. Hard skills: In the "hard skills" category, respondents mostly referred to general business acumen and systemic thinking. As one of them described it: "*A good chair understands the general laws of business and sees the big picture; it allows him to frame questions properly and to achieve the required level of detail during discussions.*" Interestingly, many incumbent chairs did not consider industry knowledge a must. One said: "*For a chair to enable the board to make decisions it's better to have 'an empty head'—to have no opinion on the subject matter. When you are an industry expert, it's hard to achieve.*" This view contradicts the findings of some earlier studies. For example, a survey of 117 early-stage high-tech firms in Norway established that a chair's industry experience has a moderating effect on the board's service role.[4] Some authors argue that industry knowledge is a prerequisite for adequately performing as a board leader and maintaining effective relationships with the CEO.[5] Others claim that

---

[4] Knockaert, M., Bjornali, E. S., and Erikson, T. (2015). Joining Forces: Top Management Team and Board Chair Characteristics as Antecedents of Board Service Involvement. *Journal of Business Venturing*, 30 (3), pp. 420–435.

[5] Brickley, J., Coles, J. and Jarrell, G. (1997). Leadership Structure: Separating the CEO and Chairman of the Board. *Journal of Corporate Finance*, 3, pp. 189–220.

industry knowledge increases a chair's status and therefore that person's legitimacy and ability to influence board members.[6]

EIGHT ORIGINAL PRACTICES

We now present eight (one from each country) of the most original chair practices we encountered in the course of our research, each example reflecting cultural specifics in some way. We are grateful to the authors of the country chapters, who helped us to select them.

The UK: Written agreements between large shareholders and boards defining the rules of engagement for both parties. The UK is known as a country of unwritten rules, yet we came across this approach in a number of cases. The respondents explained that it comes from their previous negative experiences with large active shareholders who tried to bend corporate governance rules in their favour. Some chairs tried to make such agreements legally binding, others did not. One said: "*Just having it on paper helps to cool some hot heads when all of a sudden they want to tell the board what to do.*" Board independence is one of the top priorities of British chairs and they use formal agreements to reinforce it.

The Netherlands: "*Polderen*". *Polderen* is a traditional Dutch approach to decision-making in a context with multiple stakeholders. It comes from politics but has spread to other situations where people with diverging views have to make a decision. Usually it is translated as "willingness to compromise" or "search for consensus". Board chairs who practise *polderen* allow the discussion to take as long as is needed to make a decision—and often nudge directors towards a compromise. In the Netherlands, where equality and consensus are the norm, chairs ensure that all decisions are made unanimously. As one chair put it: "*It is better to postpone a decision when things are too complex; a bit more reflection on the topic often helps.*" This implies that voting hardly ever takes place in the boardroom.

Switzerland: "No-surprise" agreement between the chair and the CEO. In Switzerland the relationship between the chair and the CEO is critical both for board and for company effectiveness, since chairs often

---

[6] Hayward, M.L.A., Rindova, V.P. and Pollock, T.G. (2004). Believing One's Own Press: The Causes and Consequences of CEO Celebrity. *Strategic Management Journal*, 25, pp. 637–653; Shropshire, S. (2010). The Role of the Interlocking Director and Board Receptivity in The Diffusion of Practices. *Academy of Management Review*, 35 (2), pp. 246–264.

engage with various external stakeholders and speak on the company's behalf. A number of chair- and CEO-respondents reported that they make an informal pact: the CEO reports all company problems to the chair as soon as they arise—and only after that do they become known to the rest of the board or other stakeholders. The pact also implies that neither party will bring any undiscussed items to the board. This practice comes from the Swiss culture's emphasis on reliability and predictability.

Denmark: Structured questionnaire for shareholders. In Denmark—where almost every company has significant shareholders and the national culture values transparency, openness and consensual decision-making—one of the top priorities for a chair is to establish working relationships with the major shareholders. We found that they balance engaging-asserting strategies—in order to maintain a dialogue and at the same time to keep major shareholders away from the boardroom. One respondent had designed a questionnaire for shareholders on key issues: strategy (pace of growth, organic growth vs. acquisitions, geographical presence, market positioning); financials (dividends, investments, IPO); and "emotions" (pride in ownership, brand, etc.). This allowed him to capture shareholders' expectations, document them and make them a solid foundation for future chair-shareholder discussions and board decisions.

Italy: Informal meetings with external stakeholders (regulators, bankers, suppliers, etc.). Italy has a reputation for being one of the most regulated countries in Europe, yet it is a high-context culture, where people have to "read between the lines". Here informal one-on-one encounters play an important role in enabling individuals to understand each other's positions, clarifying mutual expectations and preparing decisions to be made in formal settings. The image of a chair is an important asset, which the company uses to find potential clients or negotiate deals with bankers. Chairs meet their stakeholders over coffee, lunch, dinner or even summer holidays. It is an important element of their work: "*Face-to-face meetings are very much part of the Italian culture. We need to sit at the same table and look at each other to reinforce the trust and sense of sharing goals.*"

Germany: Making careful adjustments to meet with worker representatives. In order to appear on an equal footing with employee representatives, German chairs may choose down-to-earth meeting locations, wear casual clothes or arrive in a modest car. German board leaders operate in a system of corporate governance that is highly socially oriented and cooperative. Manoeuvring between the interests of large shareholders, employee representatives and other stakeholders is one of the most challenging tasks German chairs face. Nevertheless, equal treatment is embedded in German culture. German chairs understand that different types of stakeholders need different approaches and adjust their behaviour, tools and practices accordingly.

Turkey: Rehearsing upcoming board meetings with the CEO. Turkey is a hierarchical and, like Italy, high-context culture, which translates into significant informal, behind-the-scenes work on the part of a chair. Rehearsing a board meeting and coaching a CEO for it is a distinctive practice that reflects Turkish culture. This tactic is designed to ensure a smooth-running meeting, to develop the CEO, to strengthen the chair-CEO relationship and to reinforce the informal hierarchy. For the chair, the CEO's performance is his own performance, so the former tries to make sure that the latter is fully prepared—diving deep into the details. As one chair-respondent put it: "*Since I groomed and promoted the CEO, he consults me as he would do with an older brother, and I mentor him.*"

Russia: *Razgovor po dusham*, translated literally as *heart to heart*. In practice, this is a one-to-one, straight-talking encounter behind closed doors between a chair and a board member. It takes place when the former wants to alter the behaviour of the latter. Chairs resort to this practice when less-powerful signals to deviant directors fail to produce results. At the same time, in a conflict-tolerant Russian culture, such an approach does not inflict any deep wounds and, no matter how emotional the heart to heart, the pair continues to interact and cooperate in a professional manner. "*There are no conflicts, no disruption, just different opinions,*" as one chair explained.

References

Brickley, J., Coles, J. and Jarrell, G. (1997). Leadership Structure: Separating the CEO and Chairman of the Board. *Journal of Corporate Finance*, 3, pp. 189–220.

Hayward, M.L.A., Rindova, V.P. and Pollock, T.G. (2004). Believing One's Own Press: The Causes and Consequences of CEO Celebrity. *Strategic Management Journal*, 25, pp. 637–653.

Knockaert, M., Bjornali, E. S., and Erikson, T. (2015). Joining Forces: Top Management Team and Board Chair Characteristics as Antecedents of Board Service Involvement. *Journal of Business Venturing*, 30(3), pp. 420–435.

Larcker, D. and Tayan, B. (2011). *Corporate Governance Matters*. Upper Saddle River (New Jersey): Pearson Education, p. 133.

Shekshnia, S. (2018). How to Be a Good Board Chair. *Harvard Business Review*, March–April 2018, pp. 96–105.

Shekshnia, S. and Zagieva, V. (2016). Chair Survey 2015. Available from: https://www.insead.edu/sites/default/files/assets/dept/centres/icgc/docs/chair-survey-2015.pdf [Accessed 3 December 2018].

Shropshire, S. (2010). The Role of the Interlocking Director and Board Receptivity in The Diffusion of Practices. *Academy of Management Review*, 35 (2), pp. 246–264.

CHAPTER 11

The Future Role of the Chair in Europe

Filipe Morais and Andrew Kakabadse

This final chapter offers a forward-looking view that emerged from our research on how the chair's role and functions will evolve over the coming decade. As is often the case in the corporate governance domain, such changes will be evolutionary rather than revolutionary, but their impact will be felt across multiple dimensions.

In this chapter we identify changes pertaining to (1) the chair's demographic profile, (2) the role, tasks and capabilities of the high-performing chair in light of key developments and (3) the impact of technology on the way in which the chair works.

This chapter focuses on identifying and discussing the three main drivers of the role and required capabilities of high-performing chairs over the next decade: (1) shareholder activism and engagement and sustainability, (2) the increased frequency of business disruptions and (3) board leadership of corporate culture.

These factors will combine to make the chair's role not only more challenging and demanding, but also more important and indeed pivotal.[1]

---

[1] Kakabadse, A., Kakabadse, N. and Barratt, R. (2006). Chairman and Chief Executive Officer (CEO): That Sacred and Secret Relationship. *Journal of Management Development*, 25(2), pp. 134–150.

F. Morais (✉) • A. Kakabadse
Henley Business School, Henley-on-Thames, UK
e-mail: f.morais@henley.ac.uk; a.kakabadse@henley.ac.uk

© The Author(s) 2019
S. Shekshnia, V. Zagieva (eds.), *Leading a Board*,
https://doi.org/10.1007/978-981-13-3197-8_11

217

The chair will sit at the apex of the corporate governance system overseeing a more complex, more uncertain and ambiguous environment. As the next decade progresses, the chair's position will rise to prominence at the top of our organizations, eclipsing that of the CEO.

We begin by discussing some of the demographic trends we can currently observe regarding the chair position—and which we envisage continuing in the next decade. Next we discuss the three key factors that we believe will come to shape the chair's role and define the capabilities required to be effective in that position. A section then follows on how new technology in the boardroom will affect the chair's role. The chapter concludes by considering the balance of the chair's role in terms of monitoring versus stewardship.

Chair Attributes: Who Will Occupy the Role over the Next Decade?

In ten years' time there will be more female chairs in European companies than there are today, yet they will remain in a minority everywhere. The legislative and regulatory pressures felt across Europe in recent years[2]—although perceived by many as insufficient—mean that more women will have the required board experience to become board chairs. A relatively recent study carried out by Credit Suisse Research Institute,[3] on over 3000 large companies globally, shows much progress in Europe compared to other world regions. The average female director representation in the sample was 24.4% in Europe, compared to just over 15% in the US. The trend differs from country to country in Europe, whether as a result of quotas or through voluntary compliance: as of now, even in countries such as the UK, where voluntary compliance is working relatively well, the

---

[2] International Finance Corporate (2015). A Guide to Corporate Governance Practices in the European Union. Available from: https://www.ifc.org/wps/wcm/connect/c44d6d-0047b7597bb7d9f7299ede9589/CG_Practices_in_EU_Guide.pdf?MOD=AJPERES [Accessed 3 December 2018]; Jourova, V. (2016). Gender Balance on Corporate boards: Europe is Cracking the Glass Ceiling. European Commission Fact Sheet. Available from: http://ec.europa.eu/newsroom/document.cfm?doc_id=46280 [Accessed 3 December 2018].

[3] Dawson, J., Kersley, R. and Natella, S. (2016). The CS Gender 3000: The Reward for Change. *Credit Suisse Research Institute*. Available from: http://publications.credit-suisse.com/tasks/render/file/index.cfm?fileid=5A7755E1-EFDD-1973-A0B5C54AFF3FB0AE [Accessed 3 December 2018].

number of women in chair positions in the FTSE 100 is very low, although there has been good progress at the non-executive level, with 35.3% of these roles held by women.[4] In addition, 24% of board committees in the FTSE 100 are now chaired by a female director.[5] Such progress will translate into some of these directors attaining the board chair position in the next decade, not just in the UK but in other European countries as well.

As far as age is concerned, chairs will continue to be older than executives, with many professionals in their 70s and even 80s continuing to lead boards. The increase in time and effort demanded by the role—as well as the new capabilities that complexity and technology will necessitate—may mean that there will be more chairs in their 40s and 50s.

Board leaders' backgrounds will be more diverse than they are today, but the CEO/general management route will remain the main career path for the job.

"Celebrity chairs"—those chairing boards on account of their personal prestige alone—will almost disappear. Prestige will secure a chair position only if accompanied by capability and a clear contribution to governance and performance.

Overall, the profile of the chair will change slowly over the next decade to include more women, younger people and fewer celebrities. In addition, although CEO/general management will remain the main avenue, a wider range of backgrounds will be considered, with the role increasingly addressing topics such as stakeholder engagement, sustainability and corporate culture.

Chair Work: Three Key Factors Shaping the Role

A number of factors will influence the nature of the role and the capabilities required to be a high-performing chair. These factors also mean that chairing a board will require a greater time commitment, with fewer chairs therefore occupying more than one such position. Chairs will be busier and their focus will be split between running the board (including their relationship with the CEO) and engaging with shareholders and a variety

---

[4] Vinnicombe, S., Doldor, E., and Sealy, R. (2018). The Female FTSE Board Report 2018: Busy Going Nowhere with the Female Executive Pipeline. Cranfield University. Available from: https://30percentclub.org/assets/uploads/UK/Third_Party_Reports/2018_-_CranfieldFemale_FTSE_Board_Report.pdf [Accessed 3 December 2018].

[5] Ibid.

of other stakeholders. Chairs will find themselves more frequently called upon to lead through a particular crisis or disruption. They will need to pay more attention to their task of overseeing corporate culture and creating the right conditions for the board to function as an effective steward of the appropriate culture for the business. These factors are discussed in greater detail in the following sections.

Shareholder Activism, Engagement and Sustainability

The push by European authorities for increased shareholder rights and a stronger shareholder voice in the affairs of corporations—as exemplified by the Shareholder Rights Directive (SRD)[6] and the UK Stewardship Code[7] (due to be revised)—means that chairs will have to pay greater attention to the voices of shareholders and act as effective bridges between shareholders, the board and management. Emerging policy and regulation is advocating improvements in dialogue between companies and investors, for example, through the creation of stakeholder advisory panels and annual reporting on how companies engage with stakeholders.

The potential for improving the effectiveness of corporate governance is high, but it could also be a recipe for tensions at the top if not handled carefully. PricewaterhouseCoopers' (PwC's) annual corporate director survey indicates that, while shareholder engagement has become more common in recent years (54% of the 884 directors of public companies surveyed state that their board is involved in direct engagement with investors), not all corporate directors view this as beneficial, with 21% reporting that they derived no valuable insights from such engagement.[8] Chairs will therefore become the focal point of governance, and their ability to reconcile competing agendas and build trust is going to be stress-tested to the maximum. They will have to create meaningful and proactive

---

[6] European Parliament (2017). Directive (EU) 2017/828 of the European Parliament and the Council of 17 May 2017. *Official Journal of the European Union*, L 132. Available from: https://eur-lex.europa.eu/legal-content/EN/TXT/PDF/?uri=CELEX:32017L0828&from=EN [Accessed 3 December 2018].

[7] Financial Reporting Council (2012). The UK Stewardship Code. Available from: https://www.frc.org.uk/getattachment/d67933f9-ca38-4233-b603-3d24b2f62c5f/UK-Stewardship-Code-(September-2012).pdf [Accessed 3 December 2018].

[8] PricewaterhouseCoopers (2016). The Swinging Pendulum: Board Governance in the Age of Shareholder Empowerment. PwC's 2016 Annual Corporate Directors Survey. Available from: https://www.pwc.es/es/publicaciones/consejos-y-buen-gobierno/2016-annual-corporate-directors-survey.pdf [Accessed 3 December 2018].

engagement with investors and manage the frustrations that this process may bring for the various parties. However, a more recent report[9] suggests that, in considering a range of chair tasks, only 36% of respondents consider chairs to be very effective at communicating with shareholders (46% view them as somewhat effective and 24% as ineffective), with this competence scoring lowest of all categories of chair task effectiveness.

Chairs will have to engage with shareholders over a great range of topics beyond financial performance and executive remuneration. The pressure for firms to strategically integrate, monitor and disclose material environmental, societal and governance (ESG) issues is increasing[10] but is yet to be taken seriously, even by those boards whose firms report on sustainability.[11] This will change. The head of engagement for a large institutional investor recently told us:

> *Concerns over climate change and how these concerns are being integrated in investees' strategies is growing in the investment community; there is also a renewed push for better assessing social impact, one of the aspects of ESG that often got forgotten. I think this will become very relevant over the coming years—as firms and investors learn how to effectively engage and mind-set change starts to build.*

For many chairs, this will represent a shift in mind-set and practice. Their thinking will need to become more holistic, boardroom debate will need to move from traditional ways of looking at value creation to include social and environmental considerations; perhaps a non-executive director will need to have specific responsibilities for sustainability; an executive committee may need to report directly to the board; and CEO perfor-

---

[9] PricewaterhouseCoopers (2018). The Evolving Boardroom: Signs of Change. PwC's 2018 Annual Corporate Directors Survey. Available from: https://www.pwc.com/us/en/governance-insights-center/annual-corporate-directors-survey/assets/pwc-annual-corporate-directors-survey-2018.pdf [Accessed 3 December 2018].

[10] KPMG (2017). ESG, Strategy and the Long View: A Framework for Board Oversight. Available from: https://assets.kpmg.com/content/dam/kpmg/lu/pdf/lu-en-esg-strategy-framework-for-board-oversight.pdf [Accessed 3 December 2018].

[11] Kiron, D., Kruschwitz, N., Haanaes, K., Reeves, M., Fuisz-Kehrbach, S. and Kell, G. (2015). Joining Forces: Collaboration and Leadership for Sustainability. *MIT Sloan Management Review.* Available from: https://sloanreview.mit.edu/projects/joining-forces/ [Accessed 3 December 2018]; UNEP (United Nations Environment Programme) (2014). Integrated Governance: A New Model of Governance for Sustainability. Available from: http://www.unepfi.org/fileadmin/documents/UNEPFI_IntegratedGovernance.pdf [Accessed 3 December 2018].

mance and incentives will need to be designed to reflect investors' ESG concerns. Sustainability performance is not just another fashion concept that will fade with time. It is here to stay and will be a tremendous source of competitive advantage in the not-too-distant future.

Greater shareholder involvement also means that chairs will be under closer scrutiny and face removal if they fail to take due and balanced consideration of shareholder concerns. There is the possibility that the length of chair tenure will be reduced over the coming decade: as the role grows in importance and influence, and is subject to greater scrutiny, only the most outstanding chairs will have a secure place.

More Frequent and More Complex Business Disruptions

Business disruptions are becoming more frequent and more complex. Since the turn of the millennium, we have witnessed technological innovations disrupting entire industries (e.g. music, transportation); more frequent reputational crises fuelled by social media; systemic and global financial meltdowns; prolonged recessions; and continuous political instability. The world has become a riskier place according to 56% of respondents to the World Economic Forum Global Risks Report 2018.[12] The report highlights key fundamental concerns: the increased risks of extreme-weather events; political and economic confrontations between major powers; cyberattacks; and the persistent underlying weaknesses of global financial systems.[13] At the corporate level, CEOs appear more optimistic with 57% believing that global growth will improve (but only 45% for the European Economic Area, seemingly the least optimistic of all world regions). In Europe, CEOs identify lack of availability of key skills (51%), over-regulation (48%) and political uncertainty (42%) as the top three threats to their organizations' growth prospects.[14]

Navigating these increasingly turbulent waters, developing crisis management skills and bringing together different parties to reach shared solutions are tasks that are increasingly likely to fall to the chair. The uncertain

---

[12] World Economic Forum (2018). The Global Risks Report 2018: 13th Edition. Available from: http://www3.weforum.org/docs/WEF_GRR18_Report.pdf [Accessed 3 December 2018].

[13] Ibid.

[14] PricewaterhouseCoopers (2018). 21st CEO Survey: The Anxious Optimist in the Corner Office. Available from: https://www.pwc.com/gx/en/ceo-survey/2018/pwc-ceo-survey-report-2018.pdf [Accessed 3 December 2018].

business landscape will see corporations more frequently shifting consensus at the top on how they should be governed and directed, and strategic tensions will likely be exacerbated.[15] Chairs have long been depicted as playing a greater role during upheaval and disruption.[16] A recent large US study showed that, in contexts of high complexity and resource scarcity, chairs account for up to 9% of variation in firm performance over and above the variation explained by the CEO.[17] The coming decade will see more chairs called upon to step up and lead directly from the board in times of upheaval—as these disruptions will require more collaborative leadership, as opposed to an archetypal strong, dominant CEO saving the day. Chairs will be required to equip their boards with the capabilities they need to face different types of threats, both by ensuring a diverse board composition with the right mix of skills and experiences and by developing scanning and sense-making processes to enable effective directional responses to emerging issues. Chairs will also need to ensure that their board comprises individuals who know how to operate in a time of crisis or disruption—skills that have often been acquired in addressing extreme circumstances elsewhere. Finally, chairs will need to ensure that their board can raise uncomfortable issues and vigorously debate them on a regular basis: setting the tone for robust debate about tension-generating topics while ensuring board cohesiveness will be all the more challenging in the years to come. Chairs that combine this capability with an evidence-based approach, along with proficiency in stakeholder engagement and a long-term focus, will be better equipped to succeed in turbulent times.

Shaping Corporate Culture

Peter Drucker has been credited with the quote "culture eats strategy for breakfast", an idea which has become the subject of much debate. It is an

---

[15] Morais, F., Kakabadse, A. and Kakabadse, N. (2018). The Chairperson and CEO Roles Interaction and Responses to Strategic Tensions. *Corporate Governance: The International Journal of Business in Society*, 18(1), pp. 143–164.

[16] Mizruchi, M.S. (1983). Who Controls Whom? An Examination of the Relation between Management and Boards of Directors in Large American Corporations. *The Academy of Management Review*, 8(3), pp. 426–435; Parker, H. (1990). The Company Chairman: His Roles and Responsibilities. *Long Range Planning*, 23(4), pp. 35–43.

[17] Withers, M.C. and Fitza, M.A. (2017). Do Board Chairs Matter? The Influence of Board Chairs on Firm Performance. *Strategic Management Journal*, 38(6), pp. 1343–1355.

assertion that is increasingly recognized by regulators,[18] with organizational culture cited as the basis of the 2008 financial meltdown along with other corporate failures. An early report by the Financial Reporting Council[19] showed that boards acknowledge the responsibility of determining the purpose of the company (why it exists, beyond merely generating profit) and therefore the values and behaviours that are required to fulfil its purpose. Yet "culture" is perceived by many chairs as simply the determination of strategy: the rate of expansion, the markets in which the company is likely to succeed, the mode of entry and so on.[20]

Although regulators are paving the way for culture to feature high on board agendas, boards are yet to attach any importance to this critical governance function. Nor have they developed any means by which to fulfil their responsibility to assure shareholders and other stakeholders that the culture of the firm is healthy and conducive to sustainable business performance.

Recent research by Board Agenda and Mazars, in association with INSEAD, has revealed that much work awaits chairs in ensuring that their boards can be effective stewards of the corporate culture.[21] Boards either fail to value culture as a topic or are simply ill-equipped to handle it, yet many recognize the existence of fractures between strategy and culture. Directors generally assume that the principal ways to influence corporate culture are to set the right tone from the top, ensuring the CEO is supportive of the desired culture and making the right appointments to the board and senior management. A recent survey shows that, currently, in assessing culture, approximately 66% of directors rely on gut feeling based on interactions with the management, yet only 32% believe this is effec-

---

[18] Financial Reporting Council (2018). The UK Corporate Governance Code. Available from: https://www.frc.org.uk/getattachment/88bd8c45-50ea-4841-95b0-d2f4f48069a2/2018-UK-Corporate-Governance-Code-FINAL.PDF [Accessed 3 December 2018].

[19] Financial Reporting Council (2016). Corporate Culture and the role of Boards: Report of Observations. Available from: https://www.frc.org.uk/getattachment/3851b9c5-92d3-4695-aeb2-87c9052dc8c1/Corporate-Culture-and-the-Role-of-Boards-Report-of-Observations.pdf [Accessed 3 December 2018].

[20] Ibid.

[21] Board Agenda and Mazars (2017). Board Leadership in Corporate Culture: European Report 2017. Available from: https://www.mazars.com/content/download/914232/47476119/version//file/Board%20Leadership%20in%20Corporate%20Culture%20Report.pdf [Accessed 3 December 2018].

tive.[22] However, our own research suggests that non-executive directors' (NEDs') informal contact with a company's operations and people is an invaluable resource complementing more formal ways of assessing corporate culture. With many CEOs still feeling nervous about allowing NEDs to visit operations and talk with other layers of management, chairs need to ensure that these activities happen, so as to enable NEDs to have a line of sight into the corporation's culture. It is up to the chair to set the tone for culture—and that starts in the boardroom. One chair recently told us:

> *A wildly underplayed aspect of board performance is culture, values and behaviours. So for me the big difference is, and we know this from sitting on boards: you can have exactly the same people sitting around the board table, but with a different style of chair you will get a completely different dialogue but with the same people.*

Many leading firms with enlightened boards and chairs are actively promoting breakfasts in which NEDs meet employees from different parts of the organization, inviting employees to present to the board and enabling NED visits to operations. These companies' CEOs do not regard such practices as stepping into their territory but rather as ways in which NEDs can be more useful and bring more value to the table. One highly experienced FTSE 100 chair commented on his approach:

> *Non-executives can go into executive meetings, R&D, product marketing, visit any research establishment, any manufacturing or commercial unit, find out what's going on ... no chaperoning, and initially I said, go and be a fly on the wall but if you need to ask a question, ask a question, and that is now part of the way the company operates. And I always had that right, if you like, but I wanted to make sure all my board members did.*

In the future high-performing chairs will routinely start every board meeting by reminding board members of the purpose, values and behaviours that are integral to the firm's culture. They will be crystal clear in identifying the types of behaviours that are not tolerated and swift and assertive at addressing them if they do occur.

---

[22] PricewaterhouseCoopers (2018). The Evolving Boardroom: Signs of Change. PwC's 2018 Annual Corporate Directors Survey. Available from: https://www.pwc.com/us/en/governance-insights-center/annual-corporate-directors-survey/assets/pwc-annual-corporate-directors-survey-2018.pdf [Accessed 3 December 2018].

Technology Adoption by Boards: How Will It Change the Way the Chair Works?

The impact of technology on boards—and therefore on the work of the chair—is growing. A recent report by consulting firm Forrester (2018) indicates an increasing, albeit slow, take-up of technology by boards in Europe but also highlights growing concerns. About 45% of boards in Europe already have board-management software with one-to-one/group chat capability. Many also have minute taking, archiving and search capabilities, voting/pooling, virtual deal rooms and much more.[23] This enables board members to be more effective, as they can quickly access information, scorecards and reports in a way not possible a few years ago, allowing them to attain fresh insights and ask better questions. This is all the more important when we consider that reporting requirements are on the increase, the tracking of ESG performance being one example. However, 42% of European directors have concerns about breaches of data, fearing the exposure of sensitive information on a large scale, and over 50% of boards that use board-management software reported it as being unhelpful during a crisis in terms of responding within time constraints and assuring good communication between directors.[24]

The way board members interact will continue to change in the coming decade, and this may have profound implications. If every board activity is recorded and undertaken remotely (i.e. online), a possible outcome is that directors may be (even) less inclined to have those difficult conversations for fear of them being recorded and subsequently either leaked to the press or used against them in a lawsuit by an aggrieved shareholder or other stakeholder. Also, online communication has a greater potential for misunderstandings, in comparison with face-to-face, as behavioural language is important in conveying meaning. On the positive side, online communication may make less talkative board members feel more willing to contribute—even if handling disagreement proves more difficult. Chairs will need to be on top of this and use technology in a way that maximizes efficiency of board operations without jeopardizing relationships and quality of debate.

---

[23] Forrester Consulting (2018). Directors' Digital Divide: Boardroom Practices Aren't Keeping Pace with Technology. Too Many Boards Still Use Personal Email and Fail to Adopt Technology for Sensitive Communication. Available from: https://diligent.com/wp-content/uploads/2018/10/Global-Report-Forrester-Directors-Digital-Divide-Boardroom-Practices.pdf [Accessed 3 December 2018].

[24] Ibid.

Conclusion

In the coming decade, chairs in Europe will be required to collaborate more extensively, both internally and externally, in order to seek shared solutions to frequent and complex business disruptions.

Their focus will be divided between, on the one hand, the more traditional roles of oversight and relationship with the CEO and, on the other, a greater emphasis on stewardship in terms of shareholder engagement, sustainable performance and corporate culture. The chair will become the guardian of the long-term view of the firm and the one individual who reminds everyone—board members, executives and shareholders—of the higher purpose that the firm serves, maintaining quality of engagement and ensuring the alignment of the different and shifting interests in and around the boardroom.

Such a shift in emphasis will require chairs to become more available, which will often include leading the company through difficult situations. The skill-set of the high-performing chair must expand to include holistic thinking, political savviness, long-term vision and an ability to reconcile competing agendas and gather the support of external stakeholders.

One effect of the chair's changing role is that the profile of the senior independent director (SID) will also need to rise. SIDs will need to understand how the chair's role and prominence is expanding, and develop their skills in new domains in order to be in a position to support and/or challenge the chair when required.

The conclusions detailed earlier point to our most significant prediction all. That is, the role of chair is set to become the most important in contemporary organizations, surpassing that of the CEO. Welcome to the age of the board chair.

References

Board Agenda and Mazars (2017). Board Leadership in Corporate Culture: European Report 2017. Available from: https://www.mazars.com/content/download/914232/47476119/version//file/Board%20Leadership%20in%20Corporate%20Culture%20Report.pdf [Accessed 3 December 2018].

Dawson, J., Kersley, R. and Natella, S. (2016). The CS Gender 3000: The Reward for Change. Credit Suisse Research Institute. Available from: http://publications.credit-suisse.com/tasks/render/file/index.cfm?fileid=5A7755E1-EFDD-1973-A0B5C54AFF3FB0AE [Accessed 3 December 2018].

European Parliament (2017). Directive (EU) 2017/828 of the European Parliament and the Council of 17 May 2017. *Official Journal of the European Union*, L 132. Available from: https://eur-lex.europa.eu/legal-content/EN/TXT/PDF/?uri=CELEX:32017L0828&from=EN   [Accessed   3 December 2018].

Financial Reporting Council (2012). The UK Stewardship Code. Available from: https://www.frc.org.uk/getattachment/d67933f9-ca38-4233-b603-3d24b2f62c5f/UK-Stewardship-Code-(September-2012).pdf   [Accessed   3 December 2018].

Financial Reporting Council (2016). *Corporate Culture and the Role of Boards: Report of Observations.* Available   from: https://www.frc.org.uk/getattachment/3851b9c5-92d3-4695-aeb2-87c9052dc8c1/Corporate-Culture-and-the-Role-of-Boards-Report-of-Observations.pdf   [Accessed   3 December 2018].

Financial Reporting Council (2018). *The UK Corporate Governance Code.* Available   from: https://www.frc.org.uk/getattachment/88bd8c45-50ea-4841-95b0-d2f4f48069a2/2018-UK-Corporate-Governance-Code-FINAL.PDF [Accessed 3 December 2018].

Forrester Consulting (2018). Directors' Digital Divide: Boardroom Practices Aren't Keeping Pace with Technology. Too Many Boards Still Use Personal Email and Fail to Adopt Technology for Sensitive Communication. Available from: https://diligent.com/wp-content/uploads/2018/10/Global-Report-Forrester-Directors-Digital-Divide-Boardroom-Practices.pdf   [Accessed   3 December 2018].

International Finance Corporate (2015). A Guide to Corporate Governance Practices in the European Union. Available from https://www.ifc.org/wps/wcm/connect/c44d6d0047b7597bb7d9f7299ede9589/CG_Practices_in_EU_Guide.pdf?MOD=AJPERES [Accessed 3 December 2018].

Jourova, V. (2016). *Gender Balance on Corporate boards: Europe is Cracking the Glass Ceiling.* European Commission Fact Sheet. Available from: http://ec.europa.eu/newsroom/document.cfm?doc_id=46280   [Accessed   3 December 2018].

Kakabadse, A., Kakabadse, N. and Barratt, R. (2006). Chairman and Chief Executive Officer (CEO): That Sacred and Secret Relationship. *Journal of Management Development*, 25(2), pp. 134–150.

Kiron, D., Kruschwitz, N., Haanaes, K., Reeves, M., Fuisz-Kehrbach, S., and Kell, G. (2015). Joining Forces: Collaboration and Leadership for Sustainability. *MIT Sloan Management Review*. Available from: https://sloanreview.mit.edu/projects/joining-forces/ [Accessed 3 December 2018].

KPMG (2017). *ESG, Strategy and the Long View: A Framework for Board Oversight.* Available from: https://assets.kpmg.com/content/dam/kpmg/lu/pdf/lu-en-esg-strategy-framework-for-board-oversight.pdf [Accessed 3 December 2018].

Mizruchi, M.S. (1983). Who controls whom? An Examination of the Relation between Management and Boards of Directors in Large American Corporations. *The Academy of Management Review*, 8(3), pp. 426–435.

Morais, F., Kakabadse, A., and Kakabadse, N. (2018). The Chairperson and CEO Roles Interaction and Responses to Strategic Tensions. *Corporate Governance: The International Journal of Business in Society*, 18(1), pp. 143–164.

Parker, H. (1990). The Company Chairman: His Roles and Responsibilities. *Long Range Planning*, 23(4), pp. 35–43.

PricewaterhouseCoopers (2016). The Swinging Pendulum: Board Governance in the Age of Shareholder Empowerment. PwC's 2016 Annual Corporate Directors Survey. Available from: https://www.pwc.es/es/publicaciones/consejos-y-buen-gobierno/2016-annual-corporate-directors-survey.pdf [Accessed 3 December 2018].

PricewaterhouseCoopers (2018a). The Evolving Boardroom: Signs of Change. PwC's 2018 Annual Corporate Directors Survey. Available from: https://www.pwc.com/us/en/governance-insights-center/annual-corporate-directors-survey/assets/pwc-annual-corporate-directors-survey-2018.pdf [Accessed 3 December 2018].

PricewaterhouseCoopers (2018b). 21st CEO Survey: The Anxious Optimist in the Corner Office. Available from: https://www.pwc.com/gx/en/ceo-survey/2018/pwc-ceo-survey-report-2018.pdf [Accessed 3 December 2018].

UNEP (United Nations Environment Programme) (2014). Integrated Governance: A New Model of Governance for Sustainability. Available from: http://www.unepfi.org/fileadmin/documents/UNEPFI_Integrated Governance.pdf [Accessed 3 December 2018].

Vinnicombe, S., Doldor, E. and Sealy, R. (2018). The Female FTSE Board Report 2018: Busy Going Nowhere with the Female Executive Pipeline. Cranfield University. Available from: https://30percentclub.org/assets/uploads/UK/Third_Party_Reports/2018_-_CranfieldFemale_FTSE_Board_Report.pdf [Accessed 3 December 2018].

World Economic Forum (2018). The Global Risks Report 2018: 13th Edition. Available from: http://www3.weforum.org/docs/WEF_GRR18_Report.pdf [Accessed 3 December 2018].

Withers, M.C. and Fitza, M.A. (2017). Do Board Chairs Matter? The Influence of Board Chairs on Firm Performance. *Strategic Management Journal*, 38(6), pp. 1343–1355.

Appendix A. Research Methodology and Data Collection

To describe the work of a board chair in the European context we have relied on both qualitative and quantitative data. We use quantitative data collected through a targeted Global Chair Survey administered in 30 European countries in 2015.[1] The survey was mailed to 600 European chairs identified through the INSEAD alumni database and other sources, and we received 120 valid answers. The survey covered a variety of topics related to board leaders, such as their demographics, backgrounds, motivation, remuneration and tasks, as well as their time commitment and its allocation. On the basis of the survey we identified challenges that chairs in Europe face in performing their work, which formed the foundation for the second leg of data collection.

To identify some specific practices that board leaders use to deal with the challenges uncovered in the first stage of investigation, we assembled a team of researchers, who conducted semi-structured interviews in eight European countries. We selected these countries—Denmark, Germany, Italy, the Netherlands, Russia, Switzerland, Turkey and the UK—using a number of criteria. First, we wanted to have a compact sample reflecting the diversity of Europe. This is why our list includes both developed and emerging economies, larger and smaller nations, and countries from the north, west, south and east of Europe. Second, we selected countries

---

[1] Shekshnia, S. and Zagieva, V. (2016). Chair Survey 2015. Available from: https://www.insead.edu/sites/default/files/assets/dept/centres/icgc/docs/chair-survey-2015.pdf [Accessed 3 December 2018].

where the separation of the chair and CEO roles is the most marked, so that we would be studying the work of a professional chair who is not also the CEO of the same company—hence the exclusion of France, the third-largest European economy. In some countries from the sample (Germany, Denmark and Russia) the separation is mandatory, while others have adopted it as best practice. Third, we intended to look at the work of a board chair under different European governance models: the single-board model (Denmark, Italy, Russia, Turkey and the UK), the two-tier board model (Germany and the Netherlands) and the co-determination model (Denmark and Germany).

As one of the core research questions was whether effective chair leadership varies across national and cultural boundaries, we needed a unified approach to assess the different cultures in which our chair-respondents operate. We used our fellow INSEAD Professor Erin Meyer's methodology, as set out in her book *The Culture Map: Breaking through the Invisible Boundaries of Global Business.*[2] This model presents eight scales, showing how cultures vary along a spectrum from one extreme to its opposite. We adopted six scales (Communicating, Persuading, Deciding, Trusting, Disagreeing and Scheduling) out of the eight and placed our countries on each dimension, based on Meyer's research.

Culture map dimensions

Communicating: Low-context versus high-context
In low-context cultures, good communication is precise, simple and clear. Repetition is appreciated. In high-context cultures, good communication is sophisticated and nuanced. Messages are both spoken and read between the lines.
Persuading: Principles-first versus applications-first
In applications-first cultures, individuals begin their argument with a fact, statement or opinion and later back it up with explanations if necessary. Discussions are conducted in a practical manner. In principles-first cultures, the preference is to begin with the theoretical background or broader concept and later move to concrete statements or opinions.
Deciding: Consensual versus top-down
In cultures with a consensual decision-making style, decisions are made in group through unanimous agreements. In top-down cultures, decisions are made by individuals.
Trusting: Task-based versus relationship-based
In task-based cultures, trust is built through business-related activities. Work relationships are formed and dropped easily, based on the situation. In relationship-based cultures, trust is built through informal activities. Work relationships are built slowly over time.

---

[2] Meyer, E. (2014). *The Culture Map: Breaking Through the Invisible Boundaries of Global Business.* New York: PublicAffairs.

Culture map dimensions

Disagreeing: Confrontational versus non-confrontational
In cultures tending to open confrontation, conflict is appropriate and does not negatively impact relationships. In countries that avoid confrontation, conflicts are considered negative for a team or organization.
Scheduling: Linear-time versus flexible-time
In cultures with a linear-time approach, deadlines and schedules are strict with a focus on promptness over flexibility. In flexible-time cultures, the focus is on adaptability, time is considered as a fluid substance, and deadlines can stretch.

Adapted from Meyer, E. (2014). *The Culture Map: Breaking Through the Invisible Boundaries of Global Business.* New York: PublicAffairs

To collect data we developed a questionnaire with 35 open-ended questions, incorporating the findings of the INSEAD Global Chair Survey 2015 and existing academic theories on the work of the chair. In each country, our researchers conducted face-to-face semi-structured interviews centred on practices that chairs use to deal with 11 challenges:

- Relationship with a controlling/large shareholder
- Managing a difficult board member
- Informational asymmetry with the CEO and other executives
- Diversity in board members' backgrounds
- Relationship with the CEO/management
- Relationship with external stakeholders, such as clients, suppliers and government
- Insufficient time commitments of board members
- Level of collaboration and teamwork among board members
- Relationships with minority shareholders
- Relationships with financial analysts
- Low motivation and absenteeism of board members

Chairs were also asked about their practices for facilitating board meetings, the impact of digital technologies on their work, the planning process for chair succession and their ideas about the future of chairs' work.

Interviews lasted from one to three hours. In total the team conducted 80 conversations with chairs, who currently chair more than 153 boards between them. We also conducted 118 interviews with CEOs, directors and shareholders (or their representatives), who have significant dealings with chairs.

Given the niche nature of our target group, it would have been impossible to obtain a representative sample. At the same time we strove to achieve a high level of diversity. Selecting only seasoned board chairs (more than five years of experience in chairing boards and chairing more than two boards) in each country, we included female and male respondents who had experience in companies with different ownership structures, from different industries and of different sizes. We interviewed shareholders of three different types: controlling family representatives, private equity representatives and institutional investor representatives. We also spoke to directors who had more than five years of experience of serving on boards and had worked with at least three different chairs and CEOs who had more than five years of CEO experience and had worked with at least three chairs. All respondents spoke on the condition of anonymity but provided demographic information.

We recognize that our small sample size is a limitation of the study. Despite this fact, the overall sample of interviewees is quite large for a quantitative research project on such a niche group. The number of respondents interviewed per country varies from 5 to 15 chairs, and from 2 to 4 of each type of other stakeholders (CEOs, directors and shareholders), which limits the generalization of findings on a country level. Nevertheless, we believe that the qualitative value of many responses is significant.

Appendix B. Chairs' Challenges and Practices

Using challenges of board chairs from the INSEAD Global Chair Survey 2015 and findings from interviews, we compiled the table matching the challenges and the practices described by the participants in their interviews. The challenges are listed in the order of importance, established by the survey.

Challenge	Practices
Relationships with controlling or large shareholders	Asking shareholders to fill in a structured questionnaire about their position on key dilemmas such as growth, dividends, acquisitions, and owners' pride
	Preparing an agreement with shareholders to establish formal rules of engagement
	Organizing annual roadshows to meet with shareholders' representatives and engage them in discussion
	Conducting an annual strategy meeting with shareholders
	E-mailing to the largest shareholders to enquire whether they would like a private meeting
	Inviting the five largest shareholders and independent directors for a working dinner once a year
	Inviting representatives of large and small shareholders to the board meetings to hear their positions and concerns
	Having informal dinner with large shareholders before every board meeting
	Preparing summaries of board meetings for shareholders
	Conducting follow-up meetings with shareholders after board meetings
	Consulting with the top-25 largest shareholders on remuneration
	Personally supervising the preparation of the annual remuneration report
	Creating groups in WhatsApp for shareholders to exchange news
	Trying to be always available for shareholders
	Using shareholders' networks for recruitment, information gathering or lobbying
	Nudging shareholders to get to know corporate governance regulations through reading or attending specialized courses
	Articulating personal expectations and setting boundaries between the board and the shareholders
	Preventing shareholders from reaching out to management and directors without the chair's participation

Challenge	Practices
Managing difficult board members (special cases)	Induction interview with a director
	Assessing personality, character, communication skills and cultural fit of future directors
	Formalizing behavioural norms for directors
	Conducting a formal performance evaluation
	Conducting a 360-degree evaluation
	Recommending that the difficult board member should not stand for re-election
	Polite confrontation
	Reminding egoistic members of the collective nature of the board's work
	Repeating board rules before the meeting
	Soliciting opinions of "silent" directors before the meeting and presenting them on their behalf
	Asking for written opinions to ensure that everybody participates
	Asking every director to state his or her opinion
	Formulating one's own position before the board meeting and sending it to the other directors in advance
	Suggesting professional support to a difficult board member
	Personally coaching "timid" board members
	Involving the whole board in discussing deviant behaviour to strengthen the message
	Preparing mitigation strategies
	Postponing the discussion to reach a decision acceptable to all board members
Relationships with the CEO and management	Establishing developmental objectives for CEO
	Going on business trips together with CEO
	Having formal mentoring sessions with CEO
	Having lunch with CEO and CFO every quarter
	Having meetings with hi-pos
	Never talking to CEO's direct reports versus meeting with other executives
	Setting board meetings' agendas together with CEO
	Conducting a CEO debrief after each board meeting
	Sharing personal experiences of being a CEO
	Supporting CEO when necessary, for instance, in moments of crisis, to take pressure off CEO
	Connecting CEO with experts
	Introducing CEO to important people in business and government
	Attracting CEO's attention to potential problems and opportunities
	Providing feedback on a regular basis
	Rehearsing meetings with CEO
	Setting mutual expectations by asking "Where do you want me to contribute?"
	Planning and preparing CEO succession

Challenge	Practices
Facilitating effective board discussion	Consulting about the agenda with other directors
	Calling every director and asking if they are happy with the next meeting's agenda or would like to change something
	Defining the format of board materials
	Conducting an express evaluation at the end of the meeting
	Conducting in-camera sessions (without executives present) at the beginning or end of the board meeting
	Distinguishing between subjects that need a discussion and subjects that need a decision
	Dealing with technical and less important issues offline
	Following the "30-20-40-10" rule—30 per cent of time spent on management presentations, 20 per cent on Q&A, 40 per cent on discussion and 10 per cent on making decision—or the "30-70" rule—30 per cent of time on presentations and 70 per cent on discussion
	Forbidding or limiting management presentations
	Setting specific formats for presentations
	Verifying materials before they go to other directors
	Prioritizing important topics in advance
	Placing agenda items that require significant time and mental effort earlier and before lunch
	Giving every director the same amount of air-time
	Asking every director to state their position
	Giving the floor to the most knowledgeable director first to set the tone
	Openly encouraging directors to speak, while reminding them of the need for brevity and specificity
	Not indicating one's personal position
	Speaking the last
	Taking as little room as possible
	Outlining criteria for decision-making
	No voting
	Giving each of the conflicting parties the floor
	Writing proposed resolution on a flip-chart
	Casting a decisive vote in case of deadlock
Level of collaboration and teamwork among board members	Arranging a dinner after a board meeting
	Arranging a dinner with non-executive directors on the eve of a board meeting
	"Chair's minute" at the opening of the board: updates on developments since the last board meeting
	Convening off-site meetings with the help of facilitators
	Creating WhatsApp group chats for the board members

Challenge	Practices
Informational asymmetry with the CEO and management	Conducting board meetings at different company locations
	Encouraging directors to spend time at the company
	Attending management meetings
	Spending time in the company's office, having an office in the company
	"Chair Report"—CEO monthly update prepared for the chair
	Checking board materials before they are sent to directors
	Defining format for board materials, digital board book
	Inviting external experts and consultants
	Talking to each of the executive team members once annually in a one-on-one conversation
	Maintaining intense communication with CEO, CFO, and internal and external auditors
	Open-agenda meeting with CEO
	Assigning a board member as curator of each major management initiative
	Assigning different board members "special missions," that is, projects outside of the regular board committee responsibilities
	Creating temporary board subcommittees to address a specific issue
	Arranging meetings for improving directors' knowledge of the company and its business, including customer visits
	Inviting high-potential managers to make presentations to the board and its committees
Relationship with external stakeholders such as clients, suppliers, government	Interacting with media on a regular basis
	Participating in industry conferences
	Sharing information in local languages to reach the community
	Organizing open events on company premises and inviting stakeholders
Managing diversity in board members' backgrounds	Appointing a board member for his out-of-the-box approach
	Individual coaching of new directors
	"Round-the-table practice"—asking one director after another to state her position on a specific question
	Coaching employee representatives to help them gain the confidence to speak up
Insignificant time commitment by board members	Calling all directors a few days before the meeting to ensure participation and encourage preparation
	Obtaining time commitment from every candidate upfront
	Setting all board and committee meetings dates for the next two years
	Confronting directors who come unprepared or unfocused

Challenge	Practices
Relationships with minority shareholders	Appointing a special representative as a voice for minor shareholders in board discussions
	Providing the same data to majority and minority shareholders
	Staying on after the Annual General Meeting (AGM) to meet minority shareholders and answer any questions
	Engaging a professional communications agency to assist the board in dealing with activist shareholders
	Making adjustments to meet with worker representatives in order to appear on an equal footing with employee representatives
Planning and preparing chair's succession	Using external consultants for succession planning
	Using headhunters for benchmarking purposes
	Using shareholders' and board members' networks to identify potential candidates

Index[1]

[1] Note: Page numbers followed by 'n' refer to notes.

© The Author(s) 2019
S. Shekshnia, V. Zagieva (eds.), *Leading a Board*,
https://doi.org/10.1007/978-981-13-3197-8